Sheltered

J. Dill

First Edition

PAGE PUBLISHING
Conneaut Lake, PA

First originally published by Page Publishing 2023

ISBN 979-8-89157-175-4 (pbk)
ISBN 979-8-89157-191-4 (digital)

Printed in the United States of America

For all the ways we run, hurt, hide and heal.

And my husband, Tom, for showing me what beautiful creations come when someone takes the time to believe in another.

Chapter 1

As Sarah's best friend of eight years, Alex was, of course, exposed to her world of distracting stories frequently. Most of the time while she slumped over a cup of coffee as bitter as her regret from the night before. They were both twenty-eight and "thriving" as most millennials do in the freedom and possibility Minneapolis had to offer…Well, all the freedom that accompanied slowly chipping away at $130,000 of student loan debt with jobs that actually had nothing to do with their original dreams.

Alex and Sarah finished college together at a local private university five years earlier and found themselves wrapped up in the routines they had established. Sarah initially sought to serve unwanted puppies by becoming a freelance veterinarian. However, as one might imagine, building one's own business while single and buried under Stafford's subsidized "generosity" was less than ideal. However, Sarah wasn't the type to abandon her passion entirely in the midst of adversity. So she accepted a management position at a local animal shelter/adoption agency called "Paws" while she figured out how to build a business independently. Her job was to care for the animals and help find potential family matches, a role that Alex would come to learn showed her some of the best and worst in humanity.

They originally met senior year in their high school Spanish class. By the time the teacher had moved Alex's seat next to Sarah's, he was already in trouble for skipping class frequently to meet up and sample the "devil's lettuce" underneath hidden stairways with other senior boys who had already given up on the American dream, dismissing working for the grade as "being deceived by 'The Man,'" and "losing their individualism." Most of his friends were a part of the high school garage band Alex joined as a keyboardist. They covered a lot of basic, early 2000 punk hits; but the band was a place to feel rhythm, which he loved, however mundane at times.

The first few weeks of Spanish class, Alex didn't really pay attention to the tall girl with long, straight brown hair who was quick to answer all the teacher's group questions. He was still more interested in leaving to meet up with his "green" friends. However, as the weeks passed, Alex returned to class to find little notes written in his school agenda. The very first one was Sarah's comment on the quote he had printed and pasted on the cover from his favorite childhood TV show.

"It is important to draw wisdom from different places. If you take it from only one place, it becomes rigid and stale" (Uncle Iroh in *Avatar: The Last Airbender*).

Alex had always been a sucker for an epic hero's journey and all that the hero accomplished along the way, like Aang from the show. Of course, Alex wasn't doing his own journey any favors at the time by skipping class for what he believed then to be "essential political excursions." He thought that the green-clouded viewpoints and rantings of his band friends were more valuable than the "standardized rubbish" they were "learning" in class. Most of Alex's friends' arguments went like this: "Shit, man, Alex, if this shit were legal, I could actually sleep at night. The nights I don't smoke it, I have crazy dreams and shit. How the fuck else am I going to tackle all this anxiety?"

Alex never had an answer for any of them. He just nodded quietly and lit up beside them, content in the knowledge that he was "revolutionizing sheltered America with his enlightened ways." He didn't realize then how much he wanted to avoid responsibility. There was a pressure growing inside whose presence he was aware of but didn't understand.

When he discreetly slipped back into class after one of their "sessions," he noticed the note Sarah had written underneath his quote while he was gone…

"The only wisdom you're gaining while you're gone is how to successfully return smelling like a sack of shit."

Alex knew the note was from Sarah because he caught her smiling with satisfaction as he read the words with curiosity and apprehension plain on his face. Sarah then followed her note by tearing herself away from the novel she had been reading and sardonically pointed out that the "reefer-charged rioters weren't helping anyone by abandoning an actual education to hear themselves talk. Outside of class, there was no one to learn how to challenge them, so they could only reinforce what they already believed."

She had a point. When Alex actually stopped to think about it, their argument for legalization, at its strongest, consisted more or less of its "less harmful effects than alcohol," "It would help them focus better in school (never mind actually going to class)," and "Its 'natural' plant origins make it a healthy form of 'snacking.'"

She had heard them making the same three points at lunch often and asked Alex why he bothered wasting his time in their circling idiocy when his entertainment interests (the TV show) suggested he might actually have a brain.

"You've seen *Avatar* too?" Alex excitedly asked.

"Of course I have," she answered with a frown of disbelief, as if the idea of unawareness of the show's existence was ridiculous. "Where else would I find a hero like Zuko?"

"What do you mean, 'Hero like Zuko'?" Alex inquired, his interest piqued. "I thought everybody loved Aang? I mean, he's the Avatar."

"Of course Aang is lovable, but Zuko is easier to relate to," she replied matter-of-factly. "His sense of morality and villainous behavior is all intermingled. He feels everything at once. The pull of what he thinks he 'should' do and what he actually wants, which also happens to be what's best for everyone in the four nations."

"Best for everyone? Go on…"

Sarah smiled, happy that she had Alex's attention. "Zuko spends most of the show terrorizing the protagonist, Aang, to please his father. But you sympathize with him because of how his father has tortured him into believing he did something wrong to deserve banishment. He becomes even more easy to relate to when he chooses to crawl back to Aang, in all his shame, to ask for forgiveness and to help his heroic cause. But he also serves as a unique role model. How many of us have been brave enough to actually assign a redemptive destination to our walk of shame? Zuko does when he has to face the very people he tried to kill and eventually teams up with them to create world peace. He's best for everyone because he's seen the depths of his own cruelty and that of his culture's and found a way out of the pattern."

That conversation was the first time Alex noticed the light in Sarah's chestnut eyes as she spoke of something she cared about to another, as she shared a piece of herself. Alex had involuntarily leaned forward, almost into her as she spoke. To be fair, their desks were right next to each other, but the excitement in her words drew him in further than necessary, and he couldn't help himself as he soaked up the passion in her voice. Alex didn't speak again during that conversation after he heard her thoughts. However, the lack of response was not due to lack of interest. Rather, he was turning her words over in his mind, surprised that he had missed such an important observation in his own favorite show. She smiled adoringly as she looked at Alex for just the briefest moment, noticing that he had actually listened to what she said. She then bent back over her copy of *Jane Eyre* as her beautiful brown hair slipped off her shoulders and settled next to her cheek.

In the days after his encounter with Sarah, Alex still skipped class occasionally. But he got to the point where he couldn't help but hear Sarah's echo over the rantings of his friends ("Might actually have a brain"…"Zuko feels everything at once…"). Sarah was different. Interesting. Then, he found himself feeling as if he'd missed something important when he returned. Every time he'd leave class, he would return to another funny message written in his school agenda. Usually, the words were a twist on Sarah's favorite song lyrics telling him he'd been "hit by a smooth criminal" or some nonsense of that sort. Or that she'd stolen back the pens Alex had complained to her that Kylie Gilbert repeatedly took from him every day in first period science and claimed as her own. One day, when he returned, Sarah softly drew back a stray piece of his black, wavy hair that often curled in front of his ears and tucked one of the lost pens snuggly between his ear and face.

"There, Alex," she said, smiling, "now you're too intellectual to steal from."

At that moment, Alex concluded that his bandmates' conversations certainly dragged him around in circles and his friends weren't actually helping anyone, including themselves, by getting high under the staircase. He eventually stopped skipping class altogether and took a much needed break from getting high.

Sarah pinned Alex down to the class with her laugh and unapologetic willingness to say and do what everyone else was afraid to. Even if that fear was simply showing others that they were paying attention. She was never afraid to give hers if the cause was worthy. Alex couldn't miss a moment with Sarah, whether it was sharing her passionate ideas or telling the immature boys at school about themselves. For example, she had no problem telling Joe Robert, the boy in the desk clump behind them, that if he pulled her hair by "sneakily" slipping his tattered textbook on top of it one more time, so the hair would pull if she sat forward, she'd read the "love note" he had written inside of it to Brittany Fishbeck, the girl who sat next to him, tapping his shoulder constantly asking if he was going to basketball practice that day (she wanted to watch him). The "note" was of course made up, but the threat worked.

Alex had been in class consistently several weeks in a row. Sarah was the kind of brave he wanted to stick around. She was passionate. But she always saw others before she spoke, at least when it mattered, which is why she was sometimes second to share her voice aloud in class as she talked about the selflessness and bravery of Eva Peron or volunteered to speak aloud the recipe for empanadas solely in Spanish. Alex quietly observed her glancing around the room, searching with the hopeful eyes to see if anyone else wanted to speak first. If they did, she patiently waited and listened, filtering through her consideration of their thoughts. If they didn't volunteer to answer, she boldly raised her hand.

Sarah's copy of *Jane Eyre* wasn't the only clue that she loved to read. Her love of literature was born out of her love for listening. Sarah understood the beauty of how someone's story could change the world, and she listened to the characters' voices as she read. There were so many parts of the world that had needed saving in different time periods. Sarah knew that people could learn how to save their own world by talking about the heroes who had done it before, even if they were fictional. She knew that Jane Eyre's humble honesty and Evita's charisma were the kinds of qualities all people needed to find in themselves to make a real, positive difference.

Slowly, Alex started to do more than simply listen to Sarah. He began sharing his own voice. He also started reading *Jane Eyre* on his own and soon realized why Sarah loved the story so much. Alex became Sarah's best friend (in her mind, she was nervous at first, to ask if he felt the same companionship) the moment he shared his love for Jane's boldness and bravery: "I don't think, sir, you have a right to command me, merely because you are older than I, or because you have seen more of the world than I have; your claim to superiority depends on the use you have made of your time and experience." He could relate to those words more than most. Alex told Sarah that he understood all too well that anyone, of any age, is subject to foolish choices if they allow themselves to be owned by them no matter how old they were. Sarah knew there was more to Alex's inference, and she wanted to take the time to get to know him.

Alex had been raised by his Grandma Sandy after his parents left when he was a baby and decided to "make it" as croupiers in Vegas. His grandmother didn't speak of them often after they left, but as far as he knew, the most they accomplished was becoming addicts at the very tables they tried to deal in. Alex referenced the *Jane Eyre* quote to Sarah one day at the end of Spanish class and told her that he believed "everyone could be stupid or make mistakes sometimes, but choosing to grow from destruction and chaos rather than age into their patterns is what truly separated those worth listening to or not." As he spoke, he quietly thought about how his parents ran from responsibility and how he had followed their pattern of running in high school. He was determined to have a different story, to be there for the people he cared about. Sarah followed Alex's thoughts with the question, "Why aren't we friends? We love Spanish, laugh about all the same stupid things, find ourselves frustrated with the same people, and well, we've figured out how to listen to each other. I mean, we should be friends right? You know, the kind that actually hang out after class?"

Alex agreed. They should hang out more. Since their senior year was coming to a close, most of their hanging out consisted of after-school meetups at Alex's house where they continued to discuss novels or the symbolism in *Avatar: The Last Airbender* and similar shows of the fantasy genre. Sometimes, they'd laugh over their mutual annoyances of the hair-pulling textbook boys or the feeling that they were both just itching to move on from high school and see what else was out there.

Sarah inspired Alex's love for reading though he grew to make such love his own. He realized how reading could help him with his musical inspiration and love for writing lyrics. The more words he saw crafted by artists, the more he learned to make words his own. He especially cherished growing with Sarah and getting ideas from her through their conversations, and the discussions deepened and continued into college. In the fall after senior year, Alex followed Sarah to a local Christian suburban university where they took a few philosophy courses together. Although Sarah was not necessarily a Christian, she chose a small Christian college hoping that she might experience a more discussion-based approach to learning and build stronger relationships with the professors because of the smaller class sizes.

After class, at least a couple times a week, they would plant themselves in two puffy red leather chairs outside their English professor's office and debate the significance of Dostoevsky's influence as an author or whether or not evangelical theology was more of a cult than anything else. Sarah always mulled what she learned over deeply. She let Dostoevsky's words, as well as those of other authors, flow through her and challenge her brain, and she hated when others couldn't do the same. Sarah also found some of the same annoyances with the immature boys in college as she found in high school... Only this time, they had money and the ability to brag about their admittance into college. Sometimes when Sarah and Alex talked, she was angry at the boys in class who would challenge the professor because the professor's educated assertions didn't align with theology taught in their churches or what their fathers, as heads of the households, had raised them to believe.

Still, Sarah gently tried to draw her classmates out of themselves. When Darin, a homegrown, Midwestern, follower of Jesus, business major tried to explain to the anthropology professor that hominids "couldn't have existed because creationism doesn't allow for imperfection, God doesn't make mistakes and all beings are created for a specific purpose."

Sarah's hand immediately shot up, and she responded: "Maybe there was or is a perfect design somewhere. But that doesn't change the fact that the world evolves, for better or for worse. Don't you think that the free will of other creative beings might have influenced how the earth and its inhabitants adapted over time? What about all of the archeological evidence that has surfaced or the necessity of adaptation to survive this world?"

"That doesn't prove anything. Scientists can lie or tamper with their findings just to make a name for themselves. Suggesting that the world was influenced by anything but a perfect creator is an insult to that creator's image," Darin snapped at her in a condescending manner and turned his back toward her again, signaling that the discussion was over whether Sarah wanted it to be or not. Alex watched her slowly draw in a deep breath as she faced the front of the room again. The professor also took a deep breath, thanked everyone for their input, and went on with her lecture. Only Alex caught the disappointment resting in Sarah's eyes.

Despite the disappointment Sarah felt from her peers, she loved her professors, and her love for reading grew. Writers gave her hope where her peers (excluding Alex) failed her. She let the voices of the characters she read about slip into her veins and surface through her soul. She did her best to continue to open up and listen to others, never giving up on the significance of their stories or interests. She even tried to understand why some of the boys she attended class with clung so tightly to evangelical Christian theology and the teachings of their churches. She concluded that their misguided loyalty was most likely about power and the fear of letting go of stories they were told as children. Ultimately, though they would never admit it, as young, white, rich men, the church gave them power. They had power as "heads of households" in their families and with the assurance that "God's will" would prosper them through the American dream. However, Sarah held onto the more open-minded friends that she and Alex would occasionally meet in a biology or psychology class. Sometimes, even their jokes changed the way she saw the world. In fact, a close friend of Alex and Sarah's had a significant influence on what led Sarah to a vegetarian lifestyle and, eventually, a career serving animals.

The comment was made by a quirky college friend of Alex and Sarah's named Sammy. He occasionally joined them for their puffy lounge chair discussions. He didn't care for the critical and analytical nature of their conversations but appreciated the insight Alex and Sarah brought to the table. Sammy also enjoyed the smiles he saw on their faces when he entertained them with jokes about everyday people with everyday lives and how mundane and ridiculous their routines seemed at times. One day, after lunch, Alex, Sarah, and Sammy were comparing the buffet lines in the dining hall to farm animal feeding troughs when the subject of hot dogs surfaced. Sammy flipped back his fiery red hair and flashed a cocky smile at Sarah as he said, "Well, you know how they make those right?" ("Those" meaning the hot dogs.) Sarah's smile instantly faded as she stopped to consider where he was going with the question,

"How?" She cocked an eyebrow.

"Well," he said impishly, "they take all the nastiest, discarded parts of the pig, or maybe cow, who really knows? Then stick 'em in a tube and mass produce…" He made a clamping motion with his hands as he spoke.

Sarah's mouth dropped, horrified. It appeared that her nineteen-year-old mind had never stopped to consider the manufacturing process of America's fondest food staple.

"That's disgusting" was all she could muster as she continued to stare at Sammy in her painfully enlightened state. Sammy chuckled in satisfaction at how he had ruffled her feathers then shrugged and moved onto the more pressing topic of his football game later that day.

It's doubtful that Sammy would even remember the hot dog conversation if someone asked him later on. But Sarah not only remembered his words, she allowed the consideration to sink inside her, settle in her gut, and change her appetite. It's unclear whether it was the abhorring nature of eating combination meat parts that had been smooshed and gooshed together inside a tube or the undignified treatment of the animals who originally owned them, but Sarah never ate another scrap of meat from that day on. It wasn't the story itself or the narrator that changed her, even Sammy continued to devour hot dogs occasionally at lunch. Rather, the change resulted from how Sarah stomached his words and altered her choices. Her mind was beautiful and exhausted.

One afternoon, she rested her foot on Alex's lounge chair as she shared the second building block of her love and respect for animals. Her epitome resulted from a passage she had read in English lit from Melville's *Moby-Dick*, "Doubtless one leading reason why the world declines honoring us whalemen, is this: they think that, at best, our vocation amounts to a butchering sort of business; and that when actively engaged therein, we are surrounded by all manner of defilements. Butchers we are, that is true. But butchers, also, and butchers of the bloodiest badge have been all Martial Commanders whom the world invariably delights to honour."

"Alex," she said frustratedly as she flipped a piece of her hair back from her eyes and rocked the foot she had perched on his chair, "too long have people taken advantage of something or someone weaker than them. They take what they need then abandon the creature to its demolished fate, dead or alive. We really are all butchers, just like Melville said. Chopping beauty and life up and taking the small, dehydrated pieces that serve us. I want to make everything better." Alex raised his eyebrow at her; sometimes Sarah took on too much and had unrealistic expectations for herself.

Sarah knew what he meant by the eyebrow and continued hurriedly, "Well, you know what I mean. Everything, yes, but maybe I just start with our slice of the world here in the Midwest. People, the earth…animals. You know, revive the core of the forgotten things, heal some of the destruction? I'm switching to an animal science major." (She had been an English major before.)

Melville's take on the destructive nature of humanity combined with her disgust with consuming dead and mutilated creatures sparked Sarah's love for caring for animals. She worked at Paws throughout college to get some hands-on experience. Her original goal was to start her own veterinary clinic. However, the start-up cost of the business alone was, on average, $1,000,000, not exactly affordable for a college graduate making $12 an hour with and the obligation of $450 a month in student loan payments. However, her commitment to good causes is what drove her to finish her animal science degree despite her plans not playing out as she had anticipated. After graduating, she accepted an assistant manager position at Paws, which at least afforded her a living wage. For now, the "good cause" of caring for the abused and discarded creatures of the world and matching them with caregivers who were ready to write the animals a new story was enough to help Sarah feel that she was serving the world for the better in some way. She was able to live inside the stories of the animals and people who came through the shelter and learn from them.

Alex graduated with a general music degree. His original plan was to pursue a master's in music theory and composition at Thornton School of Music in California. He loved to create and compose and figured a school in California might actually equip him to "make it" as an artist. Unfortunately, his grandmother, Sandy, the one who had raised him, started the slow onset of dementia during his time in college. Every holiday that he drove home to stay for a few days, she appeared more confused. There were even a few times she thought he was his father and greeted him with, "Jerry, you and that girl need to stop those silly games and come see your boy. He's old enough to remember you." Disappointment furrowed in Sandy's brow, and Alex tried to set aside the sting of remembering his father's shortcomings. He did his best to gently remind her who he was. During the first year of her diagnosis, she remembered him about 80 percent of the time. However, as the second year went on, it became clear that she needed more help managing her affairs and taking care of herself.

While Alex was in high school, he worked as a barback at the Crooked Picture, the local suburban pub owned by his grandmother. She named it in honor of the memory of her favorite picture of her late husband, Jim, Alex's grandfather. The business helped support

Alex throughout his entire childhood. After graduating college, Sandy was a few years into her diagnosis, and Alex realized he was worried about her safety. Her memory was slipping enough that he wasn't confident that she would remember to turn off her stove or shut and lock her front doors. He wanted to honor Sandy by running her business, but that meant he couldn't care for her 24-7 and needed to admit her to assisted-living care.

Alex kept the name of the bar the same out of respect for his grandma though a part of the title seemed to fit him too. He wasn't quite sure why. Up until a few months into Sandy's diagnosis, she was still able to direct the managers and remain actively involved in day-to-day operations. He helped her sign the rights over to him and began spending most of his postgraduate time there once Sandy was settled into her assisted-living home. The way Alex saw the situation, Sandy sacrificed years that should've been spent in retirement to raise and support him; it was only right that he kept her business going. Remaining in the Midwest and running Grandma's business allowed Alex to feel as if he was "paying her back" for raising him. He also felt like he wasn't abandoning her because of the weekly visits he made to see Sandy at the facility. However, he couldn't help but feel the emptiness tied to putting his composition dreams on hold.

He had learned the keyboard by ear in high school, practiced with his garage band friends, and refined his skills in college. He occasionally found time to play at the bar with some of the local performers he hired for live music nights (Thursdays and Fridays) or in his limited spare time. However, playing on live nights wasn't quite the same as the vulnerability that comes with fully devoting oneself to the act of creating. As a young business owner, Alex naturally found it difficult to find space to create music while also learning to run and manage his business successfully. The closest he came to feeling the joy and passion of creating and sharing his music was when he catered to the drunken whims of a few regulars by occasionally playing a couple of originals he had written in college on the bar piano.

Chapter 2

As the years passed, Alex and Sarah had both settled into lives that were not what they had originally dreamed. They escaped the disappointing (though neither of them were able to admit they were disappointed with their circumstances) nature of their lot as obligated, debt-ridden millennials by meeting up at least once a week at Eric's Bean Shop, a tiny café, for coffee or at Alex's bar if he had too much work to do.

Philosophy wasn't the core of their conversations. Their joy was a simple connection to each other; neither was ever bored with what the other had to say. Sarah had felt Alex's ability to listen and grow, regardless of how challenging some of her statements might be. She had seen that he accepted her in the depth of her disappointment in college and had no fear of pulling him into her frustration with the worn trail left in her heart by lackluster lovers (she had dated a few in and after college). As much as she loved her books and her job, she longed for companionship and a partner to share her experiences with. Unfortunately, she was continuously disappointed, and dating frustrations soon started to grip her conversations with Alex.

Sarah didn't start dating with low expectations, rather, they slowly developed over time. She gave the men she met in college a fair shot at something real and expected the best out of them despite seeing in class how desolate the dating pool was. Occasionally, someone with a seductive or adventurous story would attract her notice.

Sarah never had a problem finding some sort of love interest, and Alex knew why. Men were intimidated by Sarah, but they were also drawn to the light in her eyes. They loved the warmth of her intellectual fire. She was real. Beautiful. Bold. Everything inside their own soul they were so desperate to know but too afraid to seek.

The end results were either swallowing her up too quickly and getting burned or dousing her flame in one fell swoop of frailty shown through an arrogant comment and running. It was the worst sort of companionship. Sarah saw the best in them and drew it out, tried to help them grow even more, and she loved them for who they were, even if she knew they could never be what she needed. They loved how she listened, how she glowed as they spoke because she truly appreciated all that they were. It didn't matter if they revealed a developed porn addiction that started young and eventually shaped them into the evangelical prophets they were in the present, or their failed math class that led them to the distinguished coding talent that was going to revolutionize the future of technology. Sarah listened to all their vain voices and encouraged them by validating their dreams.

But they couldn't do the same for her. They didn't listen. They wouldn't learn about that which fueled her passion. Alex was the only one she could really talk to about the books she loved to read so much from her college courses or what she learned at the shelter from the animals and families. Such stories were "beneath them." They didn't see the value in the everyday relationships that shape culture and build the world. Sarah always had more to learn. But her lovers never kept up with her. She soon grew tired of disappointment and started to get to know loneliness. She had expected more because she thought that men who had pursued an education would actually match her drive for using that education to better the world. Since Sarah was often disappointed, she spent many of her nights since college pretending she wasn't disappointed with men she knew were so delusional in their comprehension of the world. She never expected anything great out of them, so she never could be truly disappointed again.

Such men never knew all of Sarah like Alex did, just the pieces she decided to show them. Most of the true vulnerability she tried out only ended up causing her pain. When one becomes vulnerable and shares truth and honesty, feeling the sting of such honesty landing on a sheltered, arrogantly insecure recipient, runs deep and can only be endured for so long. Most often, Sarah chose a reflection of the type of woman they were looking for, which was easy for Sarah to figure out because of her talent for listening. Alex hated seeing her so fractured. He knew that, underneath, she still wanted more. She longed for true attraction and companionship, but she silenced and numbed that part of herself, believing she'd never find it.

Still, Sarah's love in pieces was better than everything they were. Devoting just a fraction of her soul during a forty-five-minute conversation was better than the hours they spent living as if all the world was a mirror. They only ever saw themselves, and their stories were boring, petty, and meaningful only to themselves. Sarah's very existence became a lie because she was so swept up in the dating stories she created. But even in her lies, she was more beautiful and open than their superficial, wounded ways could appreciate or even comprehend. In the midst of dating obstacles, Sarah still tried to pursue what she loved—reading, honest conversations with Alex, and pouring all of her heart and passion into the animals she worked with. She was passionate about finding them a kind home or thoughtfully coaching the other shelter employees on family interactions. She never lost herself completely; she just existed in fragments.

Chapter 3

When Alex and Sarah connected at Eric's, Sarah often spilled her secrets with regret. Many of them included the shame she felt after a night of too much wine and, consequently, too much truth sent via text to a guy she had slept with once or bided her time alongside for a few weeks. The stories she created could only be maintained for so long before some truth would spill out thanks to lowered inhibitions. Sarah always felt so ashamed after burdening the recipient with her true feelings and revealing pieces of her heart she never would have otherwise. It was a strange dichotomy because she knew she didn't really care about the men, yet she couldn't help but hope that they might understand her. If the guy was someone she was truly mildly interested in, the messages usually consisted of her frustration with their unwillingness to match her emotional maturity… An irony only if you ignore the fact that she gave them a go at an intellectual conversation while sober first.

Most of the time, though, Sarah was simply biding her time with lovers she didn't truly care for. Those drunken texts were rare, usually only when she felt something and was too tired to put her guard up high enough to listen and think first. Or when she met someone who reflected even an inch of the empathy she constantly poured out to others, even in her disappointed state. For all the time Sarah wasted with men who weren't at her level, she at least lent them a listening ear and accepted them for exactly what they were. She listened to all their egotistical stories and complaints about being "stuck" in a dead-end job that they had every resource to overcome. The only thing stopping them was their refusal to try something "hard" or unknown to try and move themselves out of whatever rut they believed they were "trapped" in. But regardless of the day's conversations, the nights always ended the same with her tangled in their arms, feeding their egos before Ubering back to her apartment shortly after. Sometimes, she would decide to date her distraction and feed the story for a few weeks to a few months, or drunken truth would get to her and she'd send a message upon arriving home while still influenced. Her defeated, pale face fell in her hands and her lovely light brown hair would cascade around her as she shared with Alex what remained of her most embarrassing memories from the night before.

"Ugh. So much wasted time. Who does that? I thought we were supposed to be over drunk texting after age twenty—no, fuck it, eighteen. I don't even know why I told him how stupid I thought he was and how beautiful at the same time. I mean, I didn't tell him I was still drunk but he could probably guess. The worst part is that I knew better. Even in my less-than-ideal mental state, I knew better. I feel like such an idiot, and I definitely regret sending him a few suggestive pictures."

Alex nodded and tried to show understanding though it was hard for him to hear Sarah's voice. He could tell that she was starting to believe that there was something wrong with her though the problem was clearly with her dates. He knew she had a moment of weakness where she let her longing for more slip through and actually shared her frustration with the guy she had been seeing over the lack of communication on his end for making plans or finally pointing out that the "memes" he sent her were actually subtly racist and not funny at all. Her words to Alex were conflicted, just as she was. She deeply wanted an honest connection with an honest, brave person and couldn't burn that part of herself out, no matter how much she distracted herself. She accepted that her honesty with this particular lover was enough to drive him away and still needed some sort of assurance that her time with him wasn't wasted.

Even in the moments where Sarah felt frustrated and ashamed, she was so beautiful to Alex. Her hands slowly slipped away from her chestnut eyes; and she brushed back her hair, so soft and light, as she stared at Alex in all her honesty, feeling relieved that he had absorbed it. Those chestnut eyes were always tired and maybe even worn, but they had a light behind them that never burned out, no matter how much of her lovers' darkness she embraced. It was the light that exposed all of their secrets but also offered them a shadow to rest in as she'd slowly close her eyes and accept whatever bad sex or joke they believed was a gift for her.

Although Alex had always seen the light in Sarah's eyes, he didn't think Sarah knew the light was there. Most of the time, she was too exhausted from spinning in her stories. "Anyway," she said as she shook her head and pinned up her smile and asked Alex about his day. Before he shared with her, he thought about how Sarah's shame and regret was likely the painful result of knowing herself too deeply. Sarah had been forced through not one, two, or three but many rabbit holes and surfaced on the other side scarred a little, but whole and bright. And she knew herself the better for it. All the men she had met and slept with were too afraid to meet her on the other side. So her consolation prize was allowing them to share their secrets. She let them whisper in her ear, and she whispered back exactly what they wanted to hear. And since Sarah was someone who listened and saw first, she always knew what it was they wanted to hear.

Chapter 4

Alex was the one part of Sarah's life that felt honest, and she leaned into her time with him more than she realized. In addition to their occasional lunches, she often hung out at his bar on Friday nights. On one particular Friday night, she was hoping to relax and talk with Alex in the little moments she could find with him while he rushed around working. Unfortunately, she was grieving the loss of a particularly loyal golden retriever from the shelter named Barry. He was dropped off after his owner passed from old age and had no close family members to care for him after she passed. Barry was a sweet animal but he was old too, and people didn't want to adopt him if they were going to lose him shortly after, so he became Sarah's partner at the shelter. She didn't even keep him caged (when he was away from potential adoptive families). Rather, she let him wander by her side while she did paperwork or checked up on the other animals.

At the bar, Sarah was wearing one of her black, lacy tank tops. Sarah always dressed up when she felt sad. Winter was just beginning to thaw into spring, and she was certainly not dressed for the weather. However, she told Alex that her outfit made her feel like she was "rebelling against the cold." If the temperature could drop and rise as slowly as it pleased, she was going to wear what she wanted. In her grief, she wanted to feel beautiful...though, of course, she always was regardless of what she wore, at least that's what Alex thought as she shared her feelings with him at his bar.

"God, he was the best, Alex," she said, defeated, as she wiped one tiny tear from the corner of her eye. "I mean, I always knew I wasn't going to have much time with him. Hell, he was already eleven when they dropped him off at the shelter. But still, time went by too fast... Routine got the best of me. I was so caught up in the expectation that he'd always be there that I forgot that losing him was even a possibility." She pushed her hair back over her shoulder and took a long sip of her gin and tonic. "Every morning, I let him out first, and I talked with him about the day ahead so he could brace himself for it with me…shots for the particularly sassy Pomeranian, plans for proactively dealing with families with toddlers who unforgivingly tugged the ears of the beagle, making sure the beagle didn't bite the toddlers in return, though they deserved it," she smirked briefly as she added that last detail. "He was always there, planning the day with me. And every evening, I finished all my paperwork with his chin on my leg. Not until today when I swatted the air did I realize the habit I had gotten into of simultaneously petting his sweet head while I worked. Now there's just an empty space beneath my desk. He was such a good dog."

Alex placed the pencil he used to keep track of bar stock behind his ear and leaned over the bar toward her. "I'm sorry, Sarah. I know how much you loved him. It really did feel like he was a staple at the shelter. Is there anything I can do?"

She looked up at Alex sadly but forced a smile as she held up her empty glass. "Just keep 'em coming. I just want to forget about it for a little while."

Alex nodded, smiled, squeezed her shoulder, then stepped away a few feet and reached under the bar for the gin. However, he was still within earshot when the blue-eyed man with the flat cap whom Alex vaguely recognized and had just served a Jack and Coke turned toward her.

"Sarah Pierce?" He raised his eyebrows as he stared and spoke expectantly and hopefully.

She dropped her glass after swallowing the particularly large gulp of gin and responded, seeming annoyed that he had interrupted the countless thoughts racing through her grieving mind and replied, "I might be, but I am more curious about who you think you are."

Alex peeked over his shoulder as he twisted the bottle top off while the blue-eyed "stranger" presented a half-cocked smile and chuckled slightly, as if he knew and expected her fearlessness and forward comments. He had two charming wrinkles around the sides of his mouth that revealed themselves when he laughed and confidently replied, "Jesse Marsh. Don't you remember me? We went to high school together. I sat in front of you in eleventh grade algebra."

She squinted at him, slowly finding some recognition. "Didn't you used to wear glasses? Yeah, I think I remember you, but you had glasses."

At that point, Alex turned back to the bar to face them and began mixing Sarah another drink. Jesse smiled at Sarah fully now, the curves of his mouth full of charm. "Yes! Got contacts since but remember, I hung out with the dudes who called themselves 'The Backwards Boys.' We used to think we were cool because we stood up to the popular jocks and dance team members. Nothing major, just passive aggressively stealing their lunch table. Or passing them the wrong assignment in math and convincing them that it was the daily work we were supposed to do." He laughed in response to his own words, relishing the memories of himself.

Alex saw on her face that she clearly didn't remember that bit, but he knew she'd humor him. "Yeah, yeah, okay, I think I remember...You guys were...funny...Anyway, it's dark in here. How did you even recognize me?"

He scooted his stool closer to her and rested his arm on the bar. Then he rolled up the sleeves of his khaki jacket, revealing a light blue and black tattoo of flames on his forearm and smiled. "Because, you were a hot nerd...rare to come by. You were beautiful and honest, someone most people were too intimidated to be near...Anyway, that's the past I guess, though some things seem to spill into the present." He looked at her and smiled as he sipped his drink. "What are you up to nowadays?"

She smiled and leaned closer to him. "I'm an assistant manager down at Paws, you know, the shelter? We take in abandoned or surrendered dogs and care for them with the ultimate goal of finding them a safe forever home...Unfortunately, safe and stable homes are way too few and far between. What about you?"

He leaned in closer to her. "You know, Sarah, you would do something like save all the world's sad, mistreated puppies. You were always going on in math about the economics of money-hungry corporations. Good for you, that's good work. The world needs more of it."

Alex slid Sarah her drink. He wanted to pull her away and back into their own conversation. He remembered Jesse Marsh too, and based on that memory, he knew he was the last person Sarah needed right now. Alex remembered Jesse as the dipshit in his English class who always interrupted the teacher, thinking he had something really profound to say. The clearest memory he had of him was when he obnoxiously raised his hand during a discussion about Fitzgerald's *The Great Gatsby*, tossed his shaggy, skater-boy hair out of his eyes, and preached, "Myrtle is the absolute representation of human instinct. Listen, she's unfiltered, uncensored desire. You know, the pursuit of all those who've fallen victim to the rhythm and routine of capitalism?" He smiled smugly after he spoke, as if he was proud of himself for gifting the world with his "revolutionary" thoughts… Though it was some of the most obvious symbolism in the story.

Alex doubted Jesse had changed much since high school. But just as he was about to rescue Sarah, one of his regulars, a middle-aged, scruffy but kind trucker named Pete walked in and plopped himself down on the stool to the other side of Sarah. "Hey Alex!" he greeted. "Been a long one today. How 'bout some Lagavulin?"

Alex was frustrated but willing to oblige. He reluctantly slid Sarah her gin and tonic as she continued to lean expectantly toward Jesse, waiting to hear his answer to her question as Alex turned back to the bar. Although he went through the motions of fixing Pete's drink, his attention was still unobviously focused on Sarah's conversation with Jesse.

Jesse sipped his whiskey, tipped back his flat cap, and responded casually, "Oh, I'm a guide at Freeman's Art Institute a little ways north of the Cities. You know that one? Kind of near the river?" Sarah nodded. "Yeah, yeah," Jesse continued, "I do class tours and private, scheduled guides of the impressionist section. You know, paintings? Been doing that for about two years. It works for now, but I'd love to travel to France and study in the Ecole du Louvre program but work just doesn't give me the time…someday."

"Freeman's though? That place is amazing!" Sarah beamed and sat up straighter as the passion grew in her voice. "We had to do a few tours there for my college humanities class, but I think that was probably before you worked there. I loved the impressionist section. Sisley was my favorite. So many people go out into nature to try to find themselves, similar to transcendentalism." Jesse smiled as she spoke. "What most artists miss about his work though is that how people see nature depends entirely on the subjects circling our minds. I especially loved Sisley's *Fog, Voisins* painting. To one person, fog could represent peace and solitude by providing the hidden shelter they need to escape from the overwhelming forces of the world. To another, fog could appear eerie and menacing if they were afraid of facing something underneath themselves." Her eyes glittered as she spoke of the analytical pieces she loved.

Jesse beamed at Sarah. "Well goddamn. How do you remember something like that so clearly with your head full of barking dogs all day?"

Alex rolled his eyes, unbeknownst to the pair, as Sarah smiled. "I read a lot. I see paintings through the same eyes that I see books. I also love that you want to study in France someday. Do you think you would ever leave Freeman's and just go for it?" she asked hopefully.

By now, Alex had served Pete his Lagavulin and was pretending to listen to a story as Jesse smiled back at Sarah and waved him over for another drink. "Another round for me, and I'll get hers too." He smiled at Sarah, and Alex was deeply annoyed. It was clear in Jesse's expression that he would probably never make it to France; the dream was a show. A willingness to actually risk the unknown is a rare quality. However, he wasn't going to relinquish an opportunity to impress Sarah in the meantime,

"Maybe, but while I'm still here with you on the same seaside, Sarah, I'd be happy to give you a private tour sometime. Might not hurt to revisit some of the pieces on a more personal level. Impressionism is all about instinct, what you feel in the moment. Sounds like you remember *Fog* pretty well, but your perception might've changed by now. See, that's the whole goal of the method. Perception changes all the time. It's why the colors and brushstrokes are so fluid. The artists saw moments as they moved. Look around at *The Crooked Picture* for example: dark except for the few red and blue lights that hit the dance floor, the small stage and the dull, yellow lights that highlight the bar.

The goal isn't to light the objects themselves but to give the patrons the impression of being seen in colors that highlight their beauty in the dark. The light at the bar is just bright enough to bounce off your eyes. Because of the light, I can see them. But my impression is of you and the way you light up when you speak of something you care about. And what I feel at this moment is the instinct to buy you another G and T in hopes that I've made enough of an impression on you to activate your instincts of wanting to dance with me."

Alex could see even in the dark that Sarah was flattered. She smiled and tipped her head down then back up as she flipped her hair in the flirtatious way only she knew how. Jesse remembered her. And that was enough. He was an artist, or at least pretended to be one while analyzing the works of actual artists. But he had succeeded in showing Sarah that he had seen something, someone outside of himself. He called her a "hot nerd." And the sad truth was, Jesse's boldness and strange honesty was more alluring and charming to Sarah than all the half-hearted attempts of academics to win her over. They weren't brave or bold enough. Jesse was never brave. Alex saw him for the coward he was from the start. But he was bold. And although Sarah was smart enough to recognize that he was missing some of the bravery and adventurous spirit she craved, she began to love him for the honesty he inspired.

The live musicians wrapped up their set before the bar closed, so Alex filled the late-night space with a DJ. By the time the DJ played "Wave" by Meghan Trainor, both Sarah and Jesse were three drinks deep, and he had convinced her to dance with him…Meghan started to sing, "I want what I can't have, still holding onto hope, drowning in my tears. This love's a sinking boat." Jesse met the light in her eyes with his own icy blue ones as he slowly and surely smiled, wrapping his fingers inside hers and steadily led her to the dance floor. Meghan continued to sing, "Take me like a wave, pull me back and forth, crash into my arms, tell me I am yours…," as he lifted her arm with all the grace of a storybook prince and twirled her around and into him. Then, he draped her arms over him and rested them on his shoulder as he gently slid his hands down her waist and rested them on her hips. He pulled her into him softly, and she pressed up against him, letting herself sink into his embrace and the melody of "Wave."

The rhythm quickly changed from slow and steady to rapid, jumping notes and their hips began to bounce and pop. "Headed to surface I'll keep you afloat, I'll keep you safe, babe. Right in the middle of heaven and hell, this world was made for us. Don't blame you at all. It was all my fault, I swear that I won't do the shit that I did before…" They swayed their hips back and forth together along with the bouncing rhythm of "Wave." The beat slowed again, and as she sang of "Waves," they swayed together slowly and fully in sync. When the rhythm bounced, they bounced off each other's beats until he lifted her right leg and wrapped it around himself as he pulled her in closer and spun her around. "I just wanna push it left, 'cause I miss the way you're dancing on me, yeah, let me pull you back in…" He slowly released her leg and spun her around so she could back into him. As she rested herself against him, he wrapped his arms around her and slowly rocked her hips to the left and right. "Once my hands have reached the shore, you pull me back in. And I shouldn't beg for more, but I don't want it to end. Just take me like a wave…wave…wave…"

As the song slowly came to a close, he brushed her soft hair off her neck and shoulder with his fingers and softly gave her one single but intentional kiss. Alex watched as Sarah melted into him as his lips brushed her beautiful bare, soft skin. The song ended and he lifted his lips, twirled her back around, and hugged her tightly. They both laughed with the sheer pleasure of each other's company.

"Well, that was some *Dirty Dancing* shit, huh?" Pete commented as he pulled his wide brown eyes away from the dance floor and back to Alex. As a matter of fact, Pete and Alex weren't the only ones who were drawn into the melody of Jesse and Sarah's connection. The entire dance floor had made a circle around them, not daring to come within two feet of their performance. The other patrons were captivated by them. Some still tried to dance but all couldn't help but stare, even after the song ended. Not until "Yeah" by Usher blasted through the speakers and inevitably broke the trance were enough eyes turned away so Jesse and Sarah could discreetly slip out the back door of the bar with Jesse's arm wrapped tightly around Sarah's waist.

"I don't know, Pete," Alex answered as the door slammed shut behind Jesse. "Seems more alcohol-fueled than artistically inspired." Alex rolled his eyes and cracked open a few IPAs for the couple who had taken Jesse and Sarah's place at the bar.

Pete narrowed his eyes at Alex and sighed. "Come on, Alex. She was beautiful out there, and he ate all of her up with his charm. Everyone noticed how they enchanted each other. You're as criss-crossed as all that navy-and-green flannel you wear. I know you love that girl. I see it every Friday when she comes in here. You're captivated by every piece of her. Doesn't matter if she's telling some sad puppy story, making a dumb sarcastic joke, or melting over those books of hers, you love every word that drops from her lips. I see you lean into her as if you need her words to stand. That dorky, half smile of yours never goes away when you're around her. Why the hell haven't you just asked her out?"

Alex grabbed the refill of seltzers from the barback, plopped the box down harder than necessary, and shrugged at him. "It's not like that with me and Sarah. She's known me for years. Every guy she's ever dated was boring, disappointing, and brief. No one's ever been this close to her for this long. She trusts me enough to stay in my life. If I go chasing after her like one of those doe-eyed, charmed idiots, she'll think I'm only interested in the secrets that lie in her pants. We're about more than that. We talk."

Pete raised his bushy eyebrows and wrinkled his mouth, clearly skeptical. "You're an idiot. I been coming here for ten years, and I've never seen you take a second look at any of the lovelies that frequent this place. What I have seen is many of them writing their phone numbers on napkins that you toss out with the leftover cherry stems from their fruity drinks. You couldn't care less about their digits because you're too concerned with which douchebag is leaving with Sarah. 'Talk.' Yeah, sure you guys talk, you talk so much you might as well be making love to each other's words. What do you think love is, son? Love is that connection that you have. It's why she talks to you so much. Sarah's the type of woman who lives her soul through her words. I've talked to her too. And with all the secrets and passions she shares with you, you might as well announce your engagement tomorrow."

Alex finished unpacking the drinks and broke down the cardboard box. "Pete, Sarah sees me as a friend. She loves talking with me, sure, but she doesn't feel anything more. And anyway, I don't have any time to have more than a casual lunch with her here and there. I gotta visit Grandma on weekends, manage all her finances, and keep this place running. People can get a drink anywhere. I gotta make sure they find something here that keeps them coming back, something like home or themselves. Comfort. Managing that kind of business doesn't just happen."

Pete shook his head in frustration and tossed back the last of his whiskey. "Yeah, and what about your music? You still writing songs on that piano you got at home?"

Alex wiped the bar down and shook his head in reply. "Nah, not often. I'm here too many nights and exhausted by the time I get home. Playing occasionally with the musicians here keeps the notes fresh enough in my mind."

A sad smile crossed Pete's face. "Yeah, you really do light up live night with that voice of yours. But, someday, you should consider going back to creating originals. I remember you scribbling lyrics down on napkins and box flaps back when your grandma ran this place. It's like your music was alive in you all the time and always had something to say. You know I listen to the radio all the time out on the road. Half the shit only makes it on there because the little pricks that 'sing' it have money and connections. Pop culture needs you, Alex. They need an artist who actually gives a shit about writing something genuine."

Alex's brow furrowed a little, and he went quiet for a moment, considering Pete's words before shaking them off and returning to his work. Pete paid his tab, slapped his cap back on, and stood up. "Well, as usual, thanks for makin' my Friday a little less lonely. I need to get in and chat with people from my hometown. Too much road and too many strangers. Don't stay here too late. You know Sarah will want to be wanting to catch up with you tomorrow morning. I doubt her night with Dousch Charming is going as well as she hopes."

Alex chuckled, hiding the fact that he hoped Pete was right. "Night, Pete. See you next Friday."

Pete might have been right about Sarah and about Alex's music. But Alex didn't care. He was more comfortable with the security of knowing she'd at least stay in his life if he remained her best friend and nothing more. If Alex tried anything else, he feared she might slip away at the thought of hurting his feelings. Alex knew Sarah cared about him more than anyone else. She cared enough to break away if she thought she might be leading him on. And Alex believed that he owed more of his loyalty, time, and energy to his grandma and the business that supported him through college than the flimsy dreams of becoming an actual composer.

Chapter 5

Alex and Sarah met for lunch the following Monday. Sarah beamed over her dark roast as she recalled the events of the weekend.

"Alex, Jesse was amazing. He lives in a duplex just outside a wildlife park. I thought he'd take me to some hipster flat in the city since he works at the museum. But no, he actually lives about forty-five minutes out of the city. When we arrived that Friday night, it didn't take Jesse long to discover my love for red wine. He actually liked it too. Most men are all about beer and whisky—you know all about that." Sarah smiled at Alex. "Anyway, he actually loved the same kind of wine I do, which was refreshing. Dry, dark, and red. He poured me a glass when we got to his place, handed the glass to me as he held his, then slipped his other hand into my empty one. Then, he winked, smiled a half-grin, and slowly led me out onto his deck. You could see deer peacefully ambling around and grazing in the moonlight. Their shadows under the bright light of the moon, coupled with the mystery of the night, might be one of the most beautiful scenes I've ever witnessed in my life. There was something so simple about gazing at their elegant forms just simply living, sheltered under the night sky.

"As we watched on his deck, we were both silent, in awe that we could witness their beauty without them freezing and dashing. Although we were quiet, he slid his hand out of mine and wrapped it carefully around my waist. I sipped the wine as I felt him tightly hug my side. All of it had a beautiful flavor. The wine gently warmed my throat as he helped me feel secure. I liked how his hand felt resting on my waist, and something about the beauty of the night brought a new comfort."

Alex cringed slightly, so subtly Sarah was unlikely to notice, at the thought of Jesse's arrogant arm around her but brushed his feelings aside and quietly leaned forward, encouraging her to continue…

"Then he slid his hand up under my ear, lightly holding my neck and kissed me. He was gentle and let my lips move with his. Nothing suffocating, we just guided each other as he grazed his tongue on mine. It was one of those deep kisses that we simply fell into. I loved the secure feeling of his hand on my neck as the tips of his fingers lightly lifted my hair. Soft and gentle is how we started, though the warm buzz of Cabernet on my lips is also probably what encouraged us inside. His hand slipped from my neck, down the side of my breast and waist, and back into my hand as he led me slowly inside and down the hallway to his room." She took a deep, relaxed breath as she remembered. "Then we just fell into it. He kissed me gently again, but when I placed my hand on his back and pulled him further into me, our mouths became more passionate, almost aggressive but with the gentleness underneath, always feeling each other first, switching back and forth between leading each other. It was the same motion when he slipped my shirt off, gently laid me down and ran his hands over my body, no doubt he felt the goosebumps. God he gave me chills. Jesse kissed my breasts all over, not just focusing on the nipples, like most, and he made it so easy to just pull his hips into mine, to just grip him inside of me, over and over again. We continued this way throughout the night, probably three or four times while we slept peacefully in between into the morning."

Sarah breathed deeply again, slowly stepping outside the memory and met Alex's eyes, a strange fire and determination in hers as she tried to explain the source of such passion. Although Alex was used to Sarah's openness, the light and fire in her eyes always startled and captivated him anew. He also couldn't help but notice that Sarah might have enjoyed her night with Jesse. For once, she was not speaking of regret.

"Peace, Alex," she continued. "It's a word people throw around so often, yet I've rarely ever experienced it. But that Friday night, Jesse offered me peace. He showed me his small slice of the world, a view I had never seen. Each night of his life, he goes to sleep with the deer just out back. He actually started sketching them with some techniques he picked up from pieces at the museum. His entire living room and the nightstand are filled with the beginnings of moonlight drawings of the deer, pieces of the light reflected in their eyes, their forms jumping, lying down, standing, reaching, their antlers outlined tall, solid, and proud in the night. He saw creation and sought to create it from his view. I've never met someone before who could see such beauty each night and then care enough to capture it for himself so he could remember. Alex, I love that he can teach me something. He showed me beauty in the moonlight—simple, peaceful, beauty."

Alex now understood why Sarah liked Jesse, despite his own reservations about him. Jesse could create, a quality Sarah had always admired and respected. Creation is funny though. The act of bringing something nonexistent into existence is beautiful. However, once that thing exists, what purpose does it serve? Good, evil, or gray? The thing that stood out to Alex in Sarah's story is that none of Jesse's sketches were finished. He had several laying around but none that were completed. He saw something beautiful and began to try to capture its memory but became distracted. Alex couldn't help but wonder, "What was distracting him?"

"Alex?" Sarah questioned, raising one curious eyebrow to see if he was still listening.

"Yeah, sorry," he quickly replied. "I was just wondering if you saw any other art around besides the sketches?"

Sarah started silently upward for a moment as she thought. "No. Not now that I think about it. I actually asked him about art school and why he had never finished. He told me that his family had been really disappointed in him for quitting. I'll be honest, at first, I thought less of him for not following through but then he said something that stuck…'Every day, I am surrounded by the beauty of actual artists. Beauty that I can learn about and share with the patrons. I think I'm happy there. Why pay tens of thousands of dollars to lose myself in the theoretical?'"

Sarah smiled and met Alex's eyes. "He's right, Alex. Who's to say more school would have led to Jesse's best self? Of course, I think it's better to fully explore something before you quit. But maybe his intuition spoke. Maybe there is something to our gut feelings in the moment. I don't know. School certainly altered my view of reality. I never imagined all that my peers or fellow 'scholars' would be so rigid and stale. At least Jesse's work exposes him to diverse perspectives. He is in the presence of all different styles of art. He faces real people and answers all their questions every day. He's not confined to the theoretical and hypothetical discussions 'intellectuals' have within classroom walls. There's a practicality to practice, right? The museum is real. Who's to say Jesse's landing there was 'wrong'?"

Alex's heart sank a little. Sarah felt something real for Jesse. Although he knew there was something off about him, he didn't want to ruin Sarah's excitement. Sarah could feel so many things at once. Maybe Jesse was a distraction, maybe he was something real to Sarah. The only thing Alex knew certainly was that Sarah was an excellent storyteller. If she wanted to wrap herself up in Jesse's world, a world fueled by her own passion, she could. She could see Jesse's story and grow to love the role she played in it, especially if his world distracted her from the disappointment she felt in so many other avenues of her life. Sarah's only real friend was Alex, and she wasn't quite over many of her broken dreams. Mostly the dreams she had of starting her business or finding friends or partners from the intellectual circles of college where she thought she would fit, only to discover that so many were just looking for a degree to reinforce what they already believed.

Alex knew better than anyone how lonely Sarah was. He felt the same loneliness. Since he believed he could never have the time to pursue Sarah the way he truly wanted to, he developed distractions of his own, mainly in the form of absorbing himself in the stories and daily tasks of his bar. He decided during his conversation with Sarah that he would keep his beliefs about Jesse—that he was a watered-down version of a true artist and more impressed with himself than any insight anyone else had to offer—buried. As he already shared with Pete, he wanted Sarah in his life. Alex had a feeling that Sarah saw some of the same red flags in Jesse that he did, but maybe she needed to lose herself in him for a little while. Alex didn't feel it was his place to stand in the way of numbing loneliness, however temporary.

Chapter 6

Alex soon discovered that Sarah and Jesse might not be so temporary. Usually, Sarah's distractions lasted a few weeks to a few months at most, but she had been seeing Jesse for eight months now and a large part of their conversations centered on that man though Sarah was more focused on what she learned from Jesse, rather than Jesse, the person, which Alex found interesting.

"I'm having so much fun, Alex," she said as she smiled brightly. "Last night at the museum, Jesse showed me this portrait of a lone sailor at sea, and it reminded me of that *Lord of the Rings* discussion you and I had at Christmas." Sarah took a deep breath as she always did before articulating something that had been circling her mind for days. Alex leaned toward her as she started to speak, noting the single, beautiful braid she had twisted into her hair. She had that braid almost every day in high school and occasionally brought it back for nostalgia's sake.

Sarah continued, "The sailor was on a small, clumsily crafted raft boat. In the portrait, you can see him pulling his sail to aim east. There is no land to the east, only deeper sea and high, violent waves. But in the other directions—north, south, and west—there are three islands. The islands aren't connected to each other, and there's no sign of anything resembling life besides identical, tall, straight palm trees grown closely together."

She paused and stared at Alex, waiting for him to nod to show that he was following; of course, he nodded back and gestured with his hands for her to continue as he said, "Got it, got it. No land to the east, yet he runs that way, but there are islands in the other directions with tall palm trees, your favorite." Alex grinned at Sarah, and she blushed at his adding an important detail about her interests before she continued.

"Okay, now, remember how we were talking about Tolkien's line, 'Not all who wander are lost?' Before, I felt ashamed when we talked about that quote, but I didn't fully understand why. Something I saw in the portrait helped me understand why that line always stirred so much anxiety inside me. The sailor made me realize that it's impossible to wander without being lost in some way. I had always felt ashamed because every time I've wandered in my life, I always felt lost. I also felt envious of all those who could wander for the sheer pleasure of it—like they weren't running from something or trying to lose themselves. But the more I looked at the deep blue of the ocean circling the narrow islands with their narrower trees, the more I realized that all who wander must be lost. Think about the meaning of the word. To wander means you've lost sight of where you're headed, you're exploring without a clear destination. And there are so many ways to wander. Wandering is aimless. Wandering is confusion, maybe even desperation. You might stumble into something interesting along the way, but that's all it is, something simple, superficial, and interesting in one, small insignificant moment. In those moments when we are just moving, leaving one place to lose ourselves in another, we are lost. Aimless movement is so empty." She took a breath, noting that she still had Alex's attention and continued.

"The sailor in the painting may have known how to steer his ship, but he had no intention of docking anywhere. I think everywhere he could have gone, he may not have liked what he would find and he knew it. He would rather have risked the danger of the open, unknown water than build a shelter on an island where he couldn't move. He wandered because the only alternative was sinking." She exhaled and looked down, relieved that she had an understanding and empathetic place to release her thoughts.

Alex nodded thoughtfully then replied, "And there are so many ways to be lost. Maybe the sailor saw something in the east that no other had. He aimed with the intent to discover the mystery. Uncharted waters can go many ways. He may not have been willing to acknowledge the truth the wind and raging sea were telling him, that he was clearly stumbling into danger. Waves always warn. They are clear with their intentions. Maybe only desperation or a small hope of discovery pushed him from land."

Sarah nodded back and was about to respond when Alex couldn't help but ask, "Did you and Jesse talk about the painting? What did he think?" Alex was sure he already knew the answer but couldn't help but surface his thoughts for Sarah to acknowledge.

She leaned back quickly and glanced up slightly before she spoke slowly, carefully choosing every word, "Well, I didn't go into heavy detail. He didn't have the context of our LOTR discussion. He said the painting was probably more about sailing or the dangers of nature itself. He didn't think much about the sailor..." She hesitated, searching for more words. "I mean it was mostly something I looked at while I passed the time waiting for his shift to finish. He has too many paintings to worry about explaining to too many people. He can't go into extreme detail on each one." Sarah took a deep breath but changed the subject before Alex could ask more questions. "So how's your grandma doing? I haven't heard you talk about her in a while."

It was clear to Alex that Sarah wanted to avoid diving into Jesse's commentary, or lack thereof, on her thoughts. He wondered if Sarah realized that she was more engaged in her insights about Jesse's world than Jesse himself. Each time Sarah shared a story about Jesse, she was more interested in the world he exposed her to than the man himself. As if she saw more depth around him than he even cared to notice. He began to think that Sarah might be the one desperately hoping to discover something new, yet safe and exciting, in the waters surrounding Jesse. Yet Alex couldn't shake the feeling that something dangerous may lie ahead, least of which may be how exhausted she might feel about trying to engage her partner in a conversation he simply wasn't capable of.

"Alex?" She gently but insistently interrupted his thoughts and forced the subject change again, clearly not wanting him to focus on Jesse anymore. "I asked how your grandma was doing. It's been a while since you've shared anything about her."

"Oh." Alex shook his head slightly and tried to refocus, guilt creeping up on him. "Truthfully, I haven't been to see her in a while.

Bar's been busy. Last I checked, she was grateful for the extra help with meals and daily chores. But it was also clear that she missed our home. She kept asking about the white Crock-Pot lined with tan flowers that I donated because there was no electric cooking allowed in her room. She insisted she wanted to make that 'beanless beef chili I loved eating when I came home to visit from college in the fall.' She knew I 'needed the comfort food.'" Alex looked down sadly for a moment after he spoke.

Sarah interjected thoughtfully, "Sandy was used to taking care of things—most of all, you. I have a feeling that, despite her confusion, she knows she cannot independently care for you as she used to. I wonder if the chili is something she could grasp onto, a familiar recipe that she's made for you a thousand times and knows would be hard for her to mix up?"

Alex replied, "You are probably right. That chili has been one of my favorite meals since I was a kid. It's just so hard for me to see her reaching for who she was when it's physically impossible for her mind to ever allow that level of independence to exist again." He looked to the side quickly, trying to hide the sadness in his eyes. He wasn't afraid of Sarah knowing, but her acknowledging his pain, as she would, meant that he would have to see and feel it too.

Sarah came to the rescue. "Alex, there are pieces of her that will always be untouchable, pieces that no disease could ever reach. Something inside us can always grasp on tightly to ourselves. Despite pain, trauma, lies, and sickness, our true selves always have a way of refusing to drown. Pieces are not the same as her being whole, and I am so sorry you have to see her that way. But maybe there is more of her that you can hold on to while she's still here than you think. Maybe there's something new in your relationship with her that you could discover."

Alex turned back to Sarah, gratitude and stubbornness in his eyes; he couldn't let the sadness take hold too deeply. He had to stay whole for his grandmother and the life she built for him. "Thank you, Sarah. It's so easy to become lost in grief. I know she's still here, but God, sometimes her presence makes the pain so much worse.

She is here, but she's not herself. I need to figure out how to accept her this way."

Sarah smiled. "Maybe start with a visit this week. One step. See how you feel in the moment...And you know I'll be there to check in with you on Friday, wouldn't miss live night."

Alex nodded and stood up from his chair, Sarah followed, and they hugged tightly. She rubbed his back gently for a moment, the way only those who truly care for us do and told him she would see him soon. As she walked out the door of the café, he watched her toss her hair gently behind her shoulder as she confidently opened the door to brace the world. Sarah was nothing if not resilient, which meant that she was also right about his needing to build a little resiliency of his own and start with step one, a visit.

Chapter 7

Alex wrote best when it rained. Finding time to himself was becoming more and more difficult as he managed the bar and grew more business because of musician's live night. Quiet was becoming a stranger. However, he found himself needing a quiet moment out on the porch at Ramell's Corner, the assisted-living home where his grandmother lived. He took Sarah's advice and chose to visit Sandy the following Tuesday afternoon before the bar's happy hour rush.

Alex tried to make conversation with his grandmother, but he had a hard time helping her settle on a topic that would, well, settle her. Sandy had always been a worrier for Alex's whole life. When she took him on vacation to her sister's winter home in San Diego, she didn't even want Alex to walk around the block of the retired, gated community alone. "These old people"—such as herself—"can't see well at dusk anymore, Alex. Take a flashlight and let me follow you with my car so there's some kind of barrier." When Grandma Sandy made her mind up about how she was going to approach a situation, that was that. There was no point in Alex arguing. So even though he wanted to take the walk to get some space from Sandy and her sister for a few minutes, he found himself feeling oddly stalked by his grandmother.

Of course, Sandy's worry came from a good place. Maybe it would be more accurate to describe her worry as anxiety, assuming the worst possible scenario from a simple walk around the block. But Alex knew she loved him and wanted to do whatever she could to keep him safe. Sandy also knew that her own son (Alex's father) had hurt him by leaving, an action she could never fully protect Alex from. She never stopped trying to keep Alex safe the best way she knew how.

Alex recalled some of these California memories as he tried to help his grandmother do the same. "Remember our first spring break trip, Grandma? I was almost finished with college that year, and we wanted to make a point of touring San Diego's Japanese Garden. You wanted to see all the colors of koi fish and close-up views of the bonsai trees' thick trunks." His grandmother's eyes were a beautiful, deep blue, but as the disease took a deeper hold over her body, they became glossed over with a pale confusion, and she didn't look at Alex quite the same way.

"What? No, Alex. I don't think we stopped there. That garden was too close to the city. I hate downtown traffic. I wouldn't have taken you there. The exhaust from all those city cars would have stuffed your nose right up. No, we planted that willow tree in the backyard instead." Sandy was clearly flustered as she spoke. She leaned forward in her chair, and the worry that often presented itself in her pinched eyebrows had become more of a permanent crease. She frowned after she spoke as if she was upset with Alex for suggesting something so "dangerous" and inaccurate.

Alex realized that Grandma had confused the willow tree they had planted in their backyard when he was eleven with the bonsai they had visited in his early twenties. Alex loved stories. He knew the power that positive memories had to draw people back into themselves and feel a sense of familiarity and comfort, even if they were in uncomfortable and desolate surroundings such as an assisted-living home. He knew the staff there cared well for his grandmother and made her as comfortable as possible. However, there is a sad emptiness that accompanies losing one's home and the sense of security accurate memories hold. His grandmother was not the strong, thoughtful woman she once was and watching her succumb to a disease that was chipping away at her from the inside out was, at times, too painful to bear.

Alex tried to process his disappointment that his attempt at pulling Grandma out of the disease's stronghold with one of his favorite memories with her was interrupted by Sandy's frustrated suggestion that "they just sell this place on Oakland and move back to the 'Bridgewood house.' The neighbors there were so much more friendly and helpful." Sandy gestured around her when she said,

"This place," implying that she thought she was currently living in the Oakland house where Alex grew up with her and planted the willow tree. The Bridgewood house was where Alex's father had grown up with Sandy and her late husband. Both homes were named for the streets they were built on.

Alex's heart broke at the confusion his grandmother felt. He had never heard her confuse her physical location in that manner, and he didn't understand it. He wondered, "How could someone think they were in a physical place that they were not? She was surrounded by different furniture, different walls, and most importantly, a grown grandson, not her own young child (Alex's father) or Alex as a child. Why couldn't she recognize him? Why didn't she understand where she was?" He found himself at a loss for words to give his grandmother in such a moment. His eyes subtly filled with tears, and he decided he needed to step outside and take a breath so he could understand himself and how to comfort her. "Grandma"—he tried to stop his voice from shaking—"let me see about those cookies you like from the cafeteria quickly. Maybe I can grab a few M&M-flavored ones for us to share. I'll be right back…" He barely finished the last sentence before a single tear spilled from his eye, and he rushed out of her room.

He tore down the hallway of the memory care wing, entered the access code to exit, his fingers fumbling over the stainless steel number keys as he quickly shut the door behind him so the other memory-care patients couldn't wander and potentially put themselves in danger. He then dashed into the lobby and came to a halt onto the porch.

The rain had started to pour heavily, reminding him of the sound of the heavy waterfalls he had heard at local state parks. Alex didn't have many chances to wander outside, but when he did, he loved exploring nature and listening to the sound of water. It was well into June and a beautiful bright green had settled into the trees. The water droplets that had landed on the leaves made them appear as if the green were glowing. And the light wind the rain had brought with her lightly tugged at the branches and tossed the leaves in wild directions. Alex found an empty rocking chair, grateful that the porch was vacant, and soaked up the sounds. As Alex tried to focus on the sights and sounds around him, he was suddenly aware of the pencil he had tucked behind his ear. He kept it there so often that his senses stopped recognizing its presence unless he was trying to focus on it or needed to use it. The habit began because Sarah had suggested it as a solution to stop "The Pencil Thief" they went to high school with. In the present, the quirk certainly served a business purpose. He could easily tally inventory and keep stock. However, the ultimate reason for keeping up the habit is that having the utensil so easily accessible allowed him to keep his musical dreams alive, even in a simpler form and, of course, always reminded him of Sarah.

Since Alex had stopped the majority of his composition to handle his grandmother's affairs and the bar, he rarely found time to write. However, he could not help but feel inspired by the rain. And in his most emotional moments, writing lyrics to the melodic sounds that filled his head comforted him when Sarah wasn't around to listen or the pain of his emotions had no place to land. He kept the poems and lyrics he wrote in a notepad, tucked away, waiting to be put to music and shared.

The wind and the rain helped Alex feel connected to something bigger than himself. He didn't know what religion or spirits he believed in, but he always felt that there was something greater out there when he experienced the peace that accompanied the freedom and wildness of wind and water. Moments that the weather provided and emotions he felt pushed him into the creative energy that he couldn't entirely abandon. His throat felt as if it was packed with stones as he pushed the tears that welled in his eyes back and pulled a small notepad from his pocket. He needed to name the pain that he felt while watching his grandmother suffer. He desperately searched his mind for the words needed to give a voice to his feelings. "Lost, glazed, broken, empty...Confused, strange, free? Fractured, more like home, here and gone..."

I remember home.

How can the same eyes see one life so differently?
A life she's known for over half of her own
and should feel familiar.

Or is my perspective skewed?
Maybe I could understand her better
if I bent my idea of what "remembering" should be.

I remember home as warm Sundays,
sunlight beaming in the window through the afternoon.
She and I prepped lasagnas, casseroles, and macaroni salad,
ready for the busy week.

I remember home in California, vacation on the beach.
She sat in her lawn chair, under the blue umbrella, dark sunglasses half the size of her face.
My toes in the sand, squeezing the wet grains that met the reaching shore, walking alongside the fated pair, ocean and sand, protecting her fears by refusing to venture too far.

I remember a home where my grandmother knew me as I expected.
She said my name, the one my parents chose.
Her advice fit my life as I knew it,
her words and her arms, always my childhood safe space.
Maybe it's time for me to build her a new home.
Something sturdy, formed of what home should always be.

Safe.

I can remember the home of comfort and resilience she built for me.
In this new space, I will create those same feelings.

Safe.

I want her to always remember home as unconditional, with love and acceptance despite how her brain may warp her view.

I will see her as she is,
comfort her as she always has me.

Alex took a deep breath and looked to the wind in the trees, his anxiety released to his words and the wind's wildness. Then, he gently closed his eyes and took another long, slow breath. The poem helped him accept the pain, to feel his disappointment and longing deeply. Once he understood the source of his tears, he found a safe place for them to land and was able to move forward. He decided then to get to know his grandmother as she was now and build the emotional shelter she needed in her relationship with him, putting his own disappointment aside. She was his family, and she needed his acceptance of her illness.

Alex stood up slowly and walked back to the memory care wing, quickly swiping two M&M cookies from the cafeteria along the way. He found his grandmother anxiously fiddling with her own fingers, clasping them together tightly, then releasing them as her eyes darted toward the door. Her expression relaxed as he entered, and she smiled when she saw the cookies in his hands.

He pulled up one of the small chairs from her kitchenette table, gently handed her one of the cookies, and asked her, "What would make this place feel more like the Bridgewood home?"

Chapter 8

At the shelter Friday afternoon, Sarah found herself thinking about her last conversation with Alex as she filled out intake paperwork for a new four-year-old Labradoodle.

Was it strange that Jesse didn't have much to say about the painting? Did he ever have much to say about any of them? she thought. *His job required him to have surface knowledge of most of the art in the museum, which he did, and that knowledge was impressive in itself. There were a lot of pieces. But were pieces enough for me? Part of the reason I liked him so much was his knowledge of art and the methods that created them. Jesse could speak so beautifully about pieces of each painting he described at the museum. He had even taken the time to begin his own sketches, the deer pieces that he had lying around his home. Each one had such a beautiful story. Jesse had to have surface knowledge for his job. Maybe he could only take in so much information so he could continue to share with the public without feeling overwhelmed? Art is about depth, though, as so many things are.*

Sarah turned these concerns over in her mind for several minutes then asked herself one final question before she determined she'd move on and focus on her paperwork. This particular question was one that she had been afraid to even think around Alex, for fear she might share with him and hear the answer that began to form in her own head…*Is Jesse even capable of thinking critically about anything? Well, truly critical, like he wasn't putting on a show*? The true answer lurked in the pit of her stomach, and she forced it to remain there. She allowed into her consciousness the decision that she was still interested enough in the story he offered her life, one of art, nature, small adventures, and at least the beginning of creation. That was enough to motivate her to stay.

In the meantime, Sarah would focus on the depth of thought and creation that was in her control, naming this new Labradoodle drop-off. She was a stray that had been wandering a nearby suburb for a few weeks until a sixteen-year-old visiting a friend on one of her first official, licensed drives in her mom's car almost ran the doodle over. The girl burst into the shelter holding the frightened animal, flustered and exasperated as she stared at Sarah desperately, "I'm so sorry! She's a stray, I think. I feel like such a terrible person. I almost ran over her with my mom's car. She just sat cowering on the side of the road after I swerved. I couldn't just leave her."

Sarah quickly took the dog off the teen's hands and met her big brown eyes with her own. "Thank you. I also want you to know that I am quite confident that you are not the first person to almost hit this little girl. It's okay. Take a breath." Sarah watched as the girl attempted to slow her breathing, hand on her chest. Then she continued, "You might just be the first person to do something about her wandering the streets." Sarah smiled at the concerned girl and continued, "Most people go about their routines, any event or circumstance outside the ordinary often fails to turn their attention into action. You couldn't help that this stray wandered in front of your car. However, you chose to stop, interrupt your routine for thirty minutes, and bring her here. Because of your choice to put your plans aside, even for a few short minutes, this little lady has a safe place to sleep tonight and will hopefully never be in a situation where she is wandering into danger again."

Sarah remembered how the girl looked at her with relief. She relaxed her shoulders and thanked Sarah for calming her anxiety before petting the scruffy dog behind the ears and exiting. Sarah finished the intake report and returned to the top of the form. "Name:__________________" it read. Sarah twisted her back to look behind her at the doodle. By now, the dog had relaxed and was laying on the floor chewing on one of the shelter's many rawhide bones. She decided to name her in honor of the girl who had dropped her off... though she didn't ask the girl's name with the intention of helping her feel comfortable. It was clear that the girl was nervous enough about having almost hit the poor dog. Giving too much information about herself might spin her further into anxious thoughts. Animals could be dropped off anonymously; the shelter's owners' primary concern was that the creatures were safe.

Sarah remembered that the girl wore bright colors, a bright orange shirt that fit beautifully with her dark skin. The color reminded Sarah of her favorite flower, well, technically it was a shrub and then, she thought of the name "Azalea" or "Zay" for short. Sarah followed the rest of the intake protocol (checking for injury, illness, and identification). When she determined that the animal had no identifiable owner and seemed to be physically unharmed, except for needing to put on a little weight, she walked her to the quarantine area and passed the information on to the overnight vet. Although she was happy to help the dog and comfort the girl, she couldn't help but be excited about her evening. She was planning on meeting Alex early at the bar before the live night's rush began. Sarah found herself feeling extremely eager to catch up with Alex. A force, maybe guilt or the need to justify her being with Jesse, propelled her out of work that afternoon; and she couldn't wait to talk with him.

When she arrived, Sarah sat on her usual stool in the middle of the bar. It was always easiest to talk to Alex here as she could catch him as he rushed back and forth from one end to the next. Alex smiled wide when Sarah sat down. She ordered mozzarella sticks, her favorite, which was always on the house for her. She also ordered a side of asparagus…greens to balance the melted cheese she loved so much. The bar was still fairly empty at 3:15, and Alex had his manager, Gabe, prepping for the night rush so he was able to pull up a stool beside Sarah for a while. He wanted to tell her how he had taken her advice about step 1 with his grandmother and how he started to form a solution for how to communicate. However, Sarah seemed anxious to speak first, and she started the conversation by trying to atone for Jesse or what seemed like his shortcomings in their last conversation. Alex listened patiently. He may not have been the biggest fan of Jesse, but he knew how active Sarah's mind was, and he was always eager to know where she had been circling.

Sarah took a deep breath as she began, "I couldn't help but think about the questions you asked me on Tuesday, Alex. You know, about what I am able to share with Jesse?" Alex nodded in recognition of the conversation and she continued, "He might not always have enough to say, but what he does share is interesting." She was both skeptical and honest about what she was saying at the same time. Alex was quiet, and she anxiously filled the space with more words.

"He shows me new things about the world. He teaches me things. He draws you know. Deer. Maybe an animal that people see fairly often but rarely take the time to actually notice, you get that, right? You're kind of the same way." Alex nodded reluctantly. "Anyway," Sarah went on, "I am drawn to him because he creates. To be fair, it's only one small fraction of who he is. But the originality is there. So few create anymore. I also know that, as an artist, you aren't one to have respect for those who don't finish their pieces. I know that when you write your songs, you take them seriously until every lyric is precise and every note is in its proper place."

Only the songs I actually perform, Alex thought. The actual writing process was a lot messier, but he liked that Sarah admired him, so instead, he raised his eyebrows in a cocky but flattered manner and smiled, soaking in the compliment. "You know me well. What is creation if not complete? Half poems and half songs are painful. All my songs are a message. What are they communicating if not complete?"

Sarah frowned slightly at first then smiled back. "I know you feel that way and I get it, follow-through and all that...You have a point and so, with what I've learned from you in mind, I asked him why he hadn't finished his sketches." Sarah looked to the side thoughtfully as she searched her mind for the best way to paraphrase Jesse's words. "When I asked him, he looked up, then into me and said, while smirking, 'I never really got over my first love, the art in the museum...Surrounded by bouncing brushstrokes at all times and at all angles and sculpted wonders captured my eyes. The more days I spent circling and sharing their beauty with the tourists, the more I couldn't walk away. The artists were brave enough to pour every piece of themselves into their art, the sharp, the odd, the exhausted. To commit your soul to a piece entirely means you can summon the strength to finish your message even into the hours you can barely lift your eyelids or your smile. I have been too captivated by turning puzzling pieces and their creators over in my mind to complete my own. I suppose I am enraptured by their commitment and beauty. I guess I need to stumble my way out of such a love to find a second, one that I have the peace and bravery to finish as they have. Even in moonlight, deer slowly graze, and I haven't the patience yet to understand them fully.'" Sarah smiled as she finished speaking like Jesse, remembering his words.

Rat bastard, Alex thought. He hadn't seen much of Jesse since the night he and Sarah reconnected at the bar. Alex was pretty certain that the vibe Jesse gave off hadn't changed much. He still seemed to speak a lot without saying much. He had to acknowledge that Jesse's words, as paraphrased by Sarah, were elegantly spoken. He could tell that Jesse was smart enough to realize that Sarah was smart and that she craved an intelligence that answered her own. Jesse was the most talented at reading people quickly and finding the words and acknowledgments that would satisfy their interest the most in the moment. That was his job. But it was all so fleeting and temporary, Alex had to wonder if Jesse could sustain his attempts at captivating Sarah long-term.

Sarah interrupted Alex's thoughts before he could reply and smiled as she attempted to eat her asparagus with a fork. Her smile brightened as the stubborn vegetable rolled hopelessly beneath the prongs. "Really, Alex, I promise that at the very least, I'm having fun. Wanna know something funny? He laughed when we had sex this past weekend." Alex raised an eyebrow and tried not to show the disgust he felt. "Yeah, I know right?" She went on, "It sounds bizarre, but it was oddly charming. Every time I'd grab on to him or pull myself closer, it was this strange sort of confident, 'Of course, we move perfectly and you'd put your leg there,' sort of laugh. It was new for me. He's never done that before, but I guess it was strange and exciting."

"He laughed?" Alex questioned. "That didn't make you feel strange? How do you know he wasn't mocking you or something?"

Sarah looked taken aback but wrinkled her brow as she considered Alex's question before answering, "I see why you asked that. I know it sounds strange, and I wondered about his intentions for a second too. But he kept going...You know, kept sliding his hands over my body and smiling as he felt me, so I guess I thought of his laughter as more joy and amusement with what we were doing, not so much mocking. It was as if the laughter encouraged him, so I just went with it."

Alex frowned slightly, not buying the explanation. It was unclear whether jealousy or justice (the desire for Sarah to see what he believed to be the truth about Jesse for her own well-being) emboldened him to ask the next question, "Are you sure he wasn't just amused with himself?"

Sarah put down her fork, giving up on the asparagus, and sat back on the barstool, offended. Underneath the offense, she was hurt, not necessarily by Alex, but by his suggestion that Jesse was "amused" during sex. Although Sarah was no stranger to sex, she had been taught, as most women and girls are, that their naked bodies are something to be desired and ashamed of all at once. She allowed Jesse to see and feel her naked skin fully. She laid herself bare in front of him, confident and insecure all at the same time. The idea that he cared more about his "clever" movements inside her body instead of the privilege she allowed him was too painful to stomach. There was a special balance that Sarah found when she gave into sex, for all the wrong reasons, but she did her best to find some semblance of control in the balance, even if the experience was disappointing.

First, she had to move past the insecurities about the size of her breasts. Each time she would remove her shirt in front of a partner, she felt embarrassed about the amount of padding on her bra and whether he would judge her for appearing more voluptuous with clothes on. Memories of her teenage years would flash through her mind sometimes as she undressed...Like that time she was walking home, only twelve years-old, barely on the cusp of puberty. Sarah was minding her own business and listening to her Michelle Branch album on her portable CD player as she walked when a group of teenage boys drove by her. For no other reason than their conditioned belief that their opinion on her body was something they had a right to share, one of them chose to roll down the window of the old, gray Buick they drove and scream out, "You're flat as fuck!" Then, they simply drove away.

As their cruel words sunk in, Sarah was ashamed as she continued to walk home alone. She felt that, somehow, her tiny breasts were an offense to others and something to be embarrassed of, to hide, lest they "offend" passersby again. Shame about her body was such a terrible feeling to internalize, but Sarah did. Too many boys (and girls) she went to middle school with had confirmed that small breasts were something to be ashamed of, and so she was ashamed. It was a mark on her beauty, a "flaw" she saw and hated every time she looked in a mirror.

Sarah grew older and more confident, but body-shaming messages that were reinforced continuously throughout her lifetime do not simply melt away. A lie that Sarah internalized as the truth took a long time to become exposed and replaced with the actual truth, that Sarah was beautiful and so were her breasts. The idea of a "one large boob size fits all" phenomenon was merely a conditioned response to what made a woman "truly sexy," not what all who were attracted to women actually felt. This truth was the other part of the balance Sarah tried to maintain. She learned as she got older and talked with more people that large breasts were not essential for sex appeal and not those who were attracted to women actually preferred them. She learned more about sexism in the media and in US culture and was able to see the slimy stereotypes as lies. Once she realized that her B-cups were actually beautiful and perky, she examined them against the rest of her body. She realized they fit perfectly with the curve of her waist, and she loved how her nipples would wake up and harden when she was aroused by a partner. Sarah tried to remember these feelings and truths of self-acceptance each time she slept with a new partner and each time she slept with Jesse. She was always fighting the lies about her body that she was told young with the truths she came to accept about herself as she grew up.

All of these memories and the balance flashed through her mind quickly as she considered what Alex said about Jesse focusing on his own movements for his own amusement instead of her. She was hurt more than she was angry, but she wasn't ready to accept what Alex said about Jesse, or to share her feelings about her body with Alex, so she responded with her perceptions of Alex's thoughts about Jesse,

"Alex, I know you don't like him because he was an idiot in high school. But I am telling you, there is more. Yes, he talks out of his ass sometimes AND sometimes he actually has something to say, well, I mean, not with his ass though. I promise there's some creativity and intelligent thoughts intermingled with the bullshit."

Alex understood that Sarah needed to feel understood at this moment. He sensed that there was some sort of pain lurking beneath the surface of her defending Jesse, a pain she wasn't ready to share or even acknowledge. He nodded, smiled, and said, "I get it, Sarah. Maybe I just haven't been around him enough. You should invite him out tonight. Maybe he'd enjoy a few of the bands I have lined up."

Sarah smiled back with relief. "Already on it. He should be here by the time the bands start at six...And I didn't forget about your grandma, Alex. I know you've got to go get ready for the night, but I hope we can talk about that soon," she said a little anxiously.

"Of course. Monday lunch, maybe?"

"Monday lunch." She smiled back with certainty.

Sarah stuck around the bar, casually chatting with Pete about his trucking route and if there were any cool places he'd seen lately. If Alex passed with a box of beer or backed Gabe up with fulfilling drink orders, she made sure to catch him in brief, casual, witty conversation. After an hour passed, Jesse had not yet arrived. Alex had ran down to the basement storage to grab a few extra mini wine samples. At this moment, Pete saw an opportunity to ask Sarah a question that had been sitting with him for a while, "Ms. Sarah, I've been meaning to ask you something a little more forward for a while now..."

She laughed and sipped her gin, feeling a little buzz at this point. "Yeah, Pete, what is it?"

"I catch up with you here almost every Friday while you're waiting for a moment to catch up with Alex, and I know you been friends for years..." Sarah stared to feel a little nervous as she saw where Pete was going with this conversation. He continued, "Why didn't you ever try for more than friends? I see how you smile at him when he passes by, and you both always got something interesting to say to each other." He looked down shyly at his beer after he spoke.

For a moment, Sarah's witty mood faded. Her smile dropped, and she became thoughtful, glancing down seriously. Sometimes, her buzzes resulted in her feeling very philosophical and insightful. She was just buzzed and comfortable enough with Pete to let a little more truth slip than she may otherwise had while sober and with someone else (Jesse). She set her glass down, looked Pete in his eyes, and replied, "How could I fall in love with Alex? Sometimes I look at him and he's such a stranger. I know it sounds crazy, how could I not recognize the mannerisms of my best friend? I find myself lost in some of his simple movements, but they carry such weight. Sometimes, when I look at him, disorientation crushes me in the ways I least expect, in the manner of how he casually pats the bar keys in his pocket when we leave lunch and awkwardly smiles at me because he knows we have to get back to our lives. Conversations honestly feel like a vacation with him, like what I wish I could do with my life all the time, but responsibilities and all that."

Pete nodded, listening. "He loves his grandma and her bar and I get that. There is a lot that weighs on Alex that he has yet to acknowledge, and it's hard for me to get close enough to fall in love in the meantime. All of our conversations are so short-lived. Drive-by love. In this stranger, I see the depths of my own soul, but I have not the energy to explore just how deep connection and desire reach. I am busy in my own way. Every day at work, I comfort strangers who have to make the decision to give up a treasured companion or rich assholes who bought a pet on a whim and wanted to dump it the second a fraction of responsibility was required. It's really a cruel trick of the universe. I hardly recognize him in his casual mannerisms because something deep inside is reaching for so much more. Sometimes, I look at him and I am drowning in how much I adore him. I am in awe of his ability to see and create, along with the wrinkles that form around his eyes when he smiles, but he has buried much of what he truly wants. I can feel him, but I am only allowed to look at the surface. The requirements of our survival have made soulmates strangers. There's a piece missing, and it doesn't feel right. Well, being with him does feel right but not without the missing piece. Maybe there's a lot of missing pieces…Alex has a lot he has to sort through, and I probably do too. I think he's forgotten a bit of who he is in the midst of so many obligations. There are pieces of himself he needs to remember before he could share them with me."

Sarah awkwardly took another sip of her drink, aware that she had just said more than she probably meant to an acquaintance in the low blue light of a bar on Friday night. But the thing about Sarah was, when she spoke from her soul, the words were out there in the air, searching for their place in the universe, even if they did not quite fit the space they were in.

Pete was clearly confused but recognized that what Sarah felt was real. Even though some of her words may have been lost on him, he sensed her disappointment with the timing of pursuing something more with Alex. He found himself able to reply with, "Well, Sarah, I suppose I can understand how life gets busy. But if there's one thing I've learned from living on the road, it's that I can make time to stop where I need to. There might be more routes to getting what both of you want than you think."

Sarah looked at Pete, considering what he said, but it was at this moment that Jesse entered and slid into the barstool on her other side. Sarah was shaken out of her thoughts and immediately averted her gaze to Jesse. Pete nodded in greeting and turned back to the bar, uninterested in engaging with Jesse.

Tonight, Jesse wasn't alone. As he put his arm around Sarah and kissed her excitedly, another young man sat on his other side. Sarah hadn't known that he was bringing anyone with him. After Jesse removed the hand that cupped her face as he kissed her, Sarah's eyes were drawn to the stranger. He had loose, feathered hair that just slightly covered his eyebrows. When he returned Sarah's glance, he tossed his black bangs to the side, revealing dark brown eyes set deeply against pale skin. Sarah couldn't help but notice that he was strikingly handsome.

Before she could introduce herself, Jesse interjected, "Hey, Sar, this is Dean. I've been meaning to introduce you two for a while. He was my best friend growing up in Ecuador. Both of us were in the same missionary family camp. He's been going back to volunteer at the church there on and off. He just came back to the States last week." Jesse leaned back slightly so Sarah could shake his friend's hand. She gripped Dean's hand firmly and couldn't help but notice that he did not return her strength; his grip was sort of a floppy medium. However, he met her eyes and smiled, revealing charming wrinkles around the corners of his mouth.

"Jess hasn't stopped talking about you since I arrived." Dean smiled. "I've been texting him on and off since I got back, and your name appears in my messages at least twice a day." Sarah smiled and brushed her hair gently behind her ears. "I hear you work at the local animal shelter," Dean went on. "How do you like it there? I would guess it's hard to convince people to adopt all those strays?"

Before Sarah could answer, Jesse offered to swap stools so they could talk more easily. He saw Alex making his way down the bar and figured he'd use their time breaking the ice to order a few drinks. Sarah accepted the swap, excited to get to know someone new, and asked Jesse to order her another gin with lime. Alex heard Dean's question and smirked as he poured the drinks Jesse ordered. Sarah loved contradicting assumptions, and he knew she'd be ready to answer Dean with carefully chosen words that cleverly challenged his thinking.

"You're right about the challenge of the adoption process, but the problem is more with the people than the 'strays.' It's actually a lot harder to find people genuine and responsible enough to commit to adopting the animals we have for more than a week. Our animals have quirks, of course, but they have good hearts and are mostly just in need of stability."

Dean questioned further, intrigued by her comment about responsibility for the pet owners, "Why is it hard to find that kind of stability?"

Sarah happily went on, "For instance, a lot of people believe adopting a dog is harder than raising one's own from puppyhood. However, the opposite is more often true. For many, adopting a dog is easier because of the perceived lack of commitment and responsibility that comes with a shelter animal. If something goes wrong, people just blame the dog. It doesn't matter if the dog tore up the carpet, peed everywhere, or was too afraid to cuddle. In the eyes of the new owner, the dog behaved a certain way because of prior damage or regression. They never stopped to observe their impact and whether they were patient enough to draw the dog out of itself and help it grow around them. They also didn't take the time to recognize that dogs react to the energy of their owners. So adopting is easier because if something goes wrong, they abandon it back, shedding any and all responsibility."

Dean sighed. "The sad part is that actually makes sense. I remember my brother adopting a shelter dog and returning it within the week because it chewed up all the carpet on his stairs...like gnawed its way up each step, as if it were rock climbing with its teeth." Both Sarah and Dean let out tiny laughs.

"Anyway, he told me that it was an outdoor dog and needed to run. My brother is not exactly an athlete, so to your point, the dog's acting out was most likely on him, though of course he would never acknowledge it," Dean replied.

Sarah smiled and answered, "Well, I appreciate that you understand. It can be exhausting trying to encourage people to commit to being a little uncomfortable for a little while. Routine is so important to most. They have a hard time creating a new one, even if that means sometime as simple as walking a dog for twenty minutes in the morning. I know everyone is busy, but it's easier to make time for the things you care about than most people think."

Dean smiled, clearly interested in hearing more of Sarah's thoughts, but she was ready to ask questions.

"Anyway, what do you do, Dean? Free time or work time? You like...stuff?" She laughed.

Dean scooted the stool slightly closer and responded, "Yeah, I like a lot of stuff, mostly mathematical things. I'm an electrical engineer. I love figuring out how and why things work...or don't work. In fact, I love when I can investigate a malfunction, especially when I can experience the pleasure of fixing it."

Sarah was not mechanically inclined at all, so she found Dean's work fascinating, something different from what she knew. She then asked him, "What was the most interesting device that you have ever fixed?"

Dean was delighted to answer. As he began his story, Alex attempted to make conversation with Jesse. His gut feelings about Jesse being untrustworthy and superficial hadn't changed, but it was clear that he wasn't going anywhere anytime soon…

"So, he said as he popped off the top of another beer and handed it to him, "you said your friend was from the missionary camp in Ecuador? I didn't know you grew up there." Jesse leaned forward and frowned in a manner that showed he believed he was about to say something serious and profound, "Yeah, yeah, lived in Ecuador until I started high school actually. My parents volunteered to teach Bible classes down there through part of a program at their church."

"Wow. You must have learned a lot about the different Ecuadorian cultures. Can you speak Spanish?" Alex asked. "Or any of the indigenous languages?"

Jesse replied, "A little Spanish, no indigenous languages. Truthfully, I was surrounded by a lot of people from the States who were also in the program, so I was raised speaking English. I picked up a few phrases here and there, but I am nowhere near fluent."

"What did you like the most about living there?" Alex asked while replenishing the ice machine.

Jesse took a sip of his beer, "Oh man, I gotta narrow it down to one thing, huh? Honestly, just being surrounded by constant beauty. That country has everything from mountains to rainforests. Every summer, my parents would take my brother and I on some sort of hike through the forests or adventure up a mountain. Usually, the trips lasted for an entire week. We would spend days staying in old haciendas, kayaking along the beaches, and visiting llama farms." Jesse smiled as he remembered and charming wrinkles formed around his eyes.

Alex had stopped filling the ice and had leaned against the bar as he listened to Jesse. "I can't believe your parents would ever want to come back."

"Everyone misses home eventually," Jesse answered. "Plus, my parents wanted us to finish our education here.

"Understandable," Alex answered. Though he couldn't help but wonder why Jesse's white parents entered someone else's country to teach them a religion they didn't ask for, yet sent their son back home for his own education...But now wasn't the time to bring that up to Jesse, so he went on, "Sarah said something about you wanting to pursue an art and archeology history program in France? That sounds amazing. Do you think you'll ever go?"

"Honestly, I don't know, Alex." Jesse sighed. "The whole reason my parents came back here was so that I could become a history and theology teacher and pursue international evangelism like they did. I've been trying to find the right middle ground for myself for a long time. I love surrounding myself with beauty. I guess that's how I grew up, but there's so many stories out there, so much to learn. It's easier for me to scratch the surface of each piece I describe to the museum visitors for now. And as for the evangelism part, I positively reach a lot of people at work. My parents certainly wish that I took a different path. Actually, pursuing the program in France would look a lot more like their life and their understanding of what life should be—traveling solo or with a partner and making some sort of difference. They have definitely not hidden their disappointment in my staying local and working an entry-level job. But maybe there's something beautiful in what the world sees as 'wrong choices.'"

Alex stopped prepping the drinks and focused on Jesse as he went on, "Everybody says, 'Find your own path.' Either that or they try to pave one for you. What I wonder is where all the guilt and regret come from? Why feel guilty about running madly and passionately down one path and crashing? Or in my case, finding a middle ground and seeking comfort? Can pain come from regret? Sure. Consequences? Absolutely. But what makes a choice 'wrong'? We are all stumbling in the aftermath of some sort of pain others caused us anyway. Can we be blamed for charging ahead in the midst of the wreckage and trying to survive? I just wish I knew regret's true source. Who can really reflect clearly when we're still dazed and dizzy from so many lies about who we 'should' have been?" Jesse paused, looked Alex deeply in his eyes, and then drained the last of his beer.

Alex's mouth had formed into a thin line of serious understanding. He responded, "I guess I can appreciate that. Here I am, years after college, and I am nowhere near the composer I thought I'd be.

Isn't that what our twenties were supposed to be for? Finding ourselves and our creativity?"

Jesse shook his head. "But what about all the obstacles? It's easy to get lost in what we think we want or what we should have been. Maybe that's where the regret comes from, guilt over a future we still see ourselves in but may never actually be. Maybe such futures were never meant to exist. I've had my obstacles as I am sure you've had yours. Nothing wrong with trying to run a business, a successful one at that, so you can pay the bills…And I'll keep doing what I can to hold on to the beautiful moments I find along my way." He glanced at Sarah. "Speaking of business, I wouldn't mind another one." Sarah was still deep in conversation with Dean. "She may want one more too. Rumor has it you're about to go on soon?"

Alex quickly glanced down at the clock on his phone. "Shit, 9:00 p.m. That is my cue. Pete and a few other regulars always like when I play one of my own before the next live musician goes on. I'm going to play one that I wrote on vacation with my grandma a few years back. Should fit in with acoustic night, though I'll be on the keyboard."

Jesse smiled. "Don't let me stop you. Nice catching up, Alex. I know you mean a lot to Sarah."

Alex nodded and gave Jesse a half-smile. Gabe took over managing the bar as Alex walked to the small prep area behind the musician's stage. He couldn't help but begin to understand Sarah's point… There was more to Jesse. Perhaps he had grown a little since high school. However, Alex kept his guard up. Jesse may have more depth than he had previously thought, but some of the same cocky tendencies were still there. Jesse was quick to respond with an excuse, however seemingly wise that excuse came across in the moment. And Alex wasn't entirely sure he cared for the company that Jesse kept. In between conversations and managing the bar, Alex had glanced at Dean several times while he was talking with Sarah. He didn't like how Dean looked at her. He leaned into Sarah close. She wasn't flirting with him, but Dean looked at her as if she was infatuated with him. He could also tell that Dean mistook Sarah's intellect and interest in learning for a vested interest in him, as most men did in their arrogance. However, unlike most men, Dean looked at Sarah with a strange intensity. He had dark, handsome eyes, but they peered into her as if he was trying to consume her. It was a gaze that was hard to explain but Alex could feel it, and he couldn't help but notice how fixated Dean's attention was on Sarah.

Alex had to put the bad vibe aside for now and focus on his song. He couldn't deny, even to himself, that he loved playing and sorely missed the sound of the keys beneath his fingers, the way a melody could bring to life human emotion as nothing else could. Relief. Music was always relief. He lingered on the joy he felt as he plugged in his keyboard and began reviewing the chords for the song in his head. Just a few minutes before he was to go on.

Sarah noted that Alex had disappeared and made a point of turning around on her barstool toward the stage. She loved when he played. He used to play around with songs often during college. They would be studying or talking together, and he'd turn toward his keyboard and experiment with chords here and there. However, there was nothing quite like Alex inside a complete song. Sarah heard his music so rarely these days, and she was eager for the opportunity. She anxiously awaited his approaching the stage and tried to ignore the fact that Dean's shoulder was brushing against hers. He had flipped around too and inched even closer to her. She was uncomfortable but felt awkward asking him to move, so she just made a point to lean toward Jesse, whose attention was also fixed on the stage, and a little on the beer Alex had left him. Although Sarah had enjoyed talking with Dean, she had no desire to be so close to him. She noticed that Jesse had ordered her another drink and decided to try her best to just continue to ignore him. She quietly sipped as she waited for Alex.

The night had been filled with two local acoustic bands playing catchy music similar to that of Dave Matthews. Alex still had a lot of connections to his college musician friends and their friends, so he was always able to find talented artists for live night. People had been dancing to the upbeat music on and off all evening and were ready for something a little slower. By this time, enough liquor had been flowing and conversation ice broken that real or false intimacy in the form of slow dances started to look pretty great to the patrons too. Alex's music style was slow, melodic, legato sounds, often played in minor chords. He played and sang long and deeply. Although Sarah was buzzed, she knew how his music could always grip her soul and draw her in. So many beautiful words. She tried to ignore Dean, pressing more deeply into the side of her arm as Alex entered the stage.

Instant clapping and cheers erupted. Alex's patrons loved when he played. And he was a performer, the shyness and fear he felt melted when he was in front of an audience. When the whistling died down and the clapping faded, Alex took a seat on a stool and brushed the keyboard with his fingers and flipped the dark waves of his hair away from his eyes. Then, he rolled up his flannel sleeves (red-and-black checkers tonight) and said a few words before he played, "First, I want to thank everyone for coming out tonight. I know our musicians are grateful for all the love." He paused for a few cheers and applause. "I'm also grateful that y'all choose to take a break from whatever journey that you're on in this place. I've been thinking tonight about all the different paths we take…" He nodded at Jesse. Jesse returned the gesture by lifting his beer in good humor toward Alex. "It's hard to know how or why we end up on a certain path in life. Figuring out how we feel about that path and what to do with our feelings and dreams, lost or found, is a complication so few of us ever really figure out how to work through. The song I want to play for you tonight is about just that, working through whatever path we're on in life and coming to terms with whether we're supposed to be on that path. More importantly if we even want to be on that path. It's called 'Wandering Warrior.'"

Alex took a deep breath as a few applause whistles escaped the crowd briefly and faded as he began to play a slow, minor melody with deep chords that couldn't help but encourage the audience to take a deep breath and sink into the lullaby.

> "Bend for me, break easily.
> Follow my road, stay numb as you grow old."
> That's what they told her

So easily.

Her stories are those of fiction.
It's easy to blend inside them if you just listen.
Hear their desires, empower their words.
Lose yourself so in loneliness.
You won't be lost.

Brace yourself, this long road's ending,
Step inside the adventure that's been waiting.
I know your heart's long been bending
Toward that rising sun you know you've won.
"In time," they said, now your joy's never ending.

She bends, she breaks.
She blends, they take pieces of her soul,
the same sad song growing old
take a breath and feel the breeze,
you can be bold from your knees.

Brace yourself, this long road's ending,
Step inside the adventure that's been waiting.
I know your heart's long been bending
Toward that rising sun you know you've won.
"In time," they said, now your joy's never ending

Brace yourself, Wanderer
Brace yourself, Believer.
Brace yourself, Broken.
Or so they called you.
Brace yourself, Warrior.

She stands again,
Remembers herself.
The rising sun a shelter for her soul.
Walk your road, feel as you grow old.

Your joy is coming,
Bend toward the rising sun.
You've won.

As Alex sang, Sarah couldn't help but feel captivated by him. From the opening line, she was enchanted. The music was beautiful, but Sarah saw passion in her best friend's eyes that had been lost elsewhere. Alex was so tied to obligatory responsibilities. Sarah admitted to herself during his song that she missed seeing him this way, swept up in his music, allowing the beauty of his own creation to take over and enchant others. Although the melody of Alex's voice held her attention, she couldn't help but hear Dean whisper in her ear that he'd "like a dance." She noted that she didn't like how he gripped a piece of her hair and placed it behind her ear so she'd be sure to hear him. However, she didn't want to miss Alex's song by averting her attention fully to Dean. Dean didn't wait for an answer but grabbed her hand in what he presented as a gentlemanly manner and led her to the dance floor. As Sarah walked, she glanced behind her at Jesse to make sure he was okay with the dance, and he raised his glass and winked at her, happy that she was getting along with his best friend.

Dean wrapped one hand tightly around Sarah's waist. He locked his other hand into hers, forcefully gripping her knuckles with his own. Mostly, they gently swayed to Alex's next song, but each time Dean occasionally twirled her around, he'd pull her closer to his hips. Sarah felt his invasive movements, but she was buzzed and the liquor only allowed her full attention to be pulled in one direction—that of Alex. She watched his fingers dance across the keys so rhythmically, so naturally, as if he was catching up with an old friend. The microphone stood on the stand and almost seemed to lean into his voice, eager to share his words with the room.

As the last note of Alex's song rang in the air, Sarah couldn't help but catch the look in Dean's eyes before she pulled her hand out of his to applaud Alex. Throughout most of her conversation with Dean that night, he had smiled at her. Now, there was a strange, cold arrogance in his stare. His gaze bored into her eyes, as if he was drilling her for a compliance she didn't understand, something that yet lacked existence. He caught her meeting his gaze, quickly smiled, flipped his wavy hair, and applauded along with her, adding in one of those loud finger whistles that pierced the room, a sound Sarah could never quite master. She shook her head and dismissed the nervousness she felt around him. She didn't want to feel so strangely around her boyfriend's best friend. Plus, she was eager to meet Alex and congratulate him on his performance.

At this point in the night, Gabe had taken over managing the bar as Alex set aside some time to mingle with the patrons. He was leaning on the corner of the end of the bar when he saw Sarah slowly weave her way through the crowd toward him. He thanked the two young women he was talking with for coming in then quickly stood up to catch Sarah's embrace. She almost leaped toward him and fell into a tight hug. "Beautiful, Alex." She beamed at him as she spoke. "God, I don't hear you play enough anymore. Sometimes I forget how your lyrics can just fuck my soul right up. 'Brace yourself, Broken. Or so they called you…Brace yourself, Warrior.' You've named such honest things."

It was too dark for Sarah to see that Alex was blushing. It wasn't the first time she complimented his music; nevertheless, her words hit hard, and he couldn't help but feel happy that he had impressed her. "Thanks, Sarah." He smiled. "Felt like the right words for tonight. There's been a lot on my mind." A sadness briefly settled over his eyes. Sarah recognized the feeling.

"Your grandma?" she asked.

He nodded.

"I wondered if maybe she had something to do with your song choice." Sarah didn't realize that Alex's song represented a few people and feelings, those about Sarah included. "I know now isn't the best time to ask, but I have been thinking about her. I know you never got a chance to tell me how the visit went."

Alex met her eyes. Somehow, it was easier to speak about his pain at night with all the noise of the familiar bar around him. "My heart breaks when I see her. She is confused and doesn't always recognize me. This disease is slowly breaking her, commanding her who to be. But she is still there, and she is becoming something new. I felt better when I realized that I can help her find hope in this life she has now. I've got to let go of what she's been to me and help her navigate this new path. The task gave me comfort I guess, even though the reality of what the dementia is doing to her brain is heartbreaking."

Sarah's eyebrows furrowed into a worried line. "I think I understand as best I can. Sandy always was so full of strength. She knew herself, she knew you. There's got to be traces of that still or a way to weave that strength into this life. And if not, she did her best to pass that strength onto you, it's there. Maybe you can give it back to her."

Alex nodded and wiped a tear from his eye quickly as Jesse found his way to Sarah and interrupted their conversation. He slipped his arm around Sarah's waist, kissed her cheek charmingly as she smiled back at him, though she looked back at Alex and was clearly still worried. "Alex, my man," Jesse said confidently as he shook his hand. "Amazing song, sir, just amazing." He pulled Sarah closer to him. "Sarah always said you had talent, but there's nothing quite like actually hearing and seeing your music for myself. You should play more often, man."

Alex didn't much care for Jesse's arm around Sarah's waist but did his best to smile in return. He met Jesse's eyes. "Well, it's like you said, 'I've had my obstacles as I am sure you've had yours.'"

Jesse smiled. "Touché, my guy. Still, I gotta make my way down here Friday nights more often to hear you play. You really are inspiring, man, makes me think about the direction of my own path." He glanced toward Sarah. "Anyway, we'll get out of your hair, looks like we've created a bit of line." Several patrons had stacked up behind Jesse and Sarah, excited to connect with Alex. He winked at Alex as he escorted Sarah out. Dean had already exited shortly after the song ended, some excuse about having to visit family early in the morning.

"We'll catch up Monday, Alex?" she yelled behind her as Jesse led her out.

"Of course," he called back then returned his gaze to the line of patrons coming to congratulate him on the performance.

Chapter 9

Sarah spent the rest of the weekend at Jesse's duplex. Most of Friday and Saturday had been spent inside. They cooked a few meals together. Jesse had a good taste for spices, and Sarah loved the creativity he poured into the pasta sauces and sandwich concoctions he made. He even played a little acoustic guitar and would string together pieces of some of her favorite soft rock songs. However, each time he played, her mind would wander back to Friday's memory of Alex singing. She smiled as she thought of the way he flipped his dark hair as his voice rang in the microphone. And his words sunk deeply in her mind, "Brace yourself, Wanderer…" She remembered how his voice hit the tenor notes hard, eager to share the glad warning. She shook her head slightly, feigning adjusting her hair out of her eyes, and returned her focus to Jesse, smiling at him as he sang, though his voice was slightly off-key.

The weather on Friday and Saturday was cool as autumn set in. However, by Sunday, the sun had come out, and it was a beautiful time for a light hike. Since Jesse's apartment was a ways out of the city, he wasn't too far from a few state parks and trails. Once he saw the sun peeking out, he suggested they set out for a walk in the late morning. Sarah loved being outside (when it was decently warm), so she jumped at the idea. As beautiful and cozy as their weekend indoors had been, she found herself feeling that fresh air might not be a bad idea. A part of her that she didn't quite understand was starting to feel cramped in his apartment all weekend.

The trail they chose was only a few miles from Jesse's place. As they walked down the dirt path together, Jesse pointed out signs that coyotes had been around or willow plants that were rare in that area. Sarah couldn't help but continue to be impressed by his knowledge of trail life. She was always too deep in thought to know the specifics of the signs of nature around her. Jesse had been out enough on his own in that area that he was familiar with the creatures who left their traces there.

The early afternoon was lit golden. Most of the leaves had turned a soft yellow, and Sarah loved watching them swirl gently to the ground. The irony of such beauty is that the leaves were dying but there was peace in their soft, spinning motion. Sarah noticed that Jesse had stopped behind her to look at some sort of tree marking, so she allowed herself to stop and relax into the motion of the leaves as they spun. She watched them peacefully for a few minutes and allowed the breeze to rest on her skin.

Suddenly, she felt a presence behind her and quickly turned. Jesse was no longer at the tree but before her, on one knee, an oak-colored wooden box in his hands. She took a quick breath and stared down at him.

"Sarah," he said and tried to meet her eyes, "I've made some choices about the direction of my life. Honestly, I've spent most of it wandering, seeking beauty. My family expected me to find roots elsewhere, to educate internationally like they did. But ever since I've been back here, in the Midwest, I've wondered why I've stayed. Sure, I've been drawn by the beauty of the museum and my apartment out here in the woods, but there was a stronger pull I couldn't quite name."

Sarah started to smile as he reached for her hand with his empty one. "Sarah, there was a reason I instantly recognized you that night at Alex's bar. You are the kind of person people remember. Your light, your passion, your fire. You are an intense force that I cannot help but embrace." He paused as a few tears filled in his eyes. "I am captivated by your beauty and your love for helping to sustain life. You care for the forgotten and abandoned things of this world and comfort those who would take them in. I crave your energy, and I will regret it forever if I don't do everything I can to make you officially mine…" He took a deep breath and opened the oaken box to reveal a singular, sparkling diamond on top of a thin, gold band. "Will you marry me?"

Sarah gripped his hand more tightly in hers and knew what her answer was. However, before she could say it, she noted that her eyes had not filled with tears as Jesse's had. His words were beautiful, they should have captivated her, but her eyes remained dry. The breeze gently touched her face as a leaf fell in relief beside her, brushing her shoulder as it landed. There could be adventure here, in this beauty with Jesse. She ignored the feeling of hardness that started to form in her stomach, along with her dry eyes, and glanced briefly at the forest around her. Then she responded with, "Well yes, don't mind if I do."

Chapter 10

Alex's eyebrows didn't come down for a good fifteen seconds after Sarah broke the news over coffee Monday morning. The lid of his mint mocha hid the fact that his jaw had dropped, but there was no mistaking his eyes. He was shocked.

"I know," Sarah said, attempting reassurance. "It's barely been a year, and I was shocked too. I had no idea his mind had even been on a commitment like that...I mean, we were exclusive and spending most weekends together but..." She stopped midsentence, took a breath, and sipped her signature dark roast, trying to gather her thoughts again.

Alex's eyes drifted to the sparkling ring on her finger then back to her expression. Sarah's brow had furrowed, and she was clearly trying to sort out her thoughts. He was too shocked by the news to let the heartbreak sink in, and he knew he had to try to help his friend sort out her feelings.

"I know you're still processing it all," he said, "but do you think this is what you want?"

Sarah unfurrowed her brow and met his deep blue eyes with her own, breathing deeply before she spoke, "Well, you know me. I can't help but see an interconnectedness in all areas of my life and my mind is spinning..." Alex smiled. Sarah continued, "Companionship is something I've built my profession on. Every day, I try to match creatures with their best caregivers, to help them find missing pieces in each other. In the empty spaces between, while the animals are waiting to find their new families, I try my best to be the temporary companion that they need. Marrying Jesse is not the same as adopting animals, but I guess I use what I know to make sense of all things in my life. The people adopting the animals need to see themselves in the creature's story. They have to envision a future where their daily life is better with the animal by their side. The people feel needed and the animals offer a new adventure. But I have to find a way to weave together the animal's past, however tragic or simple, and the customer's future. The family has to be touched by the sadness the animal has felt after leaving one life along with the excitement about joining another. Maybe there's a little bit of a hero complex there but stories are the key..."

She took a breath and sipped her coffee. "I've thought about Jesse's past and his vision for the future. Truth be told, I cannot help but notice that he's gone a little stagnant. He grew up in Ecuador, surrounded by adventure and beauty, which I find fascinating. It's a childhood I could never understand, and I love learning about his experiences...and I love creativity. He seems a little stuck, but I can feel that he hasn't let go of creating. I can feel his drive when we cook, and he loses himself in a new combination of flavors. Or when he plucks at the strings on his guitar, eager to tell a story he can't quite piece together. I can see passion in some of the drawings he has created so far...And I felt excitement on the hike where he proposed."

Alex burned inside with sadness and jealousy but forced himself to ignore the feelings. Sarah continued, "The afternoon autumn sun gently burned my skin as I looked deeply into his eyes when he asked me. There is a story with Jesse that I can see myself in, just like the stories I see at work, a match that makes sense. I don't think Jesse will stay stagnant forever. I crave adventure. You know that's why I lose myself in the stories I read and the stories I tell at work." Alex nodded. "I think I can find that adventure with Jesse. I already have small glimpses of that adventure. So...to answer your question, yes, I think this is what I want."

Alex held her gaze tightly in painful but gentle understanding. He swallowed and searched her eyes. He thought he saw a trace of sadness as she looked back at him, waiting for his reassurance...He wasn't certain but he thought he saw something else in Sarah's eyes when she looked at him. Or maybe he just couldn't shake the wishful thinking that she might return his feelings, even now. Either way, the sadness was a trace, not enough to approach the subject of his own feelings for her. And right now was not the time, she had accepted another man's proposal and she needed her friend. He could see that her shoulders had tightened in her anxiety as she waited for his response.

He smiled, trying to help her relax with an assurance of his acceptance. "If anyone knows how smart you are, Sarah, it's me. Of course, I want to make sure this is the right choice and, most importantly, what you really want. But I know you and how deeply you turn each thought over in your mind. If you accepted his proposal, you had good reason to, brevity of the situation be damned. So any idea when the wedding will be?"

She smiled back and her shoulders relaxed. "Honestly, he'd like to get married in just a few months. He wants a small, Christmas wedding…Just a few of us at the ceremony in the courthouse or with an ordained minister in one of the decorated corporate buildings downtown."

Alex frowned. "But you hate winter. I would have thought you'd want to elope to the beach."

Sarah smirked. "Well you're not wrong, Alex. Eloping would have been my first choice, but then he suggested a venue for the reception that won me over…" She looked at him playfully and smiled wider…

Alex watched her for a moment and then realized the question she was hinting at. "Ah," he said playfully in return, "Let me guess…a charming local spot, a town staple…somewhere clean and tastefully run with a flair for the creative…a place people feel like home but also flock to for a ridiculously good time. I think I know of where you speak."

"I would love to have the reception at The Crooked Picture, Alex," she said. "I think you won him over with your music on Friday night. He even mentioned something about you playing at the reception…" Alex's eyes widened in nervous apprehension. He thought maybe Jesse was playing a game. He knew how close Sarah was with Alex; if he booked their reception at his bar, he showed the world he didn't see Alex as a threat.

"Not all night," Sarah said quickly, sensing that something was off. "Just a song or two. He loved 'Wandering Warrior.' And whatever you two talked about that night must have gotten to him."

It certainly did, Alex thought but didn't say and tried desperately to focus on Sarah's words.

"After the proposal that Sunday night, he kept going back to your conversation and your song. He said a lot of things about, 'Seizing the path you're on,' and 'Embracing the reality you're in, whatever that might look like.' I think you inspire him." She winked playfully.

Alex shook his head and smiled. "Truthfully, I think he inspired himself. He talked more than I did. But I will admit, I learned a lot more about him." Alex didn't like playing games but he knew he was in one, and he had to remain supportive. "There is something to your point about a depth inside him that I missed before…And if anyone would shine a light on that depth, it's you. And of course, my bar is available for your Christmas wedding reception." Alex couldn't help but acknowledge the twinge of pain in his heart as he said the words "your wedding." He was used to his friendship with Sarah and the boundaries they had drawn, but this was a level of commitment she had never made before. The shock of Sarah's new reality was part of what pushed him through the conversation. He couldn't quite believe the engagement yet. He did his best to navigate his way through the rest of the conversation.

Sarah smiled and thanked him for offering his bar for the reception. But she was also ready to move on with the conversation at this point. As excited as she may have been about the engagement, she had spent all weekend with Jesse and wanted to simply talk with her best friend.

"I know we talked about Grandma Sandy briefly on Friday… but I really do want to hear more about how she's doing and how you're feeling." She sat back and sipped her coffee. "If you're up for the conversation that is."

"Of course," he said. "I'm about to visit her again tomorrow afternoon, so it might not be a bad idea to try to get in the right headspace now." He proceeded to fill Sarah in more about his grandmother's confusion and his plan for trying to meet her where she was at mentally. Sarah fell naturally and empathetically into their usual conversational tone as he spoke. However, underneath all their words, there was an unspoken uneasiness between the both of them. Certainly, there were feelings on both ends that were not ready to swim their way to the surface, but something else was off. Sarah was certain of her excitement about her news, but both she and Alex knew on some level that her happiness over the proposal was missing something. She was excited for the story to be told, but where exactly was Jesse in that story? What adventure would he bring to her own?

Chapter 11

The wedding was small, which meant planning happened quickly. Both Alex and Sarah hardly noticed as the three short months prior to the ceremony passed. Sarah only wanted her closest friends there, which included Alex and her close friend and manager, Jamie. She had no siblings and lost regular contact with her parents after they retired to Alaska when she moved out. They had never been particularly close, but they wanted to make it to the wedding. Unfortunately, there was a bad snowstorm that stopped outgoing flights for a week, so they couldn't make the ceremony but they promised to throw her a celebration party somewhere in the Midwest that summer.

Jesse's wedding party was small too. He only wanted Dean as his witness and his parents present. They chose the courthouse downtown for the ceremony and decided to put their celebration and decorative energy into Alex's bar for the reception afterward. Sarah had come to know The Crooked Picture as home and was comfortable with the Saturday night guests being a part of the reception.

Sarah planned most of the wedding herself. Although Jesse was all about getting married, follow-through with logistics was not at the top of his priority list. He was too preoccupied with "getting his apartment ready" for Sarah to move in though there wasn't much that needed preparation besides Sarah moving some of her furniture there. She had already been staying with him most weekends.

The morning of the wedding arrived, and Sarah and Alex were decorating the bar before it opened. Alex had planned on keeping the business closed until the reception began at 6:00 p.m., though all usual patrons were invited to the special event once it began. Alex hung several beautiful white and gold sashes from the ceiling.

They met at the disco ball in the center of the dance floor. He was arranging red and white roses on a few of the tables as Sarah hung some white string lights near the sashes for ambiance. They mostly worked in companionable silence. Although there was a strange tension between the two in the room as they worked, no one spoke of anything besides the reception plans and their usual banter. As Alex cut the stems of a few roses evenly so they rested in sync in the clear vase, he thought of the visit with his grandmother the week prior.

Grandma Sandy had told him that his music made her feel at home. In the midst of her confusion, the melodies that Alex created found a safe, untouchable space in her brain that she could not forget. In addition to piano/keyboard, Alex also played acoustic guitar. He had played for Sandy throughout his life but stopped when she was diagnosed. When she requested his music again, he reintroduced the pastime they shared by playing some of her favorite John Denver covers, along with a few of his originals. As he played, peace would wash over Sandy's face, and she would sink into the familiarity of music. The raging confusion and anxiety in her brain would settle into the serenity of the sounds as Alex's fingers confidently plucked each note. Most of his visits with Sandy started with her feeling confused about his presence or fixating on discomforts she had felt earlier in the day. "I hate the food here, Alex. These people wouldn't know actual flavor if it punched them in the face, which I have a mind to do." She frowned as she spoke and had a hard time letting go of the pieces of assisted-living life that made her unhappy. Alex did his best to listen empathetically and acknowledge her frustration. Then, he tried to help her slowly transition to the present where he could put her mind at ease and play her a song. He was only successful at easing her frustration about half the time, but the chance that he could help her refocus was worth trying.

However, a visit two weeks prior to Sarah's wedding had changed his routine. Instead of finding his grandmother sitting in the familiar floral recliner where she usually waited for him, she was standing up against an unstable kitchenette chair, struggling to speak and walk. Since she looked as if she might fall, Alex rushed to her side and tried to hold her hand to steady her and lead Sandy to whichever destination she was headed. However, as he gently grasped her hand, she leaned forward and sank her teeth into the knuckles of his index and middle fingers. Alex winced in pain and immediately tried to reposition her hand on the chair near the table. The interaction was chaotic and scary as she almost fell when he pulled his hand back, but he was able to steady her on the kitchen chair in time. Then, he tried to meet her eyes, desperate for an answer as to why she had suddenly and violently tried to bite him, but he found nothing but clouded rage when she stared back at him. There was no familiarity in her glance. He realized then that she saw the world, Alex included, as an impediment to her journey. Everything was an obstacle to where she was trying to go, whether that place was logical or not. Alex didn't understand and couldn't help her.

He immediately pressed the emergency button on her wall that would call the staff. Two aids came in and attempted to calm and steady Sandy as she tried to shake them loose and screamed as she attempted to bite them too. Alex watched and knew he should try to help, but he couldn't have felt more helpless. He desperately dashed out of the room with tears in his eyes and disbelief in his heart. His grandmother had never been violent with him before. The new routine of calming her confusion with music had worked the last few months. But she had only been confused with her words, not her body. As much as he tried to wear a bravery he did not feel by putting aside his own longing for the caregiver he had grown up with and provide her a safe space, he could not do it in this moment. Violence was something new, and he wasn't ready to face the newfound rage in the only parental figure he had ever known.

Alex had not visited Sandy since the incident. He didn't want to abandon his grandmother to her confusion, but he was not yet sure how to face her, and he didn't trust his own feelings. He could not be certain that he wouldn't be overcome by grief and anger. The neutral empathy that his grandmother needed was not something he could give her yet. In the midst of the pain of losing the grandmother he knew even further, Alex of course also felt the grief of potentially losing the love of his life to a watered-down version of the man she actually deserved. "Who is the man she actually deserves?" he asked himself. *Me? I am a failure. What dreams am I living? Who am I helping? Certainly not my grandma and certainly not Sarah if she's looking elsewhere.*

Alex's thoughts were dark, but he couldn't help but think them. *Maybe I'm not so different from Jesse. I'm not off in California, and I am definitely not a full-time composer.* He tried to shake his insecurities and remind himself that he had good reasons for staying in the Midwest and running the bar, but he couldn't help but feel frustrated and ashamed. He was shaken by the violent interaction with Sandy, and that, plus the lack of sleep since made everything else feel overwhelmingly hopeless. All he knew how to do was continue helping Sarah with preparing for her wedding. Best friend and event planner were familiar roles, he played them all the time, safe roles where he never felt like a failure.

As he helped Sarah prepare for her wedding, Alex did his best to convince himself that the familiar role of best friend was what was best for the both of them. Sarah craved adventure. He could not give her adventure when he could barely stomach moving forward with the care of his grandmother. He was also unsure if he could handle the pain of rejection if he actually told Sarah he was in love with her. Ultimately, Alex numbed himself to the truth of what it would actually mean to lose the potential for Sarah to truly be the love of his life for the rest of his life. Underneath the distraction of helping her plan the logistics, in a place he refused to feel, a part of him was aware of the finality of marriage. Sarah was committing herself to Jesse, eliminating all hopes of ever becoming more to him. All Alex was able to do for now was continue life as her best friend. At least then he would have her in his life. And as he believed a best friend would, he pushed aside his own struggles so that he could help Sarah with her special day. He decided not to tell her about the incident with his grandmother since it occurred only two weeks before her wedding. He knew that she would put planning aside and help him focus on how to move forward with his relationship with Sandy. He told himself that he didn't want to distract from her wedding, but maybe the truth was that he wasn't ready to face the solutions that Sarah might help him find.

Sarah interrupted his anxious, repetitive thoughts, "Hey, Alex…?"

He shook his head, slightly startled, and looked up at her as she continued to hang the string lights. "Yeah, what's up?" he answered.

She smiled. "I was just thinking about that time you and I talked about visiting that same beach you used to spring break at with your grandma. You know, the one in California?"

Alex winced a little at the thought of memories of that beach, when his grandmother was herself, but was happy to think about visiting with Sarah. "Yeah, I know the one. Looks like we never made it there for the visit."

Sarah frowned. "Yeah, I was thinking about that too. I know you have to spend most weekends here, and I usually end up on call Saturday and Sunday at the shelter so we've had our obstacles. I guess it's just that things are changing for me now so I've been thinking about…Well, I don't want to call them 'regrets,' but I guess adventures I wish I would've had. Jesse likes you, but I'm not so sure he'd be cool with us vacationing alone somewhere."

Alex's back was to her as he continued to arrange the flowers and his mouth formed a small, cocky smile, "What, you wouldn't want to bring him along?"

Sarah responded quickly, speaking fast, "Well no, I mean, it's not that. Of course I would." Alex wasn't convinced. "I guess it's maybe the same idea as a bachelorette party or something, you know, one last joy ride before a major commitment and change?"

Alex responded, "I know what you mean. I would have liked to have gone with you. Though I have to be honest, I've never fully understood the concept of bachelor and bachelorette parties, or at least how they play out, like you're sentencing yourself to ONE person as if the commitment is a bad thing. You and I both know how empty the dating roster can feel. I guess if I ever did do some kind of party like that for you, I'd want it to be more of a celebration and less of a penis-necklace-filled booze fest."

Sarah smiled. "I get what you mean. I don't like to think that I am signing my life away to Jesse. A marriage is supposed to be a new adventure, right? And you're right about the roster, you know more than anyone how lonely I felt. I guess I've just been thinking a lot about my life and how I am going to accomplish all my goals. When you and I talked about why Jesse never finished art school, it got me thinking about how I have yet to open my own veterinary practice. I know that I am doing meaningful work in the interim of my long-term goals of having my own clinic, but I guess I don't have any practical plan for finding the money to actually open one. Sure, I'll save on rent when I move in officially with Jesse, but it will still be years before I'd have enough to actually start the business. Plus, I'll be farther out of the city and farther from more potential business. I don't know, maybe there's something at the wildlife park near his place. Maybe I could shadow there and get some new ideas about the types of animals I could work with." She sighed. "I know I've judged Jesse for not living bigger dreams, but when I looked at myself, there's a lot of dreams that I haven't pursued. And for some reason, I've become frustrated with my own excuses."

Alex turned to face her and met her eyes, a serious look in his own. "If anyone will find a way to accomplish their goals, it's you. I know you've had your obstacles, but your opportunities aren't empty yet. A lot could change, a lot is changing. But I know you, and your drive and you will find a way to make it happen. And on that note of inspiration, I would love to take you to the beach in California anytime you are up for it. I know you're not quite comfortable if Jesse's not cool with the trip but the offer stands. Technically, I didn't throw you a bachelorette party, so think of the trip as a wedding gift from me, whenever you might be ready."

Sarah's heart sped up, and she was briefly at a loss for words. Alex had a way of looking into her and gripping her soul with his words. Sometimes, he simply captivated her because he saw her, the deep pieces of her that she wished others could grasp; she felt understood and ready to find all she hoped for with her goals in those moments where he spoke to her deeply. She found herself lost in one of those moments with him as she stood there, preparing decorations for her wedding to another man. She gulped, met his eyes, and was about to break the silence when Jesse strolled in.

"Damn, guys, looks beautiful in here." He smiled wide and cheesily as he walked over to Sarah and gently took her hand to help her down off the ladder.

Sarah was shaken out of her focus on Alex. The words she kept hidden in her throat would remain there even when the moment passed though she would try to swallow them. She smiled at Jesse. "Well, Alex is the best. We've both been at it for a few hours now, but I think we're just about done."

Alex shifted his gaze from Sarah, barely revealing any disappointment at the interruption. He had grown used to pushing his feelings aside and accepting Jesse, at least on the surface, especially since Jesse had created some sort of game by hosting their reception at Alex's bar. "Happy to help you both, not to mention it should be a good night for business. People love a party, even if they don't know the couple super well. Open bars have a way of drawing a crowd Speaking of which, how long do you want it to be open?"

Jesse's brow furrowed. "I think my parents agreed to pay for about three hours, so let's cut it around nine. By then, people will be relaxed enough that they don't mind paying for their own, right?"

"That's a fair guess," Alex said. "So nine it is." He glanced around the room. All the decorations were hung beautifully and the tables were set. He had a few extra cooks on staff that night for a light reception dinner at six. All the details were in place, and he was ready to simply focus on the task of helping Sarah enjoy her night without incident. It was clear that any other conversation Sarah and Alex might've had about the two of them just wasn't meant to happen now. Jesse made sure of that. "Well," Alex said to the both of them as he placed the familiar pencil behind his ear, "I'm going to head to the cellar to make sure we've got enough stocked for the open bar. Lots of gin." He winked at Sarah. "See you two in a couple hours at the courthouse."

Jesse smiled wide as he put his arm around Sarah and walked her out. She couldn't help but glance over her shoulder at the empty staircase where Alex had disappeared. Sarah looked down, sighed, and then forward again. She assured herself she was making the right choice. Although there was a slight nagging in her gut that went deeper than even potential feelings for Alex, she pushed the warning aside and walked on with Jesse. There was adventure with him, she knew it, and he could grow into the brief moments of brilliance she had seen in him.

Chapter 12

The wedding was quick and simple. Alex served as Sarah's witness and Dean as Jesse's. They exchanged simple vows provided to them by the judge who officiated their wedding. Sarah would have liked to have written her own, but they only had a few minutes for their ceremony and she figured she could say a few words at the reception. She looked beautiful. She wore her shoulder-length brown hair half up with a few red spray roses woven into the strands that had been pulled tightly around her head. Her dress was a beautiful white satin that clung to her hips and hung low off her shoulders. Jesse wore a brown vest over a long, white formal shirt. He kept a matching brown jacket on during the ceremony but removed it for the ride to the reception. He looked handsome. Sarah was enamored with Jesse, but she couldn't also help but notice how handsome Alex appeared in a simple black formal shirt and gray dress pants. His dark hair and blue eyes were striking.

The small wedding party went straight from the ceremony to the reception. Alex, Sarah, Jesse, Jesse's parents, and Dean all shared a limo to Alex's bar and celebrated with champagne along the way.

"Such a beautiful ceremony," Jesse's mother remarked with a toothy smile. She was a plump woman with tight curls piled on top of her head. "I like when folks keep things simple, sort of like your hair, dear." She gestured toward Sarah. "No fuss, no muss, no need for a formal updo just as long as you're content." She made a "cheers" gesture toward Sarah and took another gulp of champagne.

Sarah frowned slightly and got the impression that she was being passive aggressively insulted but smiled anyway. Her interactions with Jesse's parents had been so minimal, she didn't want to engage in any kind of conflict now.

Jesse's father, a tall, slim man with a bushy mustache chimed in, "Now of course my wife doesn't mean things were too simple. Course not, we just haven't heard much from our guy lately until this big news so anything big and flashy might've been too much."

Jesse smiled and said, "Aw, Dad, come on. You know how busy work has been lately. Not easy to just call you up and explain how I've found the love of my life." He put his arm around Sarah as she smiled a little awkwardly but also appreciated the gesture. "I'm just glad you guys could make it today."

"Sure, sure, anything for our boy." His mother smiled. "And she is indeed lovely."

Sarah felt a little awkward at being talked about, rather than directly to her, especially when her knees were practically smooshed up against her fellow passengers. Alex was about to say something when Dean, who sat on Sarah's opposite side, quickly came to her rescue by addressing her directly and changing the subject.

"Yes, Sarah"—his eyes met hers directly—"you are lovely. I've certainly appreciated the conversations I've had with you. Matter of fact, why not start the toasts early…If everyone could please raise their glasses…I know I'm Jesse's best man, and I've got plenty of words for him that I'd like to save for a brilliant speech later tonight." He winked. "But for now, I'd like to take a moment to honor his beautiful bride." His eyes subtly traced over Sarah hungrily. "From the moment I met you, I understood immediately why Jesse was so quick to make you his. You are a passionate woman who speaks into existence all the beautiful, empathetic gestures that should dominate this world. Your care and concern for others radiates through your being and one cannot help but be swept up by your charm. Jesse, you are a lucky man. Sarah, I have no doubts of your deserving my best man. Cheers to both of you." He winked again as they all raised their glasses and drank in response. Only Alex noticed the way that Dean looked back at Sarah as everyone else laughed and drank more. There was a strangeness in his dark eyes that didn't sit well with Alex. He couldn't quite name the strangeness, but he decided not to dismiss the feeling. It was going to be a busy night, but he would keep an eye on Dean if he could.

Alex's bar was fit for a party. He brought out his best champagne and cabernet and kept the excitement flowing. His gift to Sarah was bringing in her favorite local '90s and early 2000s cover band for the night's music. They played so many of her middle and high school favorites: "Real World" by Matchbox 20, "Black Balloon" by the Goo Goo Dolls, and acoustic versions of NSync's "Bye Bye Bye." The bar patrons and few friends of Alex's and Jesse's families danced all evening and kept the party vibe going. As a special gift, one that was more for Sarah than the couple, Alex himself sang "I'll be" by Edwin McCain for her wedding slow dance. The bar lights were low and blue, per Sarah's request, and they complimented the beauty of the white string lights they hung earlier that day. Alex's voice rang strong and beautiful throughout the dance floor and he played the accompanying piano notes.

Sarah tried to pull herself into Jesse as they slow-danced to breathe in the scent of his cologne, the one that smelled of pine trees and reminded her of the nature walks they took together. Jesse held her hips tightly as she draped her arms around him and kissed her deeply as they remained alone on the dance floor for the first two minutes of the song. Sarah tried to sink into his smell and the feeling of his lips. "Yes," she told herself as she pulled away and stared into his eyes, strands of deep blue like waves of the ocean, "this is a good story. He is who I want and more adventure awaits here." Jesse kissed her shoulder where the dress had exposed her delicate skin and she felt wanted and seen.

Alex sang on, "Tell me that we belong together. Dress it up with the trappings of love. I'll be captivated. I'll hang from your lips instead of the gallows of heartache that hang from above..."

Sarah's eyes were focused on Jesse, and she didn't notice when Alex looked toward her as he sang. Alex saw how the blue light reflected softly on Sarah's hair as Jesse slowly twirled her around once and pulled her back into him. They looked so in sync on the dance floor. Their bodies moved as gracefully as the night they met. For just a moment, he felt a twinge of regret at not sharing his true feelings for Sarah and about Jesse soon after she met him. *But would that have changed her mind about the man? Would she have been bitter toward Alex for creating tension in their friendship? Would she have resented him for trying to end her relationship with Jesse?* Alex did his best to ignore these questions and perform as the twinge of regret quickly turned to pain as he saw how Jesse held her.

Alex could ignore a twinge, but the pain soon swarmed his insides as his anxious thoughts tormented him, *How could Jesse match the companionship I could offer Sarah? There's a beautiful connection I know that I alone have with her.* He thought of the connection that he was sure would make him so endlessly happy if he were brave enough to accept that it could exist, even with the obstacles of life. But obstacles are terrifying. His grandmother, the bar, Sarah's passion and insistence on bravery, a quality Alex wasn't sure he was strong enough to face any of it.

The final line of the song approached as a tear formed in his eye. He remembered something he once told Pete when he asked Alex why he loved music so much and why he had never given writing up entirely. He told him, "There is power in the words I write. In songs and poems, I can name every pain, shout every joy, and scream every anger. Song gives me the power to own the emotion and the experience. All artists should feel powerful. In their words, paint, clay, and pen, they take hold of all that is human in their corner of the world." Remembering the strength he spoke of moved him to sing the last line, "I'll be the greatest fan of your life." The word *life* was sung in four syllables. He swallowed and closed his eyes as he sang. That particular line was always so strange. He was never certain what it meant, but as he sang, he felt the power of some sort of potential. The words *I'll be* and *life* rang with something new coming, something living and moving. Maybe he didn't know what the feeling was yet, but somehow, the melody and words eased the pain he felt about losing Sarah. Life was unpredictable, and she was still in his. Endings weren't always what they seemed.

Sarah sat down after the dance and took a deep breath as the cover band continued with more hits. "Whew." She glanced up at where Alex had been playing and noticed he exited the stage. Her eyes scanned the room for him, hoping to flag him down so she could thank him when Dean interrupted her search, "Beautiful dance, Sarah." She glanced across the wedding party's table at him, seeing the table's candlelight reflecting in his dark eyes.

"Thank you." She smiled back. "I know some find McCain's one and only hit cheesy, but it's one of my favorites from our high school days."

"Not cheesy at all," he replied. "Sometimes people are too quick to judge popular things. They forget that the song had an original meaning to the artist. Creative ideas can spread quickly and seem superficial, even though they're not."

Sarah appreciated Dean's understanding, but her focus was still on Alex. "I still can't believe how beautifully Alex sang. I mean, he's my best friend and I know he's talented, but sometimes, people you know best can still surprise you in certain moments."

Jesse put his arm around her shoulders. "Never doubted him." He smiled his cocky smile. "I still remember how good he was in high school. Every talent show he always brought a little more flair to the mic than anyone else, something real there I guess."

Sarah nodded. "Anyway, I was hoping to thank him but he seems to have disappeared."

"Ah, I'm sure he's just talking with the guests or restocking the bar. It's a special night you know." Jesse smiled as he spoke.

"You're right. I'm sure I'll catch him later," Sarah replied.

Sarah danced for the next hour with a few friends from work, regulars at the bar, and Jesse's friends and family. She was having a fantastic time but was bothered that she couldn't find Alex. She knew he hadn't left but was likely managing the party from afar.

In truth, Alex was taking some time to himself outside the bar. After the song, he needed air and to collect his thoughts. As much as he questioned whether it was the right time to be with Sarah (had she not, of course, just married another man), the pain of pretending his heart wasn't broken could not constantly be kept at bay. The music he played for her both saved and crippled him. He was able to release his sadness, but in that release, he was reminded of just how despondent he truly was about losing her. He knew they would remain friends, but the sense of loss slowly dug into his heart. He leaned against the brick wall on the side of the building, opposite from all the smokers, so he could be alone.

He decided then that he needed space the rest of the night. He would focus on making sure the rest of the evening ran smoothly but would stay out of Sarah (and Jesse's) direct sight line. He couldn't face her, not now. He needed time to fully accept the loss the music stirred up. He wiped the tears that had streamed silently down his face, took a deep breath, and headed back inside and down to the bar cellar to make sure liquor was fully stocked. He only had an hour or two until the night was over, and he had enough staff working to manage the floor. He tried to convince himself as he walked that he could simply continue being her friend. As long as she was still in his life, the pain would subside. But on some level, one he wasn't ready to acknowledge, Alex recognized that convincing and truly believing were two different states of mind and the former may only be maintained temporarily.

Chapter 13

Alex took the rest of the weekend to himself. He handed over management of the bar to Gabe and spent most of his time reading, hiking nearby trails, or trying to write music though nothing came to him. He hadn't heard from Sarah, which he thought was a little strange. However, he didn't look too far into the realization of her silence. She had just been married after all, and Alex's main goal was distraction. He was trying to find a way to move on and live in a new normal where Sarah was married and he would only ever be a friend.

He didn't hear from her until the following Friday, almost a week later. She called him to ask if he could meet her for coffee that afternoon. He figured she had been busy celebrating with Jesse over the last week, but he walked into the coffee shop to find a very strange, heavy expression on her face and throughout her body. Sensing that something was very wrong, he skipped ordering his drink and sat down with her at the table. She instantly met his eyes, and said, "I have no idea how to begin this conversation other than simply to tell you everything..."

Chapter 14

Sarah's Story

"The invasion started with how he held my hand. Dean pulled me toward the back of the dance floor as the band began to play another slow song."

"'You looked like you could use a break from the spotlight.' He smiled.

"Truth be told, I was exhausted and overstimulated. Although my wedding night was a blast up until then, I still needed a break from the crowd and emotions, however elated I might have been. That's why Dean's pull was so inviting. As he led me to the back of the dance floor, near the back hallway of the bar, I felt his fingers lightly trace the swollen veins on top of my left hand, my dominant hand. We were surrounded by the party noise but he touched me intimately anyway, as if we were alone. Then, he locked his fingers in mine. Tight. The liquor buzzed in my skin, but I still felt the clammy discomfort that comes with fear, fear of something wrong felt in public, yet somehow, no one else was noticing. Dean didn't care that we were so close to a crowd. He locked his fingers inside mine anyway.

"When I turned to speak to someone else, his arm slid around my waist and gripped my hip. I felt his shoulder and chest against my back as he cleverly forced me into the back hallway and into the single-stall bathroom. I must have looked like I was stumbling, and that he was trying to help steady me because no one stopped him from leaving the dance floor with me. Inside the bathroom, I was just tipsy enough to lose my balance and rely on him so I wouldn't fall as he pushed. As I stumbled, trying to catch my balance and breath, he shut and locked the door behind him…Alex, you know those chaise loungers you keep in the bathroom?"

He nodded in recognition.

"I'll never forget the sight of the red velvet one, lined with the golden-yellow frame under the low, soft lights of the restroom."

She continued, "Dean pinned my arms down on the chaise. Then, he released his right hand once I was situated where he wanted and pressed his forearm deep into my ribs and arms, holding me steady as he slowly slid my satin dress up and pulled my underwear down. He used a gentle forcefulness and whispered that he would 'Be my escape.' I felt his hot breath heavy in my ear as he spoke, 'You are a passionate woman,' hands sliding further up my legs and gripped my hips, 'So much need for control.' He pressed himself into me, 'Let me show you that you can let go…'

"He didn't need to use much force. I was in shock. I was also not completely sober. Only two thoughts ran through my mind the entire time…One, had I given him some sort of signal that this is what I wanted? Perhaps he had misread some of my thoughts and that my interest in his work meant I was interested in him? Two, how could I get out of this? No one else was around, the door was locked, and the music was loud. When I remember the invasion, I mostly hear muffled laughter, yelling, and the echoes of acoustic guitars though I couldn't name the song. I pinned a place on the ceiling to stare at. I had to focus on my thoughts so I couldn't feel his dry, scaly hands on my hips, his sick twistedness inside me…I refused to really feel how he touched me though my body sensed every inch of him. You might think that I should have yelled, screamed, or perhaps even fought him off me. Although I am a tall woman, Dean was at least four inches taller, and he had probably fifty pounds on me. I wasn't physically strong enough to fight him. And I didn't know what he might do…There was no certainty that anyone could hear me. I could only think of one thing to say to Dean, and I repeated that thing over and over again in a soft but sure and desperate voice, 'I married Jesse. No, I married Jesse, I married Jesse, I married Jesse…'

"He continued the invasion for what felt like an hour, but I think, really, it was only a few minutes. Then, he suddenly and silently let me go after one final, 'I married Jesse.' I could only think about one step at a time. My first step was to get out, to try to get to the crowd again, even if they didn't notice me before. When Dean got off me, I left the bathroom as quickly as possible. My clothes were still on for the most part, so it was a quick exit. Second step, find help. I wandered out to find you, but I couldn't see you anywhere on the floor, and I didn't have the clarity to wander too far, so I searched for Jesse. I found him laughing and drinking with a few of his museum friends on the opposite side of the bar. I did my best to pull him out of the bar before Dean resurfaced, desperate to avoid seeing him at all costs. I will still too in shock to cry or yell, but Jesse must have recognized the fear and confusion on my face because he followed me out.

"'Dean,' I said to him…I started breathing faster and felt my heartbeat race, 'Dean…' I struggled to actually say the words to Jesse. I didn't want it to be real. Not at my wedding, not my husband's best friend, this couldn't have happened to me. I didn't want to say them but I had to. What words could I find except those that described exactly what happened? Matter of fact was all I was capable of in that moment. I did my best to take a deep breath. 'He…I think he raped me, Jesse.'

"'What?' his brow furrowed as he shook his head, and it seemed like he was trying to sober up. 'He what? What do you mean? What happened?'

"'I said what happened,' I responded, 'He raped me.'

"'But how? When could that even have happened? At our wedding? Where?'

"'He was dancing with me and pulled me into the bathroom,' I told him.

"'What? Why did you go with him?' He still looked confused and was still very clearly drunk.

"'Because he's your best friend, Jesse, and it's our wedding. Why would I ever expect him to do something like that? I'm your wife. Things happened fast and I didn't understand.'

"'Okay, okay.' He rubbed my back. 'Let's just go home where it's quieter and we can think. I already lined up a cab to take us back earlier today. Should be ready to go.'"

Alex just stared deeply into Sarah at this point. His eyes full of desolate sadness and regret.

Sarah swallowed and continued, "I tried to talk to him when we got back to his apartment, but I couldn't find any more words to explain. I then attempted to go to bed so I could unwind my mind, but I tossed and turned, feeling like maybe I should make some sort of report. Jesse said he believed me but that it would be better to wait until morning before making any 'big' decisions. Despite what he said, I couldn't shake the feeling that I should make a call. I left our bed around 3:00 a.m. and stepped out on the deck, the same one where we had watched the deer in the moonlight only a short time ago. I couldn't help but compare past romance to my current crisis as I dialed the nonemergency police line.

"I don't know why I allowed my mind to wander to a time that was more beautiful. It made the present truth of what Dean had done that much more ugly. And I couldn't say why, but something about Jesse's response bothered me. He didn't think to confront Dean or go to the police. He said he believed me but just wanted to get out. If I am being honest, Alex, he looked lost, full of disbelief. I guess I felt in my gut that I had to make the right decision for myself, whether or not Jesse responded as I wanted him to. Although I wasn't even sure exactly how I wanted him to respond. How could I imagine a desired response to something horrific that I never thought would happen to me? To a crime that repulsed me and didn't feel real? Anyway, I called the police from the deck. I had to leave to meet the detective in the city where the crime occurred to start an actual investigation. I felt sober enough by that moment to drive and left our house at 6:00 a.m. Sunday to drive down here alone to meet her. I decided not to tell Jesse I was leaving. I know it sounds strange that I wouldn't say anything to my new husband before leaving, but I had this overwhelming feeling that I just had to go and that if I were to wake him up, he'd try to talk me out of it."

Alex's brow furrowed at her last statement, but he quickly released the frustration in his eyes and responded, "I'm so sorry, Sarah." He gulped, completely uncertain of how to comfort her, or if she even needed comfort in that moment. How does one follow such a story? What words are there? He tried to find some words, any words as she stared at him—a deep, unique sadness and hopelessness set deeply in her eyes. Before Alex could say any more, she interjected and pulled her gaze from his, looking to the side and up as she spoke, but not directly in his eyes.

"What words could you say? I am so trapped in my own mind, Alex, and I don't understand any of the vultures circling there or how to clear them. I feel so empty and full of disbelief. I am alive, which shows great strength, but all I feel is a crippling weakness that I am terrified of. My sense of reality is gone. In general, I have always felt that something grounded me. I couldn't even tell you what that something was. I just knew it was there and that I felt safe. The only thing I can think to describe is that I am floating. Nothing and no one anywhere can ground me. Since the attack, I feel that I have to fear everything and everyone, except those who have a clear, defined role. It was easy to trust the nurse at the hospital. She knew each step of her task and there was a clear, researched method of comforting me in the process. I trust the detective at the station, her role is to learn what happened and collect the facts. Jamie, my manager, knows what happened. She saw me disappear quickly with Jesse at the end of the wedding night and telling work is the logical thing to do I guess, if I needed time off. I'm just following a step in my mind that seemed to make sense though I couldn't tell you why. Step 1, call in sick to work and give my manager enough details to be excused. Step 2, find somewhere to stay for the week."

Alex looked confused. Sarah responded, "I'll get to that part later…Step 3, try to find something small that comforted me—per the hospital's emotional support liaison's recommendation—so I got a dark roast coffee with extra espresso in it…In hindsight, all the caffeine probably wasn't the best idea…Step 4, find Alex and tell him the whole story." She looked up and met his eyes again, tears forming but refusing to fall.

"I don't know why I told you the story. Logically, it makes sense, you're my best friend. Logically, there should be a step-by-step guide to what you should say to help me feel better. I want to feel better so that guide should work. The guide should be just like the nurse's role, medical support, or the detective's role, collect evidence. Best friend's role, comfort. But there's no answer that could comfort me. No matter how badly I want that comfort. These are uncharted waters for an experience human beings were not meant to have. We were not meant to be violated in this way. That's why we become so sick when we are, and there's nothing anyone can say or do to pull us back to safety, to give a sense of solid ground. An anchor, Alex. That's what I need. I need words that will anchor and ground me. Words that can show me I am safe again, but I have no idea what those words are. What words can counteract this new trigger that my mind and body are always in danger? I can feel around you because you are my friend. I have a real relationship with you, which makes me vulnerable. And in that vulnerability, I feel exposed to danger because my mind and body can no longer distinguish different types of hurt. I guess I would rather just be numb right now. When I am around those I can't feel, I am safe because the feelings that make me vulnerable aren't there." Two tears, tightly connected, dripped from her eyes.

"Sorry. I know that I am talking a mile a minute." Alex shook his head, trying to reassure her that he wasn't frustrated with the speed of her words, and she went on, "In the midst of such danger, I thought I could lean on my husband, however new he was. Surely, he would tell the truth about what his best friend did to me. It was vile, it was wrong. Whatever 'bond' Jesse had with Dean couldn't outweigh rape, right? But he didn't. Regardless of my role as his wife and the drive he should feel to protect me, what Dean did was simply wrong. Jesse should have felt that. He should have recognized it and told the detective what I told him the night he brought me home instead of to the hospital." She paused and closed her eyes tightly, taking a deep breath.

Before she could continue, Alex interjected, confused, "What, Sarah? What do you mean about Jesse's bond with Dean? If you don't mind my asking, what happened after you drove yourself back to the city?"

Sarah met his eyes again, a deep fury replacing the sadness in hers. "The police officer that I reported the rape to advised me to go to the hospital for an exam...I didn't know exactly what that meant at the time but I learned later." Her fury disappeared briefly and the numbness returned to her expression as she paused then shook her head and frowned as she continued, "The police officer took a report from Jesse over the phone after I left our meeting to drive myself to the hospital. When I left the hospital, I was about to drive back to our place when the detective who had been assigned to my case called me. She said that Jesse's story didn't entirely match mine. She believed me and assured me that she was going to keep the case open and investigate, but when she questioned Jesse briefly over the phone about what happened that night, he responded with, 'Oh, I'm not sure...Yeah, Sarah came to me feeling worried and saying something went down with Dean, but we were all drinking that night and she might've just misinterpreted him flirting or something.'"

Sarah swallowed and met Alex's eyes again, her expression bursting with rage. "He didn't tell her anything, Alex. Nothing of the truth and fear I entrusted to him when I ran to find him. He saw me when I was afraid, he saw me feeling confused, and most importantly, I could see in his eyes when I told him Dean raped me that he knew it was the truth, even if he wouldn't admit that knowledge. Why wouldn't he tell the detective? As soon as she told me his 'side of the story,' I decided to stay at Jamie's the rest of the week. Jesse tried to call me a couple of times but I ignored him. I don't have any words right now for such an unexpected betrayal."

She took a deep breath and relaxed into her chair. "Anyway, all I know how to do right now is function in steps. And the next one was telling you the whole story, only I'm not entirely sure why, just that I needed to."

Alex was crippled by guilt. He felt a sinking stone in his stomach, one that held the weight of the belief that he should have protected her. He should have been there. He knew. He had seen the evil in Dean's eyes, and he was so absorbed in his own feelings the night of Sarah's wedding, he didn't stop the attack. As anxiety consumed him, the only thing he could think to say was, "I'm so sorry, Sarah."

He had said it before, but he couldn't help but repeat himself. No other words found him.

Sarah met his eyes and saw the fear and shock then put on a quick smile and tried to reassure him. She knew he hadn't the words to comfort her, and she couldn't hold the grief of the crime committed against her alongside the emptiness of the reassurance she knew he couldn't give.

"It's all right, Alex. They've got professionals working with me. I'm sure they'll do their jobs. We only have a few minutes left anyway before you've gotta get ready for the happy hour rush."

Alex frowned, frustrated that he didn't have the words. He didn't want to feel like he was pushing Sarah's pain aside. But he knew that she had made her mind up to move on, and he knew it wasn't his place to force Sarah to relive her trauma for a conversation he wasn't even sure how to have.

Chapter 15

Visits with Alex's grandmother had developed into a routine that was familiar to him; a routine, that is, of inconsistency. He had mastered the technique of emptying his mind of all expectations of her. The only way to face her disease was to simply prepare himself for whatever misguided notion her brain presented to her as truth. Some days, she was adamant that they "move back to the Bridgewood house." Other days, all she could focus on was how much she "hated the dinners they served there. So full of gravy and bullshit." Alex had not previously been used to hearing his grandmother swear.

Before the disease took her brain, she was the very essence of patience and chose each word carefully. Lately, she seemed consumed by frustration or rage. He thought about what she might fixate on and emote about as he wondered how he would find the energy to endure her moods. Everything inside of him sank so deeply into grief over Sarah. He had only brief text conversations since she told her story in the coffee shop, and two weeks had passed. He hadn't asked her much about the event; he knew it was best to let her share what she was willing on her own terms. He did, however, ask her how she was doing. Most of her responses were, "I'm all right," coupled with random short stories about strange adoptive families she encountered at work. Every once in a while, she'd relate that she had to "meet with the detective again," for some evidentiary purpose.

Alex felt so powerless and strange. Every piece of him wanted to help Sarah feel whole again, to remind her of her strength. He knew that she was most likely compartmentalizing everything she felt so she could get by and do what was asked by law enforcement. But what could he do for her? He still had no words that he felt would restore and reconcile after something so vile. And he wasn't ready to forgive himself for not being there to protect her in the first place.

Alex took a deep breath as he walked into Ramell's Corner and grasped the same silver glass door handle that had become so familiar. Strangely enough, Alex found comfort in the familiarity of the unknown with his grandmother. He walked slowly down the gray-carpeted halls and entered the passcode for the "Memory Care" hallway. He knew his role with her and could easily slip into it; the grief didn't hit him as hard as it used to. Alex clutched the comfort of familiarity. The trauma of Sarah's story and the reality of the crime committed against her and all it meant for her and the disgusting truth that people like Dean (and Jesse) existed made Alex feel as if the world were shaking beneath him. He had no idea what role he needed to play in Sarah's life now.

A best friend would have protected her or warned her of what he saw in Dean and I failed to do that, he thought. Not knowing his role in Sarah's life now, coupled with his belief that he failed her, was a terrifying grief he couldn't face. At least here, with Sandy, he could play whatever empathetic role she needed him to and forget about how lost he felt with Sarah, and the part of himself that wasn't there for her.

The visit started as usual. Sandy quickly looked up at Alex as he entered and frowned. "Oh, you again." She sounded disappointed. "Last time you were here, you said you'd do something about that oversalted gravy in the cafeteria." Alex met her eyes, a serious look on his face so she'd know he was listening to her. "Well, they served that pig slop AGAIN today, and this time it spilled over from my potatoes onto my beef and I'm NOT HAPPY. The meat was salty enough, no sense adding processed goop to it."

Alex smiled slightly, there was some truth in what she said. He then told her, "You're right, that gravy is flooding the plate and has no business creeping outside the taters. I mentioned something to the kitchen staff last time I was here, but I will be sure to tell them again. They're bound to get it right eventually. They don't want any 'beef' with me, right?" He smiled dorkily, hoping he could make his grandmother laugh. She didn't. But her frown softened. Alex quickly cleared his throat and said, "Well anyway, I brought my guitar again. Would you like to hear me play something?"

Sandy smiled wide and said, "Of course. What's your name again?"

"Alex."

"Alex, Alex…I remember now. I liked the song you played last time. What was it…?" Her eyes darted around the room, searching her mind for the answer. "The one from *The Sound of Music*. What was it? What was it?"

"Edelweiss," Alex responded, smiling. She remembered the song. He was particular lately about choosing songs from the Julie Andrews movie version. He had grown up watching the movie as it was one of his grandmother's favorites. She would often sing along with the characters, which Alex loved. Her voice sounded like bad opera, deep and dramatic, as she sang along to every song. The songs always reminded him of the quiet afternoons they would spend together. He hoped the music might somehow remind Sandy of their positive memories too and bring her comfort.

"'Edelweiss,' I remember now." Sandy smiled. "I liked that one, but could we pick something else from the movie this time?"

"Of course," Alex responded as his thumbs flipped open the brass buckles on his guitar case, and he slowly pulled the instrument out.

"What about, 'Something Good?'" she suggested.

Alex was taken aback. That song was so short and played toward the end, when the time and relationships had stretched on in the movie. He usually fell asleep on the couch before part two started, but he had seen the movie through enough times that he thought he could remember the song. He smiled and replied with, "Sure I can," and began playing what he could remember of the melody.

As he began the instrumental introduction, he thought about his grandmother's song choice. The more he thought, the more he realized he wasn't actually surprised at all that she had picked "Something Good." This was one of the slowest and most melodic songs of the entire musical. He started to remember that his grandmother's voice would occasionally startle him awake as she sang along at the end. The lyrics slowly returned to him...He remembered that the song was unique, more like a short free verse poem than a formulaic song format with a bridge, chorus, etc. "Something Good" was a short story. He slowly eased into the words as his grandmother listened intently.

> Perhaps I had a wicked childhood
> Perhaps I had a miserable youth
> But somewhere in my wicked, miserable past
> There must have been something good
>
> For here you are, standing there, loving me
> Whether or not you should
> So somewhere in my youth or childhood
> I must have done something good
>
> Nothing comes from nothing
> Nothing ever could
> So somewhere in my youth or childhood
> I must have done something good...

As Alex sang, tears filled his eyes. There was a grace in the words of the song that he was not ready to fully accept. But before he could read too much into his own thoughts, he realized that his grandmother was crying too. He locked eyes with her and she said, "Alex?"

The question was stated as if she recognized him. When Alex was a child and the song came on, he fell asleep. However, his grandmother was more awake than he ever knew in the moments that the song played. She watched him as he slept soundly, happy that he was at peace. Alex had never known the regret his grandmother felt about the mistakes his father made. The regret she felt about failing her son in some way. Why would he choose to leave his child? Sandy never understood why her son walked away from Alex. It wasn't the example she set for him, and she thought she had raised him with integrity. How could Jerry run from his responsibilities instead of take care of them? she thought more than she would ever admit. Regardless of the regret and unanswered questions, Sandy felt at peace when she glanced over at Alex curled up in the chair in their den. The warmth of the afternoon sun rested on his shoulders as he breathed the deep sleep of true rest. Sandy would never know why her son made the choices he did, but she loved him; and because of Jerry, she had Alex. Alex was a creative, gentle soul, one that she was proud of. Although Alex never knew it, tears would often come to Sandy's eyes as she listened to "Something Good" while the movie played, and she took in the beauty of the little boy she was trusted to care for. All unanswered questions and regrets considered, Alex was something good, and she knew she played an important role in that truth.

Sandy remembered the moments that she watched Alex as he rested and felt full of pride as she listened to him play in the present. When the song ended, she was hit with a rush of memories. She knew herself and she knew Alex. She saw pain in his eyes that she knew ran deep and wanted to take this moment, this moment that she knew was rare but was not totally sure of the reasoning for the rarity, and help him.

"Alex?" she asked again. Before he could answer, she said, "Are you upset? What is hurting you?"

Alex was shocked. He had grown used to a cloud being over his grandmother's eyes. A mist that made it seem as if she was not truly present. When she said his name, the mist vaporized and something familiar about her returned. He didn't know what to do with himself or how to respond. He could think of no reason for this sudden familiarity, and he didn't trust it yet, so he followed Sarah's example and just took step 1: Say some sort of words back to her. "Yes, Grandma, I am Alex…Why do you think I am in pain?"

Sandy seemed surprised that he would ask her why. He had always known that she could tell how he was feeling. "Your eyes, Alex. There is a deep sadness in them. You have tears that won't fall, something that only happens when you are deeply sad and hurting but protecting yourself from the pain. What is going on?"

Step 2: Just answer the question. "I…Yes, I am in pain." Alex could not resort to anything except honesty. He was too shocked to think of a lie or follow the pattern of responding methodically to whatever she said.

"Alex," she said seriously as she wiped her own eyes and straightened her posture, trying to get into "focus mode" for helping him, "can you please tell me why you are in pain?"

Step 3: Decide if you can trust her enough in this moment to continue with honesty. Alex searched his mind for how to answer. He wasn't ready to be vulnerable about the whole story with Sarah. He didn't want to repeat the truth of what happened to her and that he failed to stop Dean. He also had no choice but to be honest. He didn't know what was going on with his grandmother. "Why was she all of a sudden talking to him the way she did before this disease snatched her mind?" he wondered. All he knew was the truth that she was talking to him as she used to, so maybe there was an honest but safe answer he was comfortable sharing. He had it. Maybe he could just tell her what happened and hide his guilt. He didn't have to say that he felt responsible. She knew how much he loved Sarah and the grief of the crime itself might be enough information. "Grandma," he gulped, "Sarah was raped."

Sandy's shoulders dropped from their serious posture as she felt the weight of Alex's grief. "Oh, honey," she replied, "I am so sorry. There are no words that I could say to compensate for the tragedy of a crime like that. I am also realizing that my time talking with you might be short too." Sandy paused, quietly and frantically searching her mind. "I'm sick, right?"

Step 4: Just keep telling the truth. "Yes, Grandma. Dementia."

Sandy sighed, pushing the painful truth of all that disease meant aside so she could talk with Alex while she was able, "Yes, honey, I think I remember now. Since my time to talk with you might be short, let me ask you this, have you been writing music or poems about anything that you're feeling?" She knew she wouldn't be there to comfort him, so she had to remind him of the one everlasting thing that would.

Step 5: No words…Alex just shook his head and looked down. He couldn't find the words to write about Sarah and the guilt he felt, nor did he have the strength to explain why to his grandmother. He wasn't even sure himself.

Sandy smiled at him. "Alex, it's okay if you haven't found the words yet. But I want to tell you this, keep writing in the thick of your pain, even if the words don't come to you immediately." Alex rubbed his forehead but kept his head down.

"Pick one word. One sentence. Start small. You've always said that you feel empowered when you can name what you feel. If you don't know how to name the feeling yet, just start searching. There is comfort in the search. Pain sometimes leads to the greatest repair and restoration because the agony of holding it in our bodies forces us to be honest. Hurt edges out lies and encourages us to search for something more in hopes that we might find the relief we are seeking so desperately. Although pain may feel crippling or even excruciating, it is honest. And I promise you, there is such freedom in honesty."

Alex had been hanging his head until now. He looked up and met his grandmother's eyes. He didn't know where or how she was speaking this truth, but he knew it was real and that regardless of the why and how, he needed to hear her words.

Sandy continued, "Knowing the traps of your own mind can be terrifying. I suppose in this rare moment, I understand that fear better than most. What a strange paradox to become aware of your own weaknesses but not have the ability to control them? I know that I cannot remember myself, just as you know how crippling your fear and anxiety can be. I know my own mind lies to me, yet now, I am powerless to stop those lies. Alex, my guess is fear of the interim between knowing your weaknesses and mastering them is why most people, your Sarah included, distract themselves. You have told me so many stories of Sarah and I have known her myself. She is a passionate woman, which is why I know you love her. Her drive and convictions are inspiring and enchanting. But I am also willing to bet that she is a victim of extreme loneliness. When there is no place for passion and drive, how can the dreamer ground themselves? Dreams are meant to be shared, and when she has found no one to share them with, I can understand how she might fear the pain and begin to lose the drive she holds in distractions."

Alex thought about Jesse as his grandmother spoke. *Perhaps one such as Jesse who was clever enough to help Sarah forget her true desire for genuine companionship.* For a moment, he forgot the jealousy he felt toward Jesse and the shame he couldn't shake. *It is no one's fault that she became involved with him and no one's fault but the man who chose to rape her that she was raped.* Alex wanted to hold on to the sense of freedom he felt, but he didn't know how, the shame still felt as if it was rotting his insides, though his grandmother's words had momentarily brought him peace.

"Anyway," Sandy continued, "don't lose yourself in grief and shame over not being able to save her. I know how that guilt might grip you. Don't be afraid to name your pain. You may feel trapped inside the lie that it was your fault that Sarah was raped, but facing that lie, telling her of your guilt, and seeing it in front of you is the only way to master the feeling and move forward. I cannot escape my own mind anymore. Eventually, I will be relieved of this crude deterioration. All I can hope for when that happens is that you will have absorbed the pieces of truth I can give you now. Know that you don't have to be afraid of facing the pain you feel and don't be ashamed of your anxiety. The anxiety you feel is your body's twisted way of protecting you from tragedy. Take the truth that I am telling you and allow yourself to heal. I can't hold onto my own words, but if you are willing to, you can help yourself and prove that even my disease cannot fully master me, just as anxiety and guilt cannot master you. There are truths and connections in this world that even the most cruel and disgusting parts of the human condition cannot snatch from us."

One tear managed to fall from Alex's eye, the only one he could allow. He gulped and gently laid his guitar inside the soft, red felt of his case. He searched for words that wouldn't find him. He sensed in that moment that maybe all he needed to do was listen…to simply see his grandmother as she was—whole again. Maybe even more whole than she ever was. Somehow, Sandy found herself in the middle of disease. She found her voice flowing, slipping through the rapid chemicals warping her brain. Maybe all Alex needed to do in that moment was recognize the strength that Sandy harnessed. To know yourself in the familiar is easy. Somehow, Sandy found herself in all the weakness that was outside her control. Every force in her mind was working against her, yet she found her voice. Alex rested quietly in her unique and rare strength.

Chapter 16

Jesse called Sarah, but not enough. There was a strangeness in the silence between the calls. When she chose to answer, he was just "checking in to make sure she was okay" but didn't ask why she wasn't coming home. Sarah didn't feel obligated to speak with him anyway. She was frozen in what to do about the fact that he refused to tell the detective the truth. She couldn't process the rape as well as the betrayal of the man who was supposed to love her more than anything at the same time. So she drifted through the days, following her step-by-step approach.

The calls interrupted her work at least every other day for the first month following the crime. She would be in the middle of helping a customer and all of a sudden, "Buzz, buzz, buzz...Buzz, buzz, buzz..." She felt the trigger of the phone vibration in the front pocket of her jeans and her stomach sank. Every time. The detective was calling with another question. As sympathetic as the detective was, Sarah's story was still a case, something on the detective's work hours, but always on Sarah's personal time. Getting the calls at work was personal. Getting the calls at her friend's house was personal. Getting the calls in the middle of the grocery store as she sifted through bags of grapes, hoping to choose one that wasn't already turning to raisins, personal. Sarah tried to develop as much of a "normal" routine as possible, but there was nothing "normal" about constantly having to relive the crime in the middle of her life.

Sarah's step-by-step process did not inform her that when one reports a crime, if the state decides if that a crime has indeed been committed, the crime becomes an offense against the state itself, not the victim. Then, the logistics of how the case is handled are outside the victim's control. When Sarah's case was opened, it was Dean

Trevak vs. the State. Not Dean Trevak vs. Sarah Pierce. Sarah began to learn that "justice" was not as simple as a report. The process left her in a constant state of exhaustion.

Since the case officially belonged to the state, and charges were developing, Sarah was responsible for information just as much as Dean…And they had to gather evidence before they could arrest him. The first call Sarah had made was to the police, a "simple" 911 dial. When she had made the call, she thought the crime would end at the report…Call the police, relate what happened, and they take it from there. However, Sarah soon learned that several follow-up phone calls and a few in-person interviews would be asked of her. When Sarah received calls from the detective, it was usually to ask more questions about the rape. Her brain naturally learned how to retell the story and continue with her day. However, she didn't realize how saying the words over and over again began to train her mind that she was constantly threatened.

The second and third times Sarah had to tell the story were probably the worst, and they both happened at the hospital. These retellings came before all of the phone calls. Sarah shared with Alex that the police officer that she initially reported the crime to advised her to go to the hospital. She followed the officer's directions after the report and went but never spoke of what happened there. When Sarah checked in, she had to tell the ER nurse why she was there. Sarah did her best to give information, but she did not fully understand why she had to go to the hospital, and it didn't even occur to her to go until the officer advised her to. Her body felt strange and violated, but if someone just looked at her, she appeared physically unharmed.

Prior to being raped, Sarah had always imagined a rape victim as someone who had been visibly beaten. Maybe the imagined victim had a black eye or blood running down her legs with ratted hair on top of her head. Sarah arrived at the hospital wearing the skirt and cardigan that she had planned on wearing to a post-wedding date with Jesse that evening. She didn't change her wedding bra; it was beautiful. The cream-colored sparkles and lace still felt like they belonged to Sarah, no matter how she was treated while wearing it.

The point was, Sarah felt strange as the automatic doors of the ER quickly slid open and the wind rushed behind her. She almost felt as if she shouldn't be there since she hadn't been beaten. Sarah experienced a strange guilt that hospitals were only for "true" rape victims. Not that she really understood what "true" meant in this case. Regardless, she walked slowly up to the check-in counter. The nurse was busy on the phone but eventually ended the call and looked up at her with tired, busy brown eyes and waited for Sarah to speak.

Sarah slowly said the words a second time, "Um…I am here because I was sexually assaulted." The nurse's gaze instantly softened as she took a sympathetic breath and looked at Sarah. Before she could respond, Sarah quickly continued, still feeling like she didn't have a right to be there, "Um…the police officer I spoke with said I should come…" As if that somehow gave her the authority to care for herself, an authority she didn't believe she had in that moment.

"Okay, honey," the nurse responded gently, "I need your name and insurance card if you've got it." Sarah reached into her tiny black purse and pulled out the card. "Thank you. You can sit right over there. Do you need a blanket or some water?"

"No," Sarah said as she quietly walked to the waiting room chair. She heard the nurse say over the staff radio that they needed to "call a SANE nurse in." At first, she didn't know what that meant, but she learned later when the "SANE nurse" finally arrived at the hospital an hour later and called her back to the examination room.

It was the first question Sarah asked, before she had to tell her story the third time. A tall nurse with brown hair and big, brown eyes, similar to Sarah's called her back and gently asked her to put on a hospital gown. After giving Sarah some privacy to change, she reentered the room and was about to explain how the exam was going to work. But Sarah said first, "So what does 'SANE nurse' actually mean?"

The nurse closed her lips together in a sympathetic look before answering softly, "Sexual assault nurse examiner. My training is specifically designed to collect, um, the evidence the courts might need and to help you feel comfortable." She paused and then spoke quickly, "Well, as comfortable as possible."

"Oh...," Sarah said. She understood why the nurse paused awkwardly. There was nothing comfortable about the concept of collecting crime evidence from her own body. Just the implication of that... The crime happened on and in her body. She was the scene. She had an odd picture in her mind of being wrapped in caution tape. Somehow, the thought made her smile a little. Any kind of control over what happened to her, even her own joke about the situation was somehow comforting.

"Anyway," the nurse went on gently as Sarah met her eyes, "I want to tell you about how this process works so that you know what to expect."

"Okay," Sarah said as she took a deep breath and braced herself to try and process the illogical (the concept of a rape examination) logically.

"So first and foremost, my name is Rachel." She smiled and went on, "My number one job is to make sure that your body is okay and to give you any medication I can to prevent pregnancy and treat potential STDs, though unfortunately, not all can be prevented or treated..." Fear punched Sarah in the gut briefly as the anxiety of a potential STD or pregnancy from this horrific event became a possibility in her mind. Up until the nurse mentioned both, she had not even considered that it could happen. The mind can only process so much...Being raped is unnatural and sick enough. Comprehending the idea that an STD or pregnancy could follow was such cruel fuel to add to the fire. A million fears whirled through her brain, but Sarah tried to process each piece of information one at a time as the nurse went on.

"So, I have different medications I am going to give you, with your consent, but I will explain them each as they are administered. In terms of the exam, I will collect the evidence at the same time that I check to make sure that you have no long-term injuries or damage." Each word she said was loaded with heartbreaking connotations and the nurse knew it. She stated each word carefully because she was probably legally obligated to but understood that there was nothing logical or strictly scientific about what she was saying.

"Basically," as she hastily wrapped up, "I need to make sure that your body is safe now and collect everything I can so the courts can nail the bastard." Although the last statement might be considered unprofessional by some, the nurse sensed that Sarah needed to hear it. She smiled thoughtfully down at Sarah as she lay there and proceeded to lay out and organize the examination tools. Right as Sarah was about to respond, stating she understood everything, someone knocked lightly on the door.

The nurse approached the door and opened it. Sarah heard the voice of an adult woman but couldn't see anyone. "Hi, I am the support advocate from the county. I am here for the victim."

The nurse nodded and looked at Sarah before allowing the woman to enter. "Sarah, when victims of assault enter the hospital, country representatives are contacted to sit with them and provide emotional support. Someone…Sorry, what's your name?"

"Natalie," she said softly.

"Okay thanks. Natalie is here. She's not a therapist or anything, and it's one hundred percent your choice if you'd like her to come in or not."

Sarah didn't expect any kind of advocate to come. SANE nurse, emotional support advocate appointed by the county, there were protocols in place at the hospital and people who were contacted when rape was committed. Sarah processed all of this information quickly as she thought of her response. "Was it a good or bad thing that the hospital had rape protocols in place?" she wondered. "The protocols meant that rape happened enough times that they had to come up with a system of support and evidence collection…Along with people whose specific roles and training were to work with rape victims." At first, that knowledge seemed like something negative. But then Sarah went on to think there must be something good about the fact that hospitals and the county were trying to put resources in place so that victims could be supported and evidence could be collected. Again, justice is complicated.

"The end goal was justice, right?" Sarah decided that no perfect system could exist for rape, but there was progress. She could report the crime to the authorities, go to the hospital for medical care, and now she had the option for emotional support. Why not take it? The world should be a place where rape didn't exist at all. The sad truth was, however, that it does exist and probably would for a while, Sarah thought. So why not accept the progress and help that was offered? She realized her thoughts were becoming repetitive.

"Sure. She can come in," Sarah said then watched as a tall, thin blond woman entered. Natalie looked to be in her late thirties or early forties. Her hair was styled into a pixie cut, and her eyes were blue and kind. She looked at Sarah with empathy, trying to understand what she needed rather than with judgment or pity. Sarah didn't want to be pitied. Nothing about her being at the hospital meant weakness. Her presence meant strength, and Natalie's arrival might help her figure out the next step in the survival process.

Natalie sat down in the visitor's chair beside Sarah's hospital bed as the nurse began the exam. At first, she was quiet and smiled softly, giving Sarah the space to speak or not if she chose. The nurse started with the basics—checking vitals. She then said that she needed to do a blood draw to check for any kind of abnormalities in Sarah's system. The blood draw could also determine if there were any drugs or alcohol that might have been in Sarah's system when the crime occurred. As the nurse explained what the blood draw was for, Sarah thought to ask if the courts would consider that alcohol was in her system when the assault happened. Sarah asked the question, and Rachel responded with, "Yes, they could do a mathematical trace if this blood draw picks identifies traces of alcohol. Depending on how much is left, they could potentially calculate how much may have been in your system at the time of the assault."

Sarah was in the hospital just twelve hours later, and she wasn't sure the blood draw would pick up on anything, but any possible evidence that could prove she did not give her consent to Dean was worth trying to collect. Sarah hated blood draws. As the nurse wiped the middle vein of her right arm with the alcohol swab, prepping, she thought it would be a good time to distract herself by talking with Natalie. She didn't know where to begin or if she was supposed to talk about what happened so she just started asking Natalie questions about herself.

"So you're a volunteer with the county?"

"Yes," Natalie responded kindly. "We go through background checks and fill out applications stating why we would like to help support victims and if they trust us, and our motives for helping, we work on an on-call basis. Of course, we have to check in every three months to make sure we are still stable enough to support victims. Usually, that just means an interview with my supervisor and a drug test…Not that the mechanics of the work are why I do it."

Natalie's last response opened the door to what Sarah was truly curious about, why she wanted to volunteer to sit with victims. She politely asked her, "Why?" as she felt the jab of the needle sliding into her vein and winced as she posed the question.

Natalie sighed. "Well, I'm an accountant and heard about the program through a coworker. I spend all day managing money for people who seem to have too much. My work helps me support my son's behavioral and medical needs (good money and benefits) but having conversations with those who are unsympathetic to the world's serious problems gets old…"

Natalie met Sarah's eyes, deciding if she could continue. When she saw the serious and open-minded look on Sarah's face, she went on, "I know I can never understand all the pain and hurt that exists in the world. However, my son has an autism spectrum disorder, and I know the pain tied to that well. Each day, I watch him struggle to process information. He is strong and smart but so much of this world is a contradiction to the way his mind and body perceive truth. Unless someone tells him in matter-of-fact, straightforward terms, he has a hard time understanding. The noise of the school makes his head hurt and causes him to seclude himself, leading to an isolation he doesn't actually want but needs."

She paused and took a deep breath as the nurse finished filling and capping five vials full of Sarah's blood, each to be sent to the lab for separate tests. "Anyway," Natalie went on, "sometimes, the world has a way of making everything in your body feel and brain feel 'wrong,' and it's not your fault. I imagine that rape victims might've had some similar feelings. I wanted to share what empathy I could with victims who needed to be seen and told."

She looked seriously into Sarah's eyes. "That the wrongness they feel, the strange contradiction to nature screaming inside their bodies is not their fault. Sometimes the world is simply cruel to those who possess something unique or beautiful inside of them. And truth be told, I also need a break from my story. Sometimes I need to just focus on someone outside of the rich people I manage money for and my son's struggle. I love him, but I am also exhausted by the difficulties he endures and managing the way his mind works. I am human. Like all humans, I just need a break from my own story once in a while, and if I can help someone else while taking that break, all the better."

Sarah swallowed in appreciation and admiration. She tried not to focus on the fact that the nurse was sliding the sleeves of her gown up and asking her to turn on her side so she could check for bruising. As Sarah processed what Natalie said, she realized that what she needed most was the same thing as Natalie, to live in someone else's story, not answer questions about her own. Learning more about Natalie might help her escape the story she had to tell three times now. Realizing that Natalie might not want to talk about the stories she was escaping, Sarah went on to ask more about her role as an emotional support advocate.

"I am really just here for whatever the clients need. I have some specific training regarding questions/topics to avoid and what kind of behaviors to show, but each client is different and I give them the space to show me what they need."

Before Sarah could respond, Nurse Rachel gently interrupted and told Sarah that she needed to see her hands. As she gently lifted the right one, she looked at Sarah and said, "I need to swab underneath your nails with a Q-tip." Sarah looked at her questioningly though the logical part of her brain pieced the answer together. Rachel saw the question in her eyes and said, "They can test to see if you have any remaining skin cells from scratching in self-defense."

"Ah," Sarah responded as Rachel began to dig the Q-tip under her thumb. She was gentle but thorough. The Q-tip didn't hurt, but the implications of the nurse's movement with the tool somehow made the process painful. Sarah knew she hadn't scratched Dean, but the reasoning behind the process of the exam was overwhelming. She allowed Rachel to do her job, telling herself that anything and everything gathered would help her case, and did her best to focus on the questions she asked Natalie. Most of them were about the history of emotional support advocates, when and how they started, how she felt about working with her clients, and general information about the volunteer job. Natalie answered each one patiently and kindly, and Sarah felt so grateful that she was there to distract her. Natalie was there without judgment and offered only kindness and openness to whatever Sarah needed. However, Sarah was forced to stop her questions and focus on the exam because of what the Nurse Rachel asked her next.

"So I know that this is going to be hard to answer, but it will help us collect the best evidence possible to support your story. Do you remember him ejaculating on you anywhere? If so, I can swab those specific places, and we can soak up as much DNA as possible." Rachel asked the question as empathetically and gracefully as she possibly could, which Sarah was grateful for.

Sarah paused before answering and laid her head back to rest against the hospital bed. She was propped up to almost a sitting position as she prepared to answer. Sarah didn't pause because of a struggle to remember. Sarah remembered very clearly where Dean had ejaculated. She felt the small, sticky droplets on her inner thigh as if they were stones that would forever weigh that part of her body down. Not only did she remember the location, she also recalled the exact moment his semen splattered on her skin, unwelcome and assuming. She heard his smooth and cruel voice in her head, "You are a passionate woman," he echoed cruelly. His semen pushed out of his body and onto hers as he said those words, as if he got off on "giving her the passion she desired."

The bright lights of the bathroom and his hot breath burned her memory as she pointed to the middle of her inner right thigh and the nurse swabbed the exact spot. Sarah felt humiliated and disgusted as she thought about the remains of Dean's semen on her skin. Then, she was quiet for a moment as she felt the Q-tip slowly circling around her thigh. After looking up and taking a breath, she continued with her questions for Natalie.

Natalie's warm presence and willingness to empathize with whatever her clients needed made all the difference during Sarah's exam. She appreciated Natalie's openness. Had she followed a rigid set of questions and responses, Sarah might have been overwhelmed and pressured by a formula that didn't fit. She needed to simply listen to Natalie and ask questions that had nothing to do with her exact experience. Getting to know Natalie helped Sarah feel less like a victim and more like herself.

The exam lasted a total of two hours. The fingernail and thigh swabs were two of the worst parts, alongside the Pap smear. The nurse had to check the inside of Sarah's vagina to make sure there was no tearing or damage. She also gave Sarah an antibiotic and a Plan B pill to prevent potential pregnancy. Great, Sarah thought, on top of everything else, her moods and period cycle were fucked for the next three months. Sarah had to take Plan B on a couple occasions prior to the current incident, and each time, she ended up getting her period for almost an entire month, then it came late the following month, and then regulated a month after that. That particular pill was never as simple as a "seventy-two-hour life cycle."

Overall, Sarah was grateful for the people, Natalie and Nurse Rachel, who made the retelling of her story bearable. They also made the indignity of a sexual assault exam feel more humane, if that was truly even possible. However, Sarah experienced one more gut punch before leaving the hospital and returning to her manager's place. The nurse said she had to keep Sarah's lacy bra as evidence since she was wearing it the night of the assault. Sarah asked if she would ever get the bra back. Sure, there was a negative energy imprinted on its fabric but Sarah still felt beautiful in the bra and wanted the clothing to still remain hers. She asked Rachel if the bra would ever be returned to her.

Rachel looked at Sarah sympathetically and said, "No. I'm sorry, Sarah. They have to keep it locked away as evidence in the event that the case were ever reopened."

Sarah's stomach sank as she did her best to compose her expression and responded, "Okay, I understand." However, she also wondered what she was supposed to wear home if the state was keeping her bra. Before she could think too long on the question, Rachel interjected, "I have some clothing donations with me so you have something to wear home."

Sarah was grateful that she could choose something. However, they were all gray/white sports bras, which always felt unflattering to her small chest and were too tight underneath her breasts. They were nowhere near as beautiful as the $84 lacey bra she had spent a large fraction of her "cushion" money on for her wedding, something elegant that was supposed to be hers. Instead, she had to watch Nurse Rachel pick up her beautiful wedding lingerie with gloved hands and place it in a plain, tired brown paper bag, then slap a label on it.

Sarah walked out of the hospital just as strangely as she walked in. She had an hour or two to kill before her manager expected her back at her house for dinner. *What on earth would one do in the empty space after such an exam?* she wondered. *What could possibly make sense?* What could help Sarah feel like she had pieces of herself returned to her after Dean violated her insides? After displaying them again for the state and medical process to rake over and collect? The truth was, nothing could truly return those pieces to Sarah because they were taken. However, she could continue her step-by-step process of rebuilding herself after. As she started her car and heard Owl City's "On the Wing" begin playing from her list of saved favorites, an idea occurred to her. Owl City always helped Sarah feel more like herself because the band often sang of the ocean, a relaxing place in Sarah's mind and reality that she longed to live near permanently.

Sarah found herself driving to the lingerie store at her local mall. Her choice may seem strange, but the endeavor made perfect sense to her. Sarah wanted to take back some of her sexuality. As much as her heart told her that she wasn't "used" or "less valuable" because of what Dean had done, she couldn't help but feel disgusting. She hated every slow, creeping memory of Dean on her skin and inside her body; and if she was honest with herself, his actions made her feel like he had taken a part of her sexuality. Going to the lingerie store and picking out some new and beautiful panties somehow made her feel powerful, as if she could still present herself sexually the way she wanted to. Dean couldn't take her now, and he couldn't control how sexually appealing she felt in the future. Buying new lingerie was a step Sarah could take in piecing herself back together in the aftermath. So she did.

Chapter 17

As shared before, Jesse called, but not enough. There was an unspoken distance between Sarah and Jesse. Underneath the trauma and grief, Sarah knew the truth about him and their relationship, and she wasn't yet ready to admit it to herself, so she mostly avoided him or provided short answers and tried to go about her life. At first, work was a successful distraction. She continued to pour herself into the stories of the animals and the people who adopted them. She also did her best to push through her life with each "buzz" indicating a call from the detective.

The detective's name was Selena and Sarah liked her. She was a short woman who looked to be in her mid to late forties. She told Sarah that she had been working in the sexual conduct crimes unit for twelve years and she would "do her best to bring justice to her case." Something about Selena's face was kind, intelligent, and matter-of-fact, all of which Sarah knew was needed for some form of justice to be accomplished. Sarah was not totally sure why at first, but from the moment she met Selena, she had full confidence that she actually had Sarah's best interest in mind and that she *wanted* a part in making sure that Dean was brought to justice and for Sarah to recover. She also took the time to actually get to know Sarah. Sarah didn't feel like a "victim" in Selena's eyes. She felt that Selena saw her for all that she was—free-spirited, intellectual, and well-spoken. Sarah also felt no judgment from Selena though she felt plenty for herself.

Sarah had lies swarming in her head about how "foolish" she was for allowing herself to trust someone like Dean and, if she was honest with herself, Jesse. Too much of the Christian college she attended and culture of shaming women for crimes committed against them infested her mind. The lies felt like truths; the assault was somehow "her fault" because she "should have" been smarter. Selena, however, consistently showed Sarah the actual truth of who she was, a person undefined by the sick behaviors committed toward her, and it was the truth Sarah knew on a deeper level than the lies, which helped her accept Selena's kindness. All of these contradictions existed in Sarah's mind at once, leaving her feeling certain of what she believed sometimes and lost at all times.

Selena informed Sarah that one of the next steps in having Dean arrested and charging him with the crime was trying to involve witnesses, which meant contacting Jesse. Sarah was informed that Jesse avoided the detective when she called and refused to talk about the situation on the first several attempts. Sarah did not call Jesse on her own to encourage him to answer the detective. She knew in her gut that he was not going to defend her, that he was not going to do the right thing and help bring Dean to justice. If he were, he would have done so by now. However, after a month of Sarah telling a consistent story and confirmation from Jesse that Dean was at least at their wedding that night, they had enough to arrest Dean and charge him with "criminal sexual conduct in the third and fourth degree." About a month and a half after Sarah had initially reported the crime, she received a phone call that Dean had been arrested at his downtown apartment. All she knew was that he was compliant when they arrested him and was being held at a county jail in the cities.

The detective attempted to connect with Jesse to get the full story a total of ten times. Thus far, she had only spoken with him once on the phone briefly. She called him seven times and showed up at his duplex apartment three times. On the tenth, which was the third time she knocked on his door, he finally answered and allowed her in. He was clearly having a small party because the apartment was filled with three other men and one woman. Selena noticed that Jesse tried to appear friendly and obliging. He asked his guests to briefly scatter into the kitchen and "Take their beers with them," as he turned down the indie rock they were listening to in the living room and invited the detective to have a seat. Jesse had on a white button-down and khaki pants, along with the gray flat cap that he wore so frequently, usually when he was in front of some kind of social audience. He smiled charmingly at Detective Selena as she leaned toward him and began to ask questions designed to gain the truth and full details of the incident Sarah reported…

"So Jesse Marsh is your name, right?" she said as she took out her pen.

"Yes, ma'am, that's correct," he said as he continued to smile.

"And Sarah Pierce is your wife?" she continued to question.

Jesse gulped but replied, "Yes, of course she is." The detective could see that the mention of Sarah's name made Jesse uncomfortable. Selena decided then that she was going to ease into questioning by cushioning his ego a bit first.

She also kept in mind that Jesse had proved himself to be dodgy. All Selena could get out of Jesse in her nine previous attempts to get the full story of his wedding night was that Dean Trevak was indeed present, and Sarah felt worried. However, he quickly hung up the phone after the admission, claiming he was on his break at work and "had to get back to it." She attempted to ask him about his job as she knew it was a source of pride for him, based on some background information Sarah provided in her own interview.

"All right," she continued. "Thank you for confirming that information. I really appreciate your help and your time, Jesse. Speaking of, I know it wasn't easy to pull yourself away from your busy job, so thank you for making the space."

Jesse cleared his throat and smiled genuinely. Selena noted the honest joy in his expression when praise was given. "Yes, yes, no problem. My job certainly is busy, but I love my work. Gives me a chance to interact with lots of different folks and keep some important history alive." The detective met his eyes and nodded. He continued as he saw he had her full attention and went on about the importance of his work. "We're especially busy post-holiday season," he said seriously, as if he was a professor lecturing. "A lot of people are beginning to see the value in the gift of art as an experience, you know?" Selena leaned in as he spoke. "I mean, materialistic things come and go, but people remember walking through a beautiful museum with a loved one." He leaned back and rested his hands on his legs. "I'm just grateful that I get the honor of guiding them."

"Of course, I get that," Selena replied. She was skeptical of how "little" free time he actually had but knew that this was a man who had a fragile but large ego, and she wanted to get him to talk by encouraging him to share about himself. Ideally, he would slip into the actual story with some truth. Clearly, he wasn't short on free time. He was having a party right then and there. It wasn't the ideal environment for an interview, but Selena knew that with a witness as slippery as Jesse, she may not have any other opportunity, so she continued, "It sounds like you are a busy guy." Jesse smiled wide. "So let me ask you this, how did you manage to get a night off for your wedding? You know, the night your wife was raped by Dean Trevak?"

Jesse's jaw dropped, and his eyes quickly transitioned from a wrinkled smile to wide tunnels of shock and fear. He shifted in his seat and searched desperately around the room for a way out of the conversation as he stammered, "Ah, well I, um…"

Selena interjected firmly before he could move or say more, "Listen, there's one of two ways we can do this. I raise my voice as I ask every detailed question that connects to you, your best friend, Dean, and how he raped Sarah at your wedding while you were in the next room so all your friends in the kitchen can hear. We both know they're already wondering why I knocked on your door. Or you can answer my questions quietly and politely from here, and they will never have to know the full nature of our conversation."

Jesse knew he had been backed into a corner. So far, he had been able to hide Sarah's whereabouts from his friends as he was full of excuses. After all, she was a driven woman. It wouldn't be out of the ordinary for her to be working longer hours or going to an overnight conference. He knew that he was never going to admit the truth of what Dean had done although he felt the truth that Dean had raped Sarah deep inside of him. He also recognized that this detective was not going to leave without at least a shred of the truth. So he had to figure out how to "protect" his friend while also satisfying the detective somehow.

He frowned, trying to appear serious, and responded, "Oh. Of course, ma'am, um, we can talk about that."

"Now, we are talking about 'that,'" Detective Selena responded firmly. "What I want to know is simple, how did Dean Trevak"—she was intentional about using his full name, clearly identifiable as Jesse's best friend—"rape your wife on your wedding night?"

Jesse's eyes grew wide and then he quickly narrowed them back down, trying to look casual. "Well, ma'am, um, I'm not entirely sure. I mean I know she"—the detective noticed that he didn't say Sarah's name—"said something happened but—"

"What did she say to you, Jesse?" Selena said.

"Well, she just said that Dean might have cornered her."

Selena raised an eyebrow. "What does 'cornered' her mean?"

"I don't know," he quickly responded. "She felt like he did something."

"How exactly did she feel?" Selena asked.

"She was afraid," Jesse said seriously. He looked down as he said it. Prior to this admission, he had met Selena's eyes, checking to see how seriously she took his responses and anticipating her next question.

"Why do you think she was afraid?" Selena responded.

"I-I don't know," Jesse said. "She might have been confused. She had a couple of glasses of wine, you know. It was a party."

The detective just nodded her head forward as if to say, "And?" but remained silent.

Jesse felt compelled to continue. "Well, I mean you know. Maybe she had a reason to be afraid, but Dean has too much to lose. He wouldn't hurt her. He's an engineer, respected in his field. Maybe she just took one of his jokes the wrong way."

"Since when does a 'joke' inspire fear? If something is actually funny, doesn't that something make the recipient of the joke laugh? You said she felt afraid. How could a 'misplaced joke' make her feel afraid?"

Jesse was finished with any shred of honesty he was going to share at this point. He reached his limit with what he was going to reveal about his friend. "Listen, Detective, I appreciate that you drove all the way out here, but the truth is that I didn't see anything, okay? Yeah, Sarah said something happened, but I really don't know what it was." Jesse side-eyed the kitchen as he spoke, conscious that the conversations in that room were quieting down and eavesdropping was beginning. He quickly looked back at Detective Selena and went quiet himself.

Selena met his eyes seriously then looked toward the kitchen, back to Jesse, and narrowed them. She knew she was unlikely to get any more information, but she made one last attempt at pulling the truth out of him.

"All right, Jesse. I can see you are busy. But don't you want to do the right thing? I mean, this is your wife. Why would she lie about Dean raping her?"

Jesse paused a moment before responding, meeting the detective's eyes again and considering the opportunity for the truth. He then heard laughter from the kitchen and quickly replied, "I've told you all I saw, ma'am. I can't speak to events I didn't see."

"What about what you know?" Selena answered.

Jesse paused again, taking in her words, but tipped his head back, held his breath, and responded coldly, "I have told you what I know."

Detective Selena pursed her lips in disappointment, took a deep breath, lightly slapped her hands on her hips, and said, "Well, that's that. I appreciate your time, Mr. Marsh." He quickly walked her out the door, grabbing his beer from the coffee table along the way as the laughter in the kitchen rose.

Chapter 18

Sarah's version of the story was always the same. Selena had called Sarah for the story a total of six times. On the sixth, the detective had enough consistency to put out an arrest for Dean. Sarah was anxious from the time she reported the crime to the month later that he was finally arrested. She wondered what would happen if Dean decided to skip town before they could find him or if he would try to hurt her if he found out she reported the crime. The consistency in Sarah's story is what confirmed law enforcement's right to arrest him on charges of criminal sexual conduct in the third and fourth degree. On a Tuesday in January, Sarah received a call from Detective Selena that both comforted her and set her on edge. Sarah was at work when she had to step out for a moment to the all too familiar buzz with the "Private Number" identification.

"Hey, Sarah," Detective Selena's voice sounded, full of hope and sympathy.

"Hi, Detective," Sarah responded simply. She had gotten into the habit of waiting to be asked questions by law enforcement rather than initiating any of her own.

"I wanted to let you know that we arrested Dean at his apartment this afternoon. He came willingly."

"That's good to hear," Sarah responded. She felt relieved but also had a strange feeling that the pain and difficulty were not over.

"There's something else," the Detective stated. "Just some information I wanted to give you. It's not easy for me to say, but I know you need to hear it."

Sarah felt stones slowly forming in her stomach. She knew that the detective had been in contact with Jesse and that their conversations were not going well or Selena would have told her already that he had corroborated her story.

"Sarah," Selena said and took a deep breath, "I want to tell you something, off the record of official business."

"All right. Go ahead."

Selena continued, "Jesse is not a good guy. I understand why you married him. He is attractive, charming, and I can see how he would be easy to have a good time with. But he's shown who he really is throughout this investigation, masks aside. When I went to gather his statement, he looked like he was having a party. I could tell he was more concerned about what his guests thought than the questions I was asking him." The stones in Sarah's stomach began to feel more deeply lodged, but she remained silent. Selena paused. "There's also the matter of Dean's jail calls. All jail calls are recorded. Dean has called Jesse a few times. Dean is full of stories about how you were 'too drunk to remember right' and how he would 'never do that to his friend' and 'you just took one of his jokes the wrong way.'" The stones sunk deeper into Sarah's stomach.

"There's one more thing. When he talked to Jesse on the phone, Jesse supported him. He responded with, 'Yeah, I know, man. I totally believe you. She probably was drinking too much, and I know she can get worked up about things.'"

The stones felt permanently lodged in Sarah's insides as tears filled her eyes but refused to fall.

"Listen, Sarah," Selena went on, "I know he's your husband and that it's a fairly new marriage. You have already been through enough pain at your own wedding, but I don't think I'd be doing right by you if I didn't say that you would be better off without Jesse. Dean committed the crime, but Jesse is more guilty in my eyes. I don't think he knows which side he's on, but he should. If you want my honest opinion, I think he's too much of a coward to actually choose. One thing you can be certain of though is that he is not supporting you like he should. I know I can't tell you what to do, but if I were you, I would remove Jesse from your life if you are able."

Sarah was in pain, but she knew Selena was right. The gratitude she felt for Selena in that moment for looking out for her outweighed her anger toward Jesse, and she was able to let Selena's support sink into her heart. "Thank you, Selena," Sarah responded. She didn't have many words, but she managed to say, "I have a lot to think about, and I know you are telling me the truth."

Selena said that she would continue to be in contact with Sarah about next steps in the prosecution process and what she needed from her. The stones in her stomach grew heavier. There were five of them in total. The first formed of grief in response to being raped. The second held the disgust she felt about the act of rape and the scar violation left all over her body. The third was one of pain. She felt hurt that Jesse didn't believe she was worth protecting. The fourth was a stone of isolation, feeling as if she had to tackle every question the detective asked and every part of the prosecution process alone because no one seemed interested or knew how to defend her. The fifth and largest stone sank in and pierced her stomach. The stone of anger. Sarah was so angry at Dean for taking her body and furious with Jesse for being a coward and failing to defend and protect her. Most of all, Sarah felt rage toward herself for allowing Jesse and Dean into her life. She had sensed that there was something off about both of them and ignored the signs to get lost in a story. All these stones sank and collected inside Sarah. The weight of anger crippling her stride the most.

Chapter 19

A few days after Dean was arrested, Detective Selena called Sarah to update her on the case. She told her that during interrogation, Dean claimed, "Sarah was under the influence of alcohol and maybe even drugs, so she made up a story about him raping her at her wedding for attention." Dean went on to say, "Come on. I'm an engineer. I have too much to lose. I've been through seven years of math and physics courses along with paying my dues as a cog in the machine to make the money I do at the company I work for. Why would I damage my image? Also, Jesse is my best friend. Why would I do that to him? She's making it up."

"So," Detective Selena went on, "we have enough to hold him in jail because your story is consistent, and so far, no one has paid bail for him to be released. It sounds like he doesn't have family or friends around besides Jesse."

The stones in Sarah's stomach turned at the mention of Jesse's name. Sarah couldn't help but ask, "So has Jesse been on any more jail calls with Dean?" Sarah had learned that law enforcement had the ability to listen to and record jail calls. Detective Selena usually shared what she learned from the calls with Sarah if she felt as if the information could help her as the victim.

"Yes," Selena said. "Dean continues to claim that you are making the rape up because you were so drunk. He also told Jesse that you were probably on some sort of drugs too."

"I have never done drugs in my life," Sarah responded. She knew she shouldn't ask about the calls anymore. They were just hurting her at this point. But something inside her anxiously wanted the information, as she believed that the knowledge would somehow protect her. Although the fact that Sarah had never done drugs was obvious,

Dean and Jesse's lies made Sarah feel backed into a corner where she was forced to defend all words said against her. She also still had this overwhelming sense that, somehow, she had done something wrong because Dean raped her and she reported the crime though she was not entirely sure what caused her to feel that way.

"I believe you, Sarah," Selena tried to reassure her. "Very little of what Dean says is consistent. Jesse is the person he calls most of the time. However, he has a close friend, Royce, from work who he calls and 'rants' to. When he talks to Royce, he says, 'You're the unprofessional one making up lies about him for attention.' He went on to Royce saying he should 'call the shelter you work at and tell them you're on drugs just to make a point.'"

The stones in Sarah's stomach stabbed at her at the mention of Dean threatening to call her place of employment. She was overwhelmed by fear that, somehow, her boss would believe Dean's side of the story and hold her accountable for his actions. Never mind the mortification of this very personal, disgusting area of Sarah's life being spread for others to gossip about. *Who knows who would answer the phone or if they would somehow think less of me if they heard something from Dean?* she thought. *What if they believe I am on drugs and I get fired?*

Sarah's anxiety about Dean calling spilled over into her words, and she interjected as Selena went on about Dean's rant to Royce about, "I'm such a good guy, you know how girls 'assume too much about compliments these days…Just look at 'em wrong and you've got a harassment case on your hands.'"

"Detective Selena?"

Selena paused. "Yes, Sarah, what's up?"

Sarah asked, her voice shaking, "Do you think Dean really would call my work? I am terrified of losing my job over this."

Selena tried to reassure her, "Sarah, perpetrators often share a lot of empty threats just to save face to their family and friends. I don't think he actually would call your job. I understand that the idea of such a call is unnerving, but I truly do believe it's an empty threat."

Selena paused and considered Selena's words, but the fear had already gripped her mind. "But he could make a call to my work from the jail if he wanted to?"

Selena chose her words carefully, aware that she had potentially instilled more worry in Sarah. "Yes, he could call your work, Sarah. However, all calls from the jail are identified as such to the recipient. Your employer would know where the call came from. I do not believe Dean wants any further knowledge out there about his current predicament. He is most likely trying to save face with his circle of buddies, which is as far as I believe the threats will go. But listen, I have to respond to another case call that just came through." She heard Sarah take a deep breath on the other end of the phone, desperately trying to calm her fearful mind. "Sarah, I truly believe he will not call your employer. It's going to be okay."

Sarah responded, "Okay, thank you, Detective Selena." Selena hung up the phone and the stones continued to pierce the inside of her stomach. In the midst of their jabs, Sarah's mind began numbing some of the pain with a pathway designed to protect her. Sarah had known for a long time that most people were disappointing. She remembered the men in college who were too cowardly to step outside of opinions catered to them, too afraid to let their egos go. Sarah did not know what stopped Jesse from telling the truth, but she couldn't help but wonder. Perhaps it was something unspoken between him and Dean, some kind of "bro code." Regardless, hearing the detective say that Jesse would not support her story or admit that Dean had raped her made Sarah feel tiny, unprotected, rejected, and vulnerable. All of these feelings became productive for her because they also sparked a fire in her heart. She felt horrible, but she also knew the truth that she was worth protecting. That her intelligence, humor, passion, and drive were above all that Jesse and Dean ever were. She felt stupid and unworthy at the same time that she felt valuable and strong. She never would have reported Dean's crime in the first place if she did not know the truth, that a crime she did not deserve was committed against her.

All these beliefs existed in Sarah at the same time, which led to her brain creating pathways that became natural for her protection. The fight against Dean was not over. She had to brace herself for every phone call from the detective that would give her more information about the prosecution, and she had to find a way to legally divorce Jesse. Jesse wouldn't fight for her. The only thing she was certain of was that Jesse was a liar, and Dean probably was too. Dean could have killed her if her mind hadn't figured out the exact words to say for her to be released. Her body flipped into survival mode during the rape, which only emboldened the survival instincts she needed now. Every move she made while Dean assaulted her elicited a reaction from him, one that could protect her or one that might motivate him to hurt her worse. Her body learned how to survive, and her mind was continuing to help her stay alive. Dean and Jesse couldn't be trusted. No one could, really. Her mind had to continue to defend her, so she allowed a pattern of thinking to form that would assume every possible character flaw that Dean or Jesse said she had so she could continue to contradict their words when they were inevitably said during the prosecution.

Chapter 20

Jesse and Sarah were not married long enough to have any shared assets. They were also both young enough (and in Sarah's case, in enough student loan debt) that they did not have large 401Ks to split. Sarah had no desire to live in Jesse's apartment (which he rented). She felt more comfortable moving back on her own, somewhere near work so she could distract herself with the familiarity of city life. The beauty of state parks full of tall evergreens and frozen rivers simply stung now. Her best memories with Jesse, those that made him seem as if his soul ran deep, were walking through the forests near his house and drinking red wine to warm themselves in the evening. Fond memories with him only brought her pain now. For her to survive the prosecution, Jesse had to become a villain and nothing more in her mind. Sarah tried to ignore the tears that would pool in her eyes when she remembered how he gently brushed her hair back behind her ear or how the moon reflected in his bright eyes when he sketched by the window at night. She hated herself for the part of her that loved him.

Maybe underneath the story she found herself in with Jesse, she knew that something was never right with him. Sarah always had a feeling that there was something or someone more out there for her. However, since that something or someone did not exist in the moment, she lost herself to stave off the loneliness. Knowing there was a part of Jesse that was cowardly and cruel also fed into her guilt. Sarah had such a hard time seeing herself as human, and she internalized the mistakes of others. She needed to see herself as she truly was. Sarah was a kind person searching for love, as many people do, who found herself with the wrong person at the wrong time. Her desire for adventure and to be loved and cared for by another was not a mistake. However, some of the lessons of her Christian college lingered; and she could not help but feel that, somehow, she deserved the degradation Dean and Jesse gave her because she had chosen to be with the wrong person.

Sarah's thinking was twisted, but the thoughts felt like truth to her. She was so divided from herself while protecting herself at the same time. She knew she could trust Alex, that he would help her feel better, but she avoided him too for a while despite his kind attempts to reach out. She gave him one-word answers when he would check in. Her mind would not allow her to feel vulnerable around anyone. The unspoken barrier between Sarah and Jesse took too much strength to hold up.

It was clear to Sarah and Jesse that their relationship was over. However, a strange silence existed between them. Sarah found an apartment near work and began living life separately. Jesse knew that Sarah was probably aware that he had not supported her story but refused to admit that truth to himself or Sarah. He was able to distract himself with his job where he felt intelligent and in control. Whenever he was home, he forced thoughts of Sarah out of his mind and filled his time with friends and parties. Underneath all of his facades, he knew that what Sarah had said about Dean was true, but he was unwilling to face any of the ugliness in himself and his best friend.

Sarah started the process of filing for divorce. She assumed Jesse would comply since she wasn't asking for anything monetary from him. Jesse also wanted to distance himself as far as possible from Sarah and the truth. If she was willing to just walk away and make the separation process easy for him, he wasn't going to fight it.

Jesse and Sarah only had one phone call between them throughout the divorce process, which only took a few months since it was mostly paperwork agreeing to avoid pursuing the other for money. The same part of Sarah that hoped for justice in her case against Dean tried to appeal to his sense of right and wrong one last time. At first, the reasoning for her phone call was to ask him to mail back his side of the divorce paperwork as soon as possible. However, hearing his voice for the first time in a while moved her to continue on.

"Jesse..."

"Yeah?" he responded quickly.

"I'm only going to ask you this once," she went on, "but I need to hear some sort of answer..." The other line was silent. "Why won't you tell the detective what Dean did? You saw me the night of our wedding. You know how terrified I was. What reason would I have to make this up? There is no part of this that has been fun for me. Do you know how invasive that exam at the hospital was? Do you know how much anxiety each call from the detectives has been? What about the lies he's threatening to tell my boss? How do I 'win' in any of this?"

Jesse paused a moment after she stopped speaking then said, "Okay, Sarah. Even if what you say is true, is it really worth Dean going to prison? Is it really worth putting on his permanent record? This report will follow him the rest of his life. Is that worth it to you?

Sarah's pain turned quickly and fiercely to anger. "What about the rest of my life, Jesse? What about what he has done to me? What about what he has done to my body? Don't you even care? I am your wife. He raped me on our wedding night with all of our friends right outside the door, with you right outside the door. Do you think that what he has done isn't going to stay with me the rest of my life?"

Jesse swallowed and held his breath. His mind had been made up about defending Dean. He was not going to say anything in response. "I have to get back to work, Sarah. I will mail you the papers this afternoon."

Sarah realized in that moment that she was never going to get the empathetic response she deserved. She shared one final thought before hanging up. "I don't understand what kind of person can know the truth about someone they were supposed to love being raped and refuse to share that knowledge. All you had to do was tell the detective that you believed me. All you had to do was tell her how afraid I was when I ran to YOU." Sarah's voice shook. "I ran to you because I thought you would defend me. Doesn't it bother you at all that Dean touched me? Doesn't it bother you that he tried to rape YOUR wife at YOUR wedding? Right underneath your nose?" If nothing else, Sarah was going to jab at Jesse's arrogance, but she knew in her heart that all her words were pointless. Jesse had made up his mind, and the battle to appeal to a conscience that did not exist was just going to overwhelm and exhaust her with anger. The stones felt hot inside her stomach now, and her whole body simply burned.

"I gotta go," Jesse said and hung up.

That was it. The divorce papers arrived at the county court a few days later. The judge signed off on everything, and her marriage was over before it even started. Sarah did her best to ignore the jabs of pain she still felt about Jesse's betrayal. However, it was soon after her divorce was final that she received a call from Selena delivering the news that a county lawyer had officially been assigned to her case.

"We are so lucky, Sarah," Selena said excitedly. "Corey Thomas is one of the best county attorneys we could have asked for."

"Yeah? He's good?" Sarah said. She didn't fully understand the criteria that made Corey "good," but she knew she felt relieved. She trusted Selena's judgment when she said Corey was good.

Selena went on. "We're still waiting for the DNA evidence from your exam, but in the meantime, Corey will help you understand your options for the prosecution. Truthfully, your case belongs to the state, and they can charge Dean as they see fit. However, we want to keep you informed as much as possible. You will probably be getting a call from Corey later this week."

"Thank you, Selena," Sarah responded. "I will keep an eye on my phone." Sarah's divorce was barely final, and now she had to continue responding to phone calls and reliving Dean's actions on the night of her wedding yet again, this time to an attorney. Thankfully, the survival pathways grew stronger and more natural as Sarah had to push aside any feelings of grief she may have held so that she was able to find the perfect, precise words to ensure that Dean saw justice.

She had stopped in the middle of the canned beans aisle and moved quietly to the side to take Selena's call. She was about to grab a can of chickpeas for three bean salad when the "Private Number" identification buzzed on her phone. There wasn't time to find a private space every time she received a phone call from the county; timing was unpredictable and on the terms of the county's processes. Thankfully, not many people shopped for the ingredients for three bean salad. However, it was perfect for Sarah. Simple ingredients and easy on the stomach. Bland foods were necessary now as the stones had taken up so much space inside her—grief, disgust, pain, isolation, and anger. Her body did not have space for much else.

But Sarah was determined to be okay. She was going to keep moving. She continued working, refusing to take a day off to rest with her thoughts. Moving was the solution to the grief. If she was constantly moving, the stones didn't jab; they only remained as a large, dull ache. She went about her grocery shopping, preparing for a weekend of movies and maybe dinner with Alex. She could keep the conversation about him if she needed to. She hadn't heard about Grandma Sandy lately and wondered how she was doing. She could ask about her and get out of her own head and the case for a while. She wheeled her cart around to the condiment aisle as she thought about seeing Alex again and accepted that her work on the case was done until she heard from the attorney.

Chapter 21

Alex was setting up the bar for the happy hour rush when he received the call. Sandy had passed away that morning. She had been sleepy but restless the night before. Her eyes were shut, and she had been moaning and jerking in her sleep. There were no clear physical causes of death besides the indication that the dementia had finally taken her brain.

Alex knew that although Sarah had been quiet when he reached out to check on her the last couple of weeks that she would be there for him now. He had no idea what to tell her besides the blatant truth. He called her and said, "My grandma's dead, Sarah."

Sarah's breath caught in her throat. Sandy had been a supportive part of her adolescence too, and her heart grieved for her friend's pain. "I'm so sorry, Alex," she responded. "What can I do?"

"Just be there with me at the celebration of life. She left enough life insurance that all the costs of burying her are covered. I just don't know that I am going to have the energy to speak to everyone at the ceremony. I know you've got a lot going on too but—"

Sarah interjected, "Alex, I can be there."

The ceremony went smoothly. Many past patrons of the bar attended and shared fond memories of Sandy. The staff from Ramell's corner attended too. She had been a positive presence to them even in her final, confused days. A few old neighbors and distant relatives came by too, and Alex played "Something Good" in her honor. The ceremony came and went quickly. Everything was a blur. Alex had planned most of the ceremony and her burial arrangements, and the only thing to do was adopt Sarah's step 1, step 2 method and take the next step that seemed to make the most sense. For now, it was accepting Sarah's offer to make him dinner at her apartment later that evening. After a few glasses of wine and deep breaths, they had both slowly opened up to each other about certain things. Both exchanged memories of Sandy, but only those that Alex was comfortable with, nothing too vulnerable. After a while, Alex needed a break from talk of Sandy, and Sarah was finally willing to open up to him about the prosecution.

"I am exhausted, Alex. I never realized how many phone calls or how drawn out this entire process would be."

"What do you mean?" he responded as he stopped pushing his pasta around his plate and met her eyes.

"Honestly, I thought reporting assault was as simple as calling the police, telling the responding officer what happened once, and that was it, law enforcement would take the case from there, and I would never have to think or talk about the rape again. But it's not that simple. I get calls from the detective every couple of days, sometimes multiple times in one day. I also have to retell the story almost every time she calls me. And now there's a county attorney involved. I guess he is the one actually defending the case throughout this whole process. I am waiting on a call from him and something tells me I will have to tell the story again."

"That's the downside about 'innocent until proven guilty,'" Alex responded. "I wish there was a better process for identifying true perpetrators quickly. Waiting for justice to be served and being dragged down in the process, constantly reminded of the crime just forces the trauma to continue."

"The trauma does continue," Sarah said. "I've gotten pretty good and numbing myself to the details of the story. I've had to… But the truth is, I can still feel how vile the crime was, almost like stones in my stomach. Each retelling is a reminder that the crime was real. It happened to me." She sipped her wine. "And Jesse has been no help."

Alex had been curious about where Jesse was at but wasn't going to ask. Sarah had her own apartment again, which made the answer fairly obvious. However, since Sarah brought Jesse up, he gently created space for her to continue. "No? He hasn't helped?"

Sarah set her wineglass down, swallowed hard, and continued, "No. Truthfully, we've already signed divorce paperwork and everything. I honestly don't want to say much about him, but he refused to acknowledge what Dean did."

"To you or the detectives?"

"Both," Sarah responded despondently.

Alex would never tell her this, but he wasn't surprised. He knew that Jesse did not have the courage in him to be honest about something as difficult to digest as rape, especially if his best friend was the one who committed the crime. If Jesse admitted that Dean raped Sarah, he would have to be honest with others and himself that his best friend was a rapist. Jesse was all about image and the easy way out and through. Admitting what Dean did would have forced him to confront himself and who he chose to surround himself with, and he wasn't willing to go there.

"I'm sorry, Sarah," Alex said. "I wish people weren't so disappointing. What Dean did was bad enough. Jesse's choice to hide the truth must be another slap in the face."

The stones jabbed at Sarah. "Well, everything is done now. I won't have to see him again, and I don't want to. Honestly, all I want is just to escape for a while. I need sights and sounds that don't constantly remind me that I am a crime victim and that my husband didn't care enough to protect me."

Alex felt a stab of guilt when he heard the word *protect*. Sandy's death had taken over his mind, but he still held the weight of his perceived failure to protect Sarah from Dean and, honestly, from Jesse too. If he had spoken up more about the both of them, maybe she would have walked away from Jesse before any of this happened. He realized that he had many things he was hoping to escape too and an idea occurred to him.

"Sarah?"

"What's up?"

"Well, I was thinking…What if we go somewhere for a little while? Maybe we can take that trip to the beach in California?"

Sarah's eyes lit up instantly. "Alex, are you serious?"

"Yes, absolutely," he responded.

Sarah paused. "But wouldn't the beach remind you too much of your grandmother?"

Alex thought for a moment. "I have beautiful memories with Grandma at the beach. For some reason, I felt like I was betraying her before if I went without her. Now, he gulped, "I guess I don't have to live with the guilt that she would be missing out…I could use an escape too. Do you want to go when the court process is over so you aren't interrupted by calls from the detective?"

Sarah responded, "Yeah, I think that would be best. I don't want to think about Dean, Jesse, or the prosecution. I have no idea which way the outcome is going to go and if Dean is actually going to be charged with the crime. They have him in jail, but that doesn't mean he's going to long-term prison. They are just holding him until he is prosecuted. I want to go now, but I think you're right to wait a little while. I have no idea how long the rest of the prosecution is going to take but, whether he is officially charged or not, I have a feeling I am going to want to leave for a while when this is finally over."

"It's done then," Alex said confidently. "As soon as everything legal is figured out, we will go. Booking a last-minute flight shouldn't be too difficult. I'll make it happen."

Sarah smiled and raised her glass. "To escaping."

Alex hesitantly smiled back. "To escaping."

Chapter 22

Attorney Corey had barely introduced himself before Sarah received a strange call from Detective Selena. Sarah remembered two primary details about the role that Corey played in her life and in the case. She did not remember much about how he introduced himself or how the case would play out exactly. She only remembered the most pivotal moments with Corey, including the strange call from the detective where she paraphrased a reaction Corey had to news Detective Selena shared. When Selena was on the phone with Sarah, she said, "Sarah, you remember that part of the exam you underwent at the hospital was to collect evidence, right?"

Sarah had not forgotten the exam, nor did she forget that her body was being treated as evidence. "Yes, I remember," she said simply though none of her feelings about being treated as evidence were simple.

"Well, we received some test results. They were checking for traces of Dean's DNA. We found a positive result for his semen on your thigh. I called Corey first. He picked up the phone and said, 'Do you have good news for me?' I told him about the DNA evidence though he already suspected we had it. Your story was strong enough already, but this evidence confirms that he was in fact in contact with you in a sexual manner. The evidence will strongly support the case."

Sarah thanked Detective Selena for sharing the news and hung up after politely saying goodbye. She was spreading the mayo on the cheese sandwich she was bringing to work and had to hold the phone to her ear with her shoulder as she continued to place the top piece of bread, pack it up in her backpack, and head out the door. Sarah was not conscious of her thoughts as she drove though they were there all the same. Sarah's conscious mind was focused on being polite to the detective, making sure her sandwich was packed and driving to work on time. However, under the surface of her step-by-step survival mode, the deeper part of her mind, the one dedicated to being Sarah, not Sarah-in-survival, was asking itself and the universe questions that Sarah was not ready to seek answers to.

Is the news that Dean's semen was found on my leg really "good"? Is "good" the right word to describe physical evidence of semen, dried and sticking to my leg like a parasite? That semen was several hours old, and it was "stuck" on me. There was enough of the dried liquid to test positive in a lab.

Her thoughts raced and bounced around. *What about the words Attorney Corey used? "Good"? He answered Selena's call with the question, "Do you have good news for me?" He considered evidence of Dean's disgusting semen on my leg to be "good news." Of course, I know that he saw the evidence as "good news" because the semen was undeniable science, something more than my word against his and Jesse's. Dean could no longer deny that I had made anything up because there was indisputable scientific evidence on my side... Corey has to see the rape as a case. Each detail has to add up to his point being stronger than the opposing side's, to weigh all the details and "evidence" with the end goal of justice. I understand him and that he needs to see my case as logical. Truthfully, I felt relieved and almost victorious when Selena shared the news with me. I knew that the DNA evidence meant corroborated the truth of the rape where Jesse's words failed. But how do I actually feel about the concept of all of it? How do I truly feel about living in a world where I rejoice in someone's dried-up ejaculation living on my skin because the evidence supports the truth that I was raped? Am I really joyful that I needed that evidence all the more because my husband refused to support my story and add his witness to the "evidence" pile? Why did detective Selena tell Corey first? Shouldn't I have been told first because I am the victim? The semen was found on MY leg. Am I only a victim at this point? The piece of evidence they can point to as proof that a crime was committed. Is this process really justice?*

Sarah's mind turned these questions and thoughts over. Her consciousness would not let her process them or seek the answers because her system was not in a place to release them yet. She had to get through the day, she had to get through the prosecution, she had to survive. If her mind allowed her to address the questions that lurked underneath, the weight of the trauma might just be too much and she wouldn't survive. Sarah's survival depended on keeping her job, providing for herself and summoning the conversational skills needed to serve families at the shelter. Although she could not address the true questions now, the part of her that longed for true justice saved them for a time when she would be ready to seek answers.

The second interaction that Sarah remembered with Corey was the advice he gave her about how to proceed with the prosecution. "Sarah," he said sincerely, "technically, this is a crime against the state at this point, and I am the state's attorney. However, you are the victim, and I, of course, want to take into account what you want. However, I have to tell you that since Dean's DNA evidence"—Sarah winced at the sound of "Dean's DNA—"came through, he has stopped his stories about your 'being on drugs' and 'making the assault up.' He is willing to confess to a lesser charge than what we arrested him for, criminal sexual conduct in the third and fourth degree."

"Why would he confess to something else?" Sarah asked.

"The charge that he is willing to confess to might not look as bad on his record. I think it's something about how he could still try to apply for another job in his field with this particular charge rather than criminal sexual conduct."

"What is the charge?"

He is willing to confess to a charge called predatory stalking," Corey answered. "'Predatory stalking is not what he actually did, but I think his lawyer advised him to go with that option."

"But how can he be charged with predatory stalking if that's not the actual crime he committed?" Sarah responded seriously.

"Truth be told, Sarah," Corey sighed and continued, "predatory stalking is a different charge. However, Dean would likely serve the same amount of prison time as a result of confessing to this crime as he would if he were actually charged with criminal sexual conduct. And if you want my honest opinion, again, I respect your wishes, but I think we should take his confession and have him charged with what he is willing to confess to."

Sarah remained silent as she processed what Corey said to her and gave him the space to continue. "Sarah, if you want to go to trial and have him charged with criminal sexual conduct, you may also have to face a lot of unknown frustrations and obstacles."

"What do you mean?" Sarah asked.

"Well," Corey went on, "you would have to show up in person and tell your story to the jury and the judge. So far, we've been able to collect everything we need over the phone."

Sarah's stomach dropped at the idea of having to show up in person and see Dean's face. She didn't want anything to do with him, and she never wanted to see him again. The thought of his face made her sick.

"Oh, yeah, that would be hard," she responded.

"The other problem," Corey explained, "is that the jury is a random selection of citizens. As much as the justice system likes to tell itself that jurors are impartial, they are all human, which means they are all also biased. They could vote against you for something as simple as not liking your shoes…" Sarah was disgusted and Corey sighed again. "I guess what I'm saying is, I will continue to honor what you would like to do when I defend this case. However, I believe our best option is to take his confession to predatory stalking. You don't have to show up in court, and there's a guarantee that he would go to prison for three years."

Sarah turned Corey's advice over in her mind for a few moments. She hated the idea that Dean could go on without being charged with an actual sexual assault crime, which is what he did. She also pictured what it would be like if he had actually stalked her, which was equally terrifying. She didn't like Corey's point about the jury making a biased decision about whether or not to charge him with the truth, that he committed a criminal sexual crime against her, but she knew Corey was right.

What if the jury thought the same thing that Jesse did? Sarah wondered. Jesse's words raked over her brain, causing her to wince as she remembered. "Is it really worth putting on his permanent record? This report will follow him the rest of his life. Is that worth it to you?"

"What if the jury liked Dean? What if they didn't like her shoes or her hair or even the sound of her voice?" Sarah shouldn't have to worry about variables that had nothing to do with the case but the truth was that she did have to worry. Biased juries were a reality. She didn't like the idea of Dean getting off on a label that didn't actually identify the heinous crime committed against her, but there was a guarantee attached to his confession that he would go to prison and serve time for what he did to her. She would have three years' time to forget about him as much as she could. The phone calls would stop, the traumatizing reminders would stop, and she could try to move on somehow.

She took a few days to consider if accepting Dean's agreement of confessing to "predatory stalking" was the outcome she was willing to accept for the case. In the end, Sarah decided she just wanted the logistics of reporting the crime to be over. She didn't want to hear his name, see his face, or have any kind of reminder of him raping her and Jesse's refusal to support her. She told Corey that she accepted his advice of moving forward with the "predatory stalking" charges. She found out after the trial that Dean was sentenced to three years in a local prison and that an order for protection (a legal document stating he could not contact her in any manner) was put in place and valid for the next five years.

Sarah felt a strange sense of relief and exhaustion. In a way, she had won a fight she never wanted to join. She reported sexual assault. Her perpetrator did not go unnamed. She would not carry the truth of the crime with her alone the rest of her life. She was proud of herself for having the courage to call the police but felt strangely empty at the same time. At the end of the day, she was still at the mercy of human judgment, in whatever form it took, for or against her. Dean judged that he could rape her at her wedding, and he was right. Jesse judged that protecting his friend's ego was more important than the safety and justice of standing up for his wife. Corey's professional judgment gave Sarah the best-case scenario inside a flawed system… and Sarah's fear of how the jury might judge her and the truth motivated her to accept a sentence that would continue to protect Dean's ego and professional future.

So did she really win the fight she never wanted to be involved in? The sentencing felt like such a hollow victory. She was genuinely proud of herself for having the courage to report the crime and see the detective/evidence process through. However, she also knew that she had made only a small step in the right direction of all that still needed to change with how women are seen and used by men.

Chapter 23

What we think we know about other people runs this world. Stories are created in our minds all the time about the feelings other people must have or the motives that drive them. Sarah was so afraid of the stories people would tell themselves about her and the truth she reported about Dean that she gave in to a lesser charge rather than take a chance. The fear that others' judgment would block the truth and send Dean walking free led to a world of even deeper lies. But lies were also what ensured Dean's conviction. So Sarah's mind continued to see the lies as safety.

The actual truth is that we know very little about what goes on in the minds of others. Sarah imagined that the jury might be filled with blond Christians, similar to those she knew in college. She pictured them looking at her long hair and age of late twenties and conclude that she was "just another millennial taking a compliment the wrong way or getting up in arms about something." Sarah would never know who would have actually sat on that jury. The hearing was a future that never was to be. However, her mind had made up that she was going to be judged by toothy, conservative Christians and that's how she "knew the trial would have played out."

Attorney Corey, though his intentions were good, played into Sarah's fear of being judged by warning her that she could be. But that was the system he was working inside of, a system of justice where the only way to win was to assume that people would imagine the worst about someone, and proactively fight to ensure the conviction could be made without that skewed judgment, which seems to defeat the purpose of prosecution and a trial. Sarah couldn't allow herself to think too much about the rape or what could have been; her mind and body were already subconsciously protecting her. She did her best to focus on the way the clouds met her at eye level, the way they only can while riding in an airplane.

Alex sat next to her. He rested his head on the back of his seat and took a deep breath through his nose as he saw Sarah staring out the window. The prosecution was over, his grandmother's celebration of life was over, and he was finally on his way to California with Sarah. He wondered what she was thinking as she stared out the window. He remembered the pictures that arrived in her mailbox the day before. Pictures of her wedding with Jesse.

His heart hurt for the betrayal she must have felt. However, he also couldn't help but remember how Jesse's hand looked as he neatly grasped her waist in the photo of the two of them on the dance floor that he (Alex) owned. Jesse was selfish and shallow. Alex knew that he wasn't right for Sarah. However, his own imagined stories and fears creeped into his mind and threatened to become the truth. He was afraid that Sarah missed Jesse, that she might not get over him despite what he had done. He saw the beautiful light brown strands of hair, tinted with red in the sunlight fall gently over her eyes. She had looked good with Jesse in the photos. His smile was charming and his cheek looked warm up against hers.

Sarah had stared at the photos for a moment before tossing them in the trash. But Alex couldn't help but think that maybe she tossed them because she saw how good she looked next to Jesse too and missed the feeling of being next to him. The truth was that Sarah felt ashamed for believing she loved Jesse in the first place. As she stared at the clouds, she thought of how peaceful her life might have been if she had simply refused to dance with Jesse the night she was reunited with him after high school and went about her business talking to Alex at the bar. She admitted to herself that she had never loved him. She lost herself in a story. He was handsome, charming, and artistic. She had loved the feeling of escaping in the woods with him. But escaping with Jesse was never truly an escape. Sarah missed important parts of who she was and compartmentalized her identity with Jesse. She could never talk with him about the thoughts that mattered most to her, the philosophies of life that she loved to turn over in her mind. These were thoughts she could only share with

Alex, and she was excited for the opportunity to talk alone with him again and just be somewhere else for a while.

Alex and Sarah both battled separately in their minds about false realities. However, they were still able to look forward to the simple joy of being together and soaking in the scenery around them.

Chapter 24

Alex and Sarah rented a two-bedroom condo on the shores of the Pacific Ocean in California. Their flight arrived late on a Tuesday night, so Sarah woke up to bright sunlight streaming through the cracks in her bedroom window. An eighty-five-degree morning had arrived, and Alex was still sleeping. Sarah brewed a pot of dark roast coffee and quietly slipped out to the balcony. She sat still in the light blue patio chair and took a deep breath. Sarah allowed her eyes to rest on the palm tree leaves as they swayed gently back and forth in the breeze. As her eyes met the trees, she could see the sun bouncing happily off the ocean as she smelled the saltwater drifting up on the wind. The beauty of warmth, salt, and light around her allowed Sarah to exist presently. She was focused on nothing but what she saw, heard, and smelled. She connected with the heat as it hit her toes. The warmth somehow helped her feel held. Sarah needed to feel present. All of her anxiety was about the pain of the past that turned into fear of the future. So many had betrayed her, how could she not believe that only a future of betrayal lay before her?

Sarah was also happy to reconnect with Alex. She regretted the distance that had grown between them after she met Jesse. There was an unspoken boundary between them ever since she and Jesse started dating. Both Sarah and Alex knew there had always been more to their friendship. There was an intimacy that connected their conversations, a level they could get to in their intellect that no one else could reach. Sarah wasn't entirely sure what continued to divide them. She remembered speaking to Pete, Alex's regular at The Crooked Picture, once of their feelings for each other. The memory was a little fuzzy because her confession was partially alcohol-induced.

"The requirements of our survival have made soulmates strangers." What did that even mean? She said the words but now that she remembered them, they sounded so ridiculous in her mind. "The requirements." What requirements? What were they both trying to survive? She had found time for Jesse, why couldn't she find time for Alex? She certainly made time to go on this trip with him and have the occasional meal, she thought.

Sarah meant something deeper when she spoke with Pete. She knew there was a clear reason she and Alex weren't together though a part of her longed for him. This exact moment wasn't the time to answer that question. She was trying to focus her mind on the trees, the ocean, and the wind—sights, sounds, and smells. She knew that here, in this moment, she was grateful for the beauty that she saw and the time she knew she had right in front of her to just be with Alex. One whole week of conversation with her best friend among the beauty she often dreamed about. She allowed herself to feel excitement for the first time since she was raped.

Slowly, she rose from the patio chair, quietly slipped through the condo, out the hotel room door, and onto the sand. She dug her feet deep into the beautiful point where the waves hit the shoreline. She watched as each wave crashed and flooded her toes all the way up to her shins then pulled away and left her feet to fully soak in the sun. Her hair fell gently down her back as the sun continued to warm her. She could just be here. She wanted to be.

Sometimes, Alex liked to imagine how his life would have turned out if he had been dating Sarah since high school. He had images of the two of them in his head holding hands by bonfires with friends and kissing in the shadows, sharing something only the two of them could know. He shared these thoughts with Sarah at dinner that evening. They found a beautiful restaurant on a dock near the ocean. Alex chose a place with live music, one of the beautiful pieces of home that he missed.

The second glass of dark red wine made his lips buzz in relaxation as he spoke of wishes. "Do you think our lives would have been simpler?"

"What do you mean?" Sarah responded as she sipped her wine too, the low lighting of the restaurant lamps floating in her eyes.

"I mean, you and I feel so tired now. We have pasts, people who have left us and hurt us." He thought of Sandy and the one or two college girlfriends he had but never quite felt committed to. "Grief takes so much energy."

"I've made a lot of decisions out of loneliness, and they've had more consequences than the brief thrill was worth." Sarah became serious for a moment.

"We probably would've had a lot more fun together," Alex tried to cheer her up.

"We've always had a lot of fun together." Sarah smiled as she spoke.

"That's because we never run out of things to talk about," Alex responded. "Speaking of, I have started writing again lately."

"Yeah?" Sarah responded, her smile widening.

"Yes. There is an empty, painful hole that Sandy left..." Sarah nodded. "Nothing seems to satiate the pain besides finding a name for how it hurts."

"I know that feeling."

"Yeah. I don't have the heart to put my hurt to music yet, but I've at least been able to describe how I feel."

"And how do you feel?" Sarah's eyes were so piercing when there was care in them. No matter how she had been hurt, she could always help the person she was looking at feel like they were the only one in the world. When she looked at Alex, he felt as though her strength held every grief and weakness he possessed. The ache of losing his grandmother didn't drag his stomach down so deeply when he was with Sarah.

"Truthfully, I've just been lost...going through the motions, trying not to feel anything. Work is a good distraction, absorbing myself in the stories of the customers." Alex took a deep breath in and folded his lips in disappointment, mostly with himself for simply not knowing what to do.

"It's hard to know what to do with yourself sometimes," Sarah responded, "or what you actually want. I went to our college because

I believed I was getting a good education and might be able to open myself up to the Christian god that so many Christians believe in. I didn't realize until I saw how hypocritical his 'people' were that he wasn't real, and neither were the dreams I used to believe in...A life of service, for both animals and people. I love the shelter and the dogs I work with, but I can't help but feel now that something is missing. I constantly want to distract myself from boredom and loneliness, like I am running or something."

"Running seems so much easier, but goddamn, it's lonely."

"Sometimes, I wish I could write like you," Sarah continued. "I have always loved to read, you know that. Why not try to create a story? Maybe put a voice to all the thoughts circling in my head."

Alex responded, "Creating makes space for all the painful, beautiful, and truthful things that don't seem to fit in a world of violence and loss. I just don't know what to do with myself the rest of the time when I'm not creating. I have to exist somehow."

"Some truths are too hard to face at the wrong time," Sarah responded. "Maybe we both haven't been ready until now."

Alex smiled. "Well, one thing I am ready for is to ask you for a dance. I meant to, before..." He didn't want to mention her wedding. "But there were a lot of distractions..."

The word *distractions* meant more to both Sarah and Alex than they wanted to admit, but they were here now, in this moment together, remembering the simple joy of being in the presence of someone each of them cared for, someone they could talk to openly. He smiled as he slowly stood up and offered Sarah his hand. Sarah reached for him, let her hand slowly sink into his, and joined Alex on the dock as the band continued to play.

The lead guitarist began the introductory solo for the cover of Jimmy Eat World's "23," and Alex glanced toward her as she stood beside him. "I felt for sure last night," the lead singer began, with the same beautiful tenor that Alex and the actual lead singer of Jimmy Eat World. "No one else will know these lonely dreams," the singer continued as Sarah turned toward Alex, a deep longing in her eyes. She needed to fall into his arms. But more importantly, she wanted to. Alex slowly reached for her hand...With his other hand, he gently grasped her waist and pulled her close, brushing his cheek against her soft, sun-kissed hair.

They slowly began to dance, just as they had at the bar occasionally on live music nights, but the knowing in the air was different, a sense had changed. Waves gently crashed as the sun set a soft orange into the ocean. Neither of them spoke, but Sarah glanced at the comforting colors of the sea and sky and sank into Alex. Although she loved how the orange of the sun bounced off the waves of the water, she let her eyes close as she rested against him. They gently moved together in perfect rhythm with the song.

The singer sang on, "It was my turn to decide. I knew this was our time. No one else will have me, like you do…No one else will have me, only you…"

Sarah breathed deeply and hugged Alex closer. She felt his hand lift from her waist and slide into her hair, stroking her head gently in a manner that gave her more comfort than any other physical touch ever had. Her eyes pinched tightly shut as she accepted the comforting pain of feeling again. While her eyes were tightly shut, a single tear dropped. She began to allow peace inside her. The feeling of relief was so painful but so beautiful at the same time. The song had reached the point of the arresting, high, and desperate guitar solo just before the chorus repeated two final times. The notes rang high, angry, beautiful, and strong, mirroring the pain Sarah had long been waiting to release. Alex was in a place to catch her here. All the jagged stones he held in his stomach that made him feel unworthy of her were washed away by the waves and sank with the setting sun.

"I'm here and now I'm ready," the singer continued. "Holding on tight. Don't give away the end, the one thing that stays mine."

Sarah and Alex grasped the deep friendship they had known since high school, a companionship that may not have been perfect, but it was true. Their connection to each other had always been real, and Sarah needed to feel how deep that connection could go tonight. The beauty and comfort of the ocean helped her slip out of her grief, and she found herself longing for Alex.

The song gently ended with the guitars slowly fading out…As they did, Sarah stepped slightly back from Alex so she could look up into his eyes. They both answered the same question each of them silently held with a small, inviting smile and gently leaned into each other for a soft but powerful kiss, a kiss that had been waiting on the edge of both of their lips for ten years. After a minute, they released each other and stepped back. Sarah looked into Alex's blue eyes, glowing with the beautiful light of the orange setting sun.

Alex and Sarah danced together until the moon rose. Then, they slowly walked back to their condo underneath the inviting moon and along the shoreline. Their fingers were intertwined as the shoreline lightly tapped the sides of their sandals, and they talked about all their favorite things, the sound of the dinner music, the Barbara Kingsolver novel Sarah had just read, and the lyrics Alex was thinking of writing for the next Live Night back home. They loved the feeling of setting all comparisons to the lives of others, all their anxieties and fears for the future aside. When Alex and Sarah spoke of the things they loved, the world's problems and insecurities had a habit of slowly melting away. Nothing else seemed to matter.

They talked on the couch together until 2:00 a.m. until happy exhaustion finally claimed them. Sarah slipped into bed with Alex that night and allowed Alex to hold her. He lay behind her and gently pulled her into himself, silently asking her if each move was okay. Until that moment, Sarah had never known that consent for touch could be quietly exchanged. Alex had always been in tune to her every feeling and nonverbal glance. He knew her. He felt for her with a sense he could not explain before resting his arm more firmly around her, wanting to comfort every hurt of her past that he wasn't there to stop. Sarah felt Alex's longing and let sleep wash over her as Alex's gentle and kind grip healed a small part of her.

Chapter 25

The next day was spent exploring. Sarah had longed to see Coronado Beach. She loved how the water reflected the skyscrapers and trees like a mirror as it draped across the sand. As she stared at the shoreline, she could see her face clearly. Everything about the curves around her eyes looked heavy. She was happy at the beach with Alex but still carried the weight of Jesse and Dean in the stones in her stomach and exhaustion around her eyes. She did her best to push out intrusive memories of Dean's cold, dark eyes above her. As soon as the vision would leave, the sound of Dean's commanding whisper entered. She could feel his hot, beer-soaked breath in her ears. She pushed that sound and sense out too but then the memory of Jesse's apathy over the phone creeped in. The betrayal of his words felt as if they would never leave her. "Is it really worth putting on his permanent record? This report will follow him the rest of his life. Is that worth it to you?" The stones turned over and over in her stomach until they became smoldering coals. Sarah simply burned.

She did her best to sink into the mirror of the ocean, to remember the comfort Alex had given her before, and to watch the beauty of him walk along the shoreline a few yards from her. She refocused her mind on the way Alex's black curls looked with the breeze running through them and the beauty of her own, albeit exhausted, face reflected in the ocean, but the burn felt impossible to ignore. Her body could not allow her to feel safe, even though she was with someone safe, in a place that held a breeze and scenery that was nothing like the place of her attack or the look of the apartment she stood in during Jesse's phone call.

In this moment, as hard as she tried to live presently, the past scorched her and she felt as if she couldn't let go. She imagined herself trying to grip each smoldering stone in her hand as her sadness and pain shifted to anger. She had to release these coals but didn't know how yet. Her thoughts were interrupted by Alex, "Hey, Sarah, come look at what I found over here!" She swallowed her grief for the moment and forced herself to walk forward. Alex had found a particularly beautiful shell, the kind that curled in on themselves and held caramel and white colors that splashed together.

"It is beautiful," Sarah responded. He offered her his hand, an invitation to continue walking along the shoreline. Sarah took it and smiled at him as best she could, the coals still burning a hole in her palms.

Alex was eager to explore California's giant redwoods. He had heard that the trees grew so tall, they were like a creature out of a fantasy novel, stretching and speaking to the air and the sky of all things green and beautiful. A beautiful truth about California is that one can drive to lovely beaches and strong redwood forests all within the span of a few hours, sometimes less. After spending one day walking along the shores of Coronado Beach and eating simple, delicious meals on patios surrounded by deep red California poppies, Alex and Sarah rested in each other's arms again that night and moved onto the redwoods in the morning.

As Alex walked through the forest, he saw Sarah a few yards ahead of him, crouching to see some of the wildflowers and small banana slugs up close. He watched how peaceful she appeared while exploring and couldn't help but notice how beautiful she looked as her hands gently grazed the flowers and her low ponytail fell over her shoulders. His eyes also searched for the tops of the trees, the place where they met the sky. The trees held a solid strength that he needed to grip. Roots were what kept Alex grounded, yet he couldn't also help but feel they held him back. He remembered wanting to study music in this very state but stayed behind for the grandmother who loved him. Too often, he felt buried in habit and routine and couldn't see himself living any other life than continuing her legacy at the bar. The trees were wider than him too. He was just a tiny living thing that barely stretched to the place where the roots grew into the trees. He felt meaningless. He did his best to control the grief he felt about

Sandy and the guilt he couldn't shake about Sarah's pain. And all the while he loved her.

He wasn't sure what the kiss, hand-holding, conversations, and sleeping beside her at night meant; and he didn't want to risk ending the closeness by asking. He knew Sarah was grieving too, and he hoped to god that the comfort she sought in him was not for the sole purpose of numbing a wound.

As his blue eyes searched the trees that surrounded him, he had to ask himself the same question, "Am I seeking only comfort in Sarah? Was he settling for the little pieces she would give him when he always wanted more?" He couldn't know for sure. They were both lost in pain, guilt, and anger. "Could love grow beside grief?" Thoughts raced through his mind as he gazed at the wonder of the wide, endless redwoods. Sarah called for him as she rounded the corner of the path, and they were no longer in sight of each other. There was so much he wanted to say as they walked together through the forest, but for now, he took a deep breath, swallowed his words, and simply followed.

Sarah and Alex spent every day leisurely exploring the vast beauties of California, including the mountains, which were last on their list. Hiking and talking were some of the best times of their lives, and they loved chasing the world's wonders together. Sarah also made a point to visit all the nature preserves in the area that she could, anxious to see the native wildlife that she could never get a glimpse of in the Midwest. They decided that on their last evening, they would cook pasta together in the condo. Homemade Cajun sauce was one of Sarah's specialties, and it was a quick and easy meal she often made for Alex at home if they weren't out to lunch. She could season and speak at the same time while occasionally sipping some wine, which worked perfectly if she needed to pause to understand one of Alex's points. However, on this particular night, she made the mistake of buying a sauvignon blanc, which sipped easily for her. Sarah was used to dry reds, which she loved, but they were strong and demanded to be slowly savored. Sarah sipped, spoke, seasoned, and stirred; and before she realized what had happened, she was drunk by the time she sat down to dinner with Alex.

Alex was drunk too. He would have a drink or two when he was out with Sarah but avoided alcohol for the most part because he almost always had to be on call in case something went wrong at the bar. But he knew this was his last night alone with Sarah before they both had to return to reality. Certainly, that meant their jobs but it also meant the realities of the separate pains they were both escaping. Up until tonight, they had avoided speaking too deeply about Jesse, Sandy, and all the feelings of frustration in between. They also had not spoken to each other of what sleeping in the same bed, holding hands, and the kiss meant. The kiss had only happened once, but it was deep, and they both knew the intimacy was real.

They were both laughing at an impression Alex made of one of his regulars who unsuccessfully hit on many women in the bar by embellishing his role as "CEO of a very important local electric company, etc.," when all of a sudden the conversation turned to other scenes in the bar that Sarah couldn't help but remember. She hadn't been back since the night of her wedding and avoided sharing any more details about how the rape felt since the first and only time she told Alex the whole story. But the alcohol buzzed in her brain and felt tingly and tantalizing on her lips and her unfiltered feelings began gushing out. "Yeah, the bar. Alex, I didn't want to tell you because I know what that place means to you, but I don't think I can ever go back again," a serious look appeared in her eyes.

Alex gulped, afraid to face his own feelings about Sarah's experience at the bar but his brain was unfiltered too, and he encouraged the conversation to continue. "It's okay, Sarah. I think I understand why you wouldn't. Truthfully, I have blocked myself from feeling anything when I look at certain rooms and objects there."

Sarah raised an eyebrow. "You mean, places like the bathroom?"

Tears filled Alex's eyes, but he fought them back as he responded. "Yes. I never thought focusing on the smell of bleach would save me from memories. I only ever thought the stuff was toxic. If Gabe is not able to get to cleaning the bathrooms, I force myself to. And no matter how much bleach I use, I never can seem to scrub an energy out of that place. There's a heaviness that just won't evaporate." He took another long sip of his wine.

"There are lots of places where that energy won't evaporate," Sarah responded. "I've been to several therapy sessions since and done my legal due diligence to see that justice was served, yet I can't stop feeling Dean in my skin or the piercing pain of Jesse ignoring me in my stomach. Now, my pain is turning to anger, Alex, and I feel it burning everywhere."

"I am angry too, Sarah." Her eyes met his, quietly inviting him to explain why. He continued, "I am angry because I should have been there."

Sarah was about to interject, telling him Dean's choices were not his fault, but Alex waved his hand back and forth and continued, "No, I should have been there. You were raped"—he winced at the sound of the words—"in MY bar, when I was standing only yards away, the same distance we've had occasionally on our hikes. How could I share the same distance with you now and feel so much joy, yet be the same distance from you months ago while that piece of shit ripped into you?" Now Sarah winced at his words. Alex's voice was raised at this point.

He saw the concern he caused her and calmed his tone, "I'm sorry, Sarah. The guilt of failing to protect you from Dean is eating me alive. I could have stopped him if I wasn't so absorbed in my own feelings. I should have."

Sarah's gaze relaxed into compassion. She didn't want Alex to feel responsible for Dean. She certainly didn't hold him responsible. The rape was Dean's choice and his alone. Alex couldn't be held responsible for not being in the right place at the right time. If anything, he was the only thing Sarah was grateful for that night. Alex had busted his ass helping her decorate, organize the food, and provide the music for her wedding, all the things that created beauty where a tragedy occurred. She felt nothing but gratitude toward him. She told him this, but he just shook his head as the tears fell from his eyes.

He couldn't control them anymore, and he couldn't believe Sarah. Too much inside him pushed a lie that he was responsible for the violation that had happened to her, just as he felt responsible for the feelings and actions of those closest to him. Alex wasn't aware yet, but he carried the responsibility of his parents leaving him too; he believed it was his fault for being so much work that they felt they had no other choice but to escape. To add fuel to the fire, he also couldn't shake the feeling that he owed his grandmother for caring for him when he wasn't hers to care for. He could never repay her no matter how many desperate hours he put into her business. The weight of every person he believed he had disappointed and burdened crashed on him in this moment as he quietly sobbed, holding his face in his hands to try to mask his sorrow.

Sarah wanted so badly to comfort him. She couldn't find the right words, but she knew she had a question. Maybe answering the question would help him to express why he felt so guilty about Dean's choice. And if she was honest, she couldn't help but feel curious. "Alex," she said gently. Alex took a breath, pulled his hands away, and grabbed his napkin to wipe his eyes. He looked at her as he attempted to dry them, giving her the space to ask.

"What do you mean you were 'absorbed in your own feelings'?" she asked as casually and carefully as she could, hoping he would be honest.

Alex felt that now wasn't the right time to tell her. He had been drinking and some feelings that he had pushed away a long time gnawed at him. He sensed that there were some about his parents, some about Sandy, and certainly, some about Sarah. He wasn't entirely sure he could sort them all in this moment, but the alcohol moved him to keep spilling words without the luxury of expressing them considerately and eloquently.

"Obviously, I love you, Sarah," he blurted out.

Sarah's eyebrows rose in shock. She suspected Alex had felt that way but was not entirely sure. He had never actually admitted any truths to her until now. There was only something unspoken between them and comments here and there from Pete…

"Obviously, you love me?" she questioned. "What do you mean obviously? And what kind of love do you mean?"

Alex swallowed, attempting to gain control of his shaky voice. "Sarah, every thought I have is of you. Every lyric I sing is fueled by a place in my heart that you hold, but I can't explain how. The conversations we have at Eric's Bean shop or at your place are the best times of my life. I always find myself looking forward to the next moment I get with you. Everything I work toward, all the time I spend everywhere, I am just waiting for the next minute, hour, or evening I get to spend with you. In you, I finally feel like I have a place. I can speak of all the things I love, music, books, poetry, and passion. No one sees me like you. The only thing I love that I haven't shared with you is, you. You have always been so disappointed with everyone. I couldn't help but believe you would be disappointed with me too. I am certainly disappointed in myself and all the dreams I have yet to live if I ever will. I never told you I loved you because I was afraid you were already disappointed in who I was. I didn't pursue music as I should have, just a sheltered version of occasionally writing and playing at a bar I own. Of course, no one would shoo me off stage there. I own the place. Even if people hated my music, they already love the casual and comfortable drinking atmosphere that Sandy started and I continued. There's no risk involved there. What if I told you how I felt and you didn't feel the same way and I just lost you? At least, before I told you, I could hold on to the happiest moments of my life without fear that you would leave if you knew the truth." He took a deep breath and gulped his wine again, desperate to move his hands somewhere. He knew this confession could come at a cost of rejection.

For once in her life, Sarah was at a loss for words. She knew that Alex cared for her, and probably loved her, but not like this. She knew Alex was likely drunk, but she was drunk too. *Did his being drunk make the words any less true?* she wondered. *Maybe he just wouldn't have said them this way or this soon…* She couldn't think clearly of what to say, so she let her body guide her. She slowly scooted her chair back, stood up, and walked toward him.

He stood up in return, tucked her hair gently behind her ear, just as he had the night they danced, then gently rested his hand on her face as he kissed her long, slow, and certain. Alex gave her the kiss of someone who was certain for once in his life, certain that he held the right hand, grasped the right waist, and shared the right piece of himself. There was home and safety in Sarah.

Yes, he thought, *I am sure I did the right thing telling her now.* He pulled her closer and began to kiss her harder when she gently grabbed his wrist, the one that supported her face.

"Wait," she said gently as she stopped kissing him. "Before this goes any further, I have to tell you something."

Alex stopped immediately, trying to respect her boundaries. He only wanted to finally reach her body the way he had imagined, hoping now that the feeling was mutual.

"Alex, I don't know if I am ready for this. I-I have to love you too if we're going to do this, and right now, I don't know if I can." Sarah didn't realize that the same feeling that was stopping her from having sex with Alex was a good sign that she actually loved him. She had spent most of her life sleeping with people to distract herself from loneliness. She realized in that moment with Alex that the men who had taken advantage of her body probably added up to way more than Jesse. Men who knew she hadn't really wanted them and slept with her anyway, taking what they wanted of her for themselves. Alex's confession had opened a scar that had formed on Sarah without her even realizing that a wound had ever been there. She had to heal from more than just Dean. She had to heal from every sexual encounter she lied to herself about. Alex offered her intimacy, he offered her something real, and she couldn't just accept that when her heart still felt so unsafe.

She hardly knew what she was thinking and certainly couldn't explain more to Alex. She only said, "I think we should stop. I can't do this until I am sure I feel the same way."

Alex was crushed. He wanted to respect her, but under the influence, he couldn't mask the pain of the rejection he felt. Pain that quickly turned to anger. The insecurities that ate at him went on the attack. "Okay fine, I get it. But I need to ask you something. Why was Jesse good enough for you? Why was a coward like that worthy of the time of someone like you? Matter of fact, someone as smart as you should have known better about him. Why couldn't you see how stupid and fake he really was?" He didn't want to say the next words, but they came spilling out as he began to raise his voice. "Why was he good enough for you to commit your time and energy to and I'm not?"

Alex's bringing Jesse up stung. Sarah was already ashamed at having given Jesse anything, especially a marriage, and Alex's question drove the stake that already poked at her heart even deeper. Sarah instantly turned from sympathetic to furious; the alcohol fueling her rage too. Alex bit her with his words, and she was going to bite back.

"Maybe Jesse is a coward, but at least he wasn't afraid to actually tell me how he felt! He asked me out as soon as he saw me. You've known me for years and never said a word about how you felt! Matter of fact, when have you ever said a word about anything you wanted?" She saw Alex's shoulders tense in pain and anger, but she continued, lost in the tunnel vision fueled by the urge to hurt back. "All your life, you wanted to study music, to become a composer, but you refused to risk your own dreams. You know that you could have sold your grandmother's business if you wanted to. You know that Sandy would want you to make a life of creating what you love. She has always encouraged that pursuit. You can say that loyalty and needing to care for her held you back, but you know the truth, you are too afraid to pursue what you love because you think you'll fail. You are so afraid to lose, you won't risk anything at all. So who really is the coward, Alex?"

Alex screamed at her before he even realized what he was saying, "The business isn't about me, Sarah! It's about my grandma, another thing you should know. If you can't understand why I won't sell, then you have no goddamn respect for her!"

Alex had never sworn at Sarah before. There was a silence in the air after the last, biting words that suffocated them both. They stood in that silence for a few seconds before he responded in a controlled but angry voice, "I'm done. Forget all this." He then stormed off to his bedroom and slammed the door.

Sarah sat in the silence that switched from rage to desperate loneliness, knowing something had broken between her and Alex. The drunkenness made that empty silence even more painful. Silent tears fell from her eyes as she slowly walked to her own room, certain that she would not feel the quiet comfort of Alex's arms that night.

She shut the door, changed into her satin pajamas, trying to feel the comfort of the silk against her skin and slipped into bed. The tears continued to stream down her face, and the alcohol made her feel as if the world was ending. She built even more protective walls in her mind. Alex was the only one who ever understood her. The part of her mind that had learned to shield her from Jesse's betrayal and proactively ensure that Dean ended up behind bars was learning new pathways, pathways of trust. But now Alex hurt her too. He was the one person she believed didn't have a vengeful or selfish bone in his body, but now it turned out that he was just as human as anybody else. And what was she to do with that knowledge? How could she tell the difference between someone genuinely battling their own demons and all the angry and selfish men who had hurt her before? Her mind concluded that the only safe response was to keep the walls up. Don't allow Alex in again and don't allow anyone. You have given chances before and you always end up disappointed, hurt, and alone. People who love you shouldn't be capable of words that hurt. Keep him at bay, as you have before, and you will stay safe. Sarah's mind spun with alcohol, pain, anger, and confusion; and it was hard to fall asleep inside the dizziness, but she desperately tried and eventually sank into restless, anxious sleep.

Alex's rage stalked him. As soon as he slammed the door, he knew he made a mistake. He should never have brought up Jesse under the influence of alcohol and when he was feeling insecure. But each time he remembered his insecurities and how inadequate he felt, his anger returned. He was angry at himself, but it was easier to direct his anger at Sarah. He knew he should just try to go to bed, but he couldn't stop pacing. So many feelings he had ignored for so long were boiling over in his skin; he had to walk them out. He paced and paced, feeling every last disappointment he had in himself and that he believed others had: "You're not a talented writer," "You don't have the stamina for music school," "You would never make it as a composer in California, there's too many other people much more talented than you," "You didn't deserve your parents' love, that's why they left," "Sandy lost all the independent years of her life caring for you, the least you could do is keep her legacy going with the business," "Sarah will never love you, you will never be brave, smart, or creative enough…" His insecurities and fears wrestled him into the night. He eventually passed out in his clothes on top of the sheets, also into a restless, anxious sleep.

Thankfully, Alex and Sarah had an evening flight home because both of them woke up in the early afternoon with wicked hangovers. Sarah was nauseated and Alex's head pounded. They both remembered flashes of their argument the night before, and the weight of the stinging words they both said to each other crushed them. Sarah replayed each hurtful word she said to Alex over in her mind, "Never said a word about how you felt!…Who really is the coward, Alex? Sandy would want…"

How could she have called him a coward? she thought as guilt began to take over her mind. She knew that Alex cared deeply for those he loved and giving his time and talents was one of the reasons she knew deep down that she actually loved him. And how could she bring up Sandy so soon after she passed? She knew Alex was still grieving, and she poured salt on his wound. The guilt of the drunken words she said the night before was too much. The depression that followed after alcohol left her brain made that guilt feel unbearable. All she could do was return to her step method. Step 1: Try to rehydrate herself with the water by her bedside. Step 2: Slowly begin to pack…

Alex woke up feeling ashamed. He didn't realize how angry he was until the alcohol and the night forced the feelings out, and the target was Sarah, the one person he felt safe with. Alex had absorbed the stories and been the safe place for so many of the strangers and regulars that he worked with. Always the dutiful, listening ear. He hadn't realized the frustration that built up inside him or the pain caused by those who had let him down. He didn't want to bring Jesse up to Sarah. He didn't want her to feel judged. He knew she already felt unnecessarily ashamed for falling for Jesse in the first place. Alex knew exactly why Sarah fell for Jesse, and he didn't blame her for it. But now, she would probably never believe that. He had targeted her in a moment of pain and weakness, and he wasn't sure their relationship could survive it. Nothing like this had ever happened to him before, and he had no idea how to navigate through the argument. One thing he did know was that their plane was taking off at 5:30 p.m., and he had to get to the airport on time. Gabe could only cover on- and off-call duties for one week. He was getting married the week after. Alex couldn't afford to arrive home late. He popped a few Tylenol and swiftly opened the door to the common space in the condo, determined to avoid speaking to Sarah because he didn't know the words to say. He would simply pack his things, arrange for a ride to the airport for both of them, and head home.

Sarah and Alex existed in a strange, painful silence. They both did their best to clean up the dishes from the night before, each one a reminder of the ugliness they had exchanged. They spoke to each other in short, detached sentences, asking and answering only the questions that were necessary.

"What time will the Uber be here?"

"Four o'clock."

"Okay, thanks."

"Did you return our condo keys to the front desk?"

"Yes."

"Cool."

Each one's coldness and matter-of-fact attitude stung the other, but they weren't sure how else to speak to each other. They had their own separate regrets about the words they said the night before. Each of them also felt equally ashamed for hurting the other. There was no easy answer to moving forward after drunken truths came out. Sarah and Alex knew that they didn't have a toxic relationship; that at its core, they were not two people seeking to hurt each other. They felt even worse because they had such a beautiful trip together before that night, yet the power of their argument sat in their hearts more heavily than the connection and beauty they had experienced together. Sarah wondered if Alex still loved her after that fight…Up until now, she thought he only loved her for the admirable parts of her he knew. He had never seen her ugly side; she had never seen it herself. How could he still love her after she purposely said words meant to sting him? Her thoughts tortured her.

Similar questions plagued Alex's mind. He never got an answer about Sarah loving him or not. He wondered if her holding back from sex was her attempt at love because she wanted sex with him to mean more. He also recognized that he could not know what trauma still flowed through Sarah's veins after Dean and might impact how she experienced intimacy, and it wasn't his place to decide when she was ready to feel intimate. Neither of them had an answer that led to moving forward, so they just stayed frozen in their pain. Avoiding each other was the answer they both nonverbally agreed to. They rode the plane silently home, said cold goodbyes and "Thank you for the trip," and each took separate cabs back to their separate homes and prepared to return to their responsibilities.

Chapter 26

Sarah had been in therapy for a while. The sessions were originally recommended by Detective Selena. Sarah was exhausted by the energy she put into "justice" for Dean and didn't want to give him any more power over her mind or the time spent thinking about him and the cruelties he had dealt. But Sarah discovered that the harder she tried to push him out of her mind on her own, the more he insisted on invading moments that were precious to her. Every other thought was of him; it didn't matter if she was connecting with families who were the right fit for the animals at the shelter, relaxing in the heat of a shower at home, or curled up reading on her couch… or when she thought of her previous conversations with Alex. Anger and sadness burned, and she still gripped the coals in her hands. She realized that both Alex and Dean had the power to hurt her, in very different ways, even when they were physically absent. Her mind raced with anxious feelings about them both

Prior to the trip with Alex, Sarah had been learning how to release the grief, disgust, pain, isolation, and rage. Her therapist encouraged her to share exactly what she was thinking for each one and then to do her best to come back and focus on the sensory information around her or count numbers in a random order. The methods were designed to help her feel safe again, to remind her body that she was safe in the present moment, that protecting herself was no longer needed. But the mind works in patterns and cannot always distinguish unique, situational factors. Nothing made Sarah feel more unsafe than being at odds with her best friend. Was he even a friend? she thought. After actually hearing him say he loved her, she had to wonder what their friendship really meant to Alex and to her. Why did it take special circumstances and alcohol for him to tell her how he truly felt? She remembered his words, "Every thought I have is of you…" "Disappointed in me too…" Why was a coward like him good enough for you?"

Sarah did her best to share her argument with Alex with her therapist, but she couldn't help but panic as she spoke. Nothing about what happened with Jesse and Dean was easy, but their betrayal fit clearly into a category: crime. When Sarah had clear answers, when she could understand, she could begin to work through all the feelings. She didn't understand the discord with Alex. She wasn't even sure how she felt. She had given answers to Pete about why they never got together, but were those answers even true? If she wanted to be with Alex, she would have, right? He has been there all along. Why wouldn't she just go for him? She couldn't come to any conclusions. Everything was too muddled. She felt too much at once. Her mind could not find a state of calm and focus. Sarah existed in a strange space between seeking truth, connection, and running. Her soul wanted to feel safe, but her mind could not help but convince her that she needed to understand every feeling, every situation, and remain one step ahead of everyone.

Alex was overwhelmed by shame as he quietly stacked cups and brought up boxes of liquor from the basement, back to his usual business at work, but nothing about the thoughts that raced through his mind felt usual. Words were his gift. When he sang, the ring and meaning of each lyric met the hearts of those who listened and helped them find something of themselves, some sort of missing piece. He caught the captivation in the eyes of bar patrons when he sang his originals on live night.

He remembered his grandmother's eyes, with a twinge of pain, as he sang, "Nothing comes from nothing, nothing ever could" from *The Sound of Music*, the last song he ever played for her. The words had brought her back to herself and back to him. They could be so powerfully healing. Words had always connected him to Sarah, from their very first interaction and throughout their entire relationship. He remembered the quote on his agenda that she responded to Uncle Iroh: "Important to draw wisdom from different places." He didn't feel so wise now. How could he have said those cruel words to Sarah?

he thought as shame grew and felt like roots determined to dig in and rot in his stomach. He loathed himself for judging Sarah for being with Jesse, but the truth was that he did judge her, whether or not he wanted to admit the truth to himself, and he had no idea what to do with that judgment. He knew he didn't want to feel it, but he had no other place to put the judgmental thoughts, so they anxiously swam through his mind and body.

Alex's whole life, he had learned how to use words carefully to encourage others or create. He never would have kept his grandmother's business going if he had not known how to connect with people through conversation...But all he could feel now was miserable failure. He was always the one in control when alcohol was around, and he lost that control with Sarah and he had no idea how to take the words back. He couldn't. They had been said, unfiltered.

You should have known better. The same voice that sang to Sarah and held her up morphed into rage that tore at her. *I don't understand how I could speak with such rage to someone I love. I don't know myself that way.* His thoughts felt like a person pacing furiously in his mind as he literally paced around the bar, unconsciously and desperately preparing for business. Alex didn't like who he was when he felt out of control. He didn't know how to accept the version of himself that wasn't exactly what everyone else needed—the helper, the musician, the bartender. These were all "easy" roles that were easily understood.

He didn't understand himself with Sarah, and he didn't know how to accept himself for who he was in all his emotions. He didn't know how to shake the shame he felt for how he spoke to Sarah, and he had no idea how to try to speak to her again. Fear of rejection crippled him. What if he reached out to her and she bit back at him again? What if he tried to restore their friendship and she refused? What would he do with himself if she were no longer in his life at all? Maybe she had actually hurt him with her words. Maybe he felt rejected and tired of being seen as just a friend.

Why didn't she choose me? he thought. He decided then that he didn't have enough answers or certainty to try to reach out. He buried himself in his work. He would focus on running the business as best he could. He knew how to be a "good" bartender and business owner. He refused to pick up his guitar or touch the keyboard. *Focus on the business*, he thought. *Sarah needs stability now more than ever, so stick to what you're good at, consistency. Maybe she will come and find you. But keep your guard up.*

Chapter 27

Sarah sat down with the therapist for her final session following the assault. The co-pays were adding up, and she had the overwhelming sense that sharing words about how she felt was more exhausting and draining than the help she could receive from releasing them. It had been several weeks since her argument with Alex, and articulating all of her feelings about the rape and discord with her best friend was more than she was able to bear. She had been desperately trudging through all of her emotions for months, and the vulnerability and honesty of survival and anger at people giving into their worst instincts yet avoiding responsibility for them was all becoming too much.

The therapist pulled out the familiar red notebook and black ballpoint pen, looked at Sarah, and asked what had been on her mind lately. Although Sarah was exhausted and nearing the end of her sessions, she did, in fact, have something on her mind…

She answered, "What role do feelings play in who we actually are?" She took a deep breath as her eyes looked up, searching for the memories that fed her thoughts. She remembered the feelings she held at her wedding as she spoke, "It was an unnameable tenseness in my shoulders and spine that numbed me, flowed through my body, and fed the instincts that ultimately led me to escape Dean. An unknowable force and feeling inside guided me, and because of that force, I'm labeled a 'survivor,' and most would say a 'survivor' is central to who I am now. In the moments Dean attacked, my feelings saved me. Now, months later, my feelings betray me. I am afraid all the time, and the same tenseness that rescued me from rape is pressuring me to believe that, now, no one is safe and who I am will never be accepted, not in this fear, mistrust, and what I perceive to be weakness.

"I have learned that I can't survive if I feel weak because there is no place for weakness in safety. The few relationships I have are twisted and confusing. The only truth I know for myself is that if I feel guarded, then I am strong and with strength comes respect and a sense of confidence. And somehow, in my mind or in reality, all this is directly tied to my identity. Feelings have saved me and betrayed me. So I have to ask again, what role do feelings play in who I actually am and how can I sort my identity and relationships out? Right now, I feel strong because I have the sense to explain all this to you, so **am I** strong?"

Sarah met the therapist's eyes as she asked the question. The therapist opened her mouth to respond but stopped as Sarah took short breaths and continued, "I haven't spoken to my best friend in weeks because I couldn't face the feeling that his anger toward me during a heated discussion meant rejection. After I left our argument, I had been avoiding him out of fear. When I made a choice out of fear, who was I then? What was I? Fearful? Weak? Dean and Jesse taught me that I can't trust anyone, especially myself. I couldn't trust my husband to protect me when I felt afraid of the man he called best friend. He was only there for me when I fed his confidence, before Dean chose to rape me and he had to face himself and those he surrounded himself with. He discovered that he was too afraid to own that he was a coward and face the ugly sides of those he knew. People only stay when they feel confident and strong and those feelings consume them.

"God, I am so lost in the question of how feelings shape our identities, and in the meantime, I don't know how to trust anyone. Alex was angry at me because I told him that he should use the money his grandmother left him to sell his business and pursue music, his actual passion. He responded to me in a loud tone and said, 'I had no goddamn respect for her if I pushed him to move on so quickly.' The look in his eyes was stern and I ran from it. I am angry that people won't own their feelings, yet I still fear the negative feelings of others."

"This does sound exhausting," her therapist responded. "It also sounds like you are putting a lot of pressure on yourself to take responsibility for the choices and feelings of others, as well as your own."

Sarah nodded. Then, she finally paused and took a deep breath before continuing, she considered what the therapist said but still had more anxious thoughts she wanted to share.

"He hasn't said a word to me since our vacation. I can guess why."

"Why?" her therapist asked.

"I am sure he feels guilty. I hoped he would reach out and try to reconcile, but I am not sure if he knows how. He raised his voice. He swore. Alex never does that. He probably knows that instinctively, I felt threatened. He might even feel worse because he knows more than anyone else about what I have been through with Dean and Jesse. I knew he would never physically hurt me, yet I still felt afraid."

"Why do you think you felt afraid?" the therapist responded. "You've always described Alex as your most trusted friend."

Sarah sat up straighter and met the therapist's eyes again. "I guess I don't know how to trust anymore, and maybe I never really did. Alex is clearly different than Jesse and Dean, yet some of my feelings of fear are the same. He showed me an anger in himself that I think he didn't even fully understand. He's spent so long hiding from how he feels and what he actually wants, only showing the tiniest shreds of truth in his music. And maybe now that I have seen people close to me at their worst, I have internalized that I am the one bringing the worst out of them, and they will associate me with that part of who they are, just as Jesse did." Tears filled her eyes as she continued, "So everything is all twisted, and now all I feel I can do is run. Feeling anything real with anyone hurts because I don't and can't know what role those feelings play in who I am and who they are and how our identities should exist in any kind of relationship."

Her therapist paused thoughtfully for a minute. "I am sorry, Sarah. I can see you are in a lot of pain. What if you tried to talk to Alex even though you are confused?"

Sarah paused. "I don't even know what I would say. My mind is always at odds with itself. I am afraid he hates me for what I said about his fear of pursuing anything he cares about."

"Why are you afraid that he hates you?"

"Because I was frustrated with him, and I didn't communicate that frustration as well as I should have."

"What's so wrong with being frustrated?" she responded kindly. "Frustration just means that you want the best and you feel like the best isn't happening. There is nothing wrong with wanting better for those you love."

Sarah was quiet for a moment. *She has a good point,* she thought. But her protective instincts got the better of her again. "But I communicated rudely, I was out of control. Sure, I think that Alex needs to be braver and go after what he wants. But I feel guilty about those thoughts because I understand why he feels obligated to keep his grandmother's business going."

"You can understand him and still want better. There is nothing to be ashamed of for wanting more for your best friend. And rarely do human beings communicate every thought they have perfectly."

Her words were starting to help Sarah soften and feel as if she could be more patient with herself.

"We've talked a lot about taking relationships in steps. Sometimes the first one is just reaching out. It's okay to try to connect with Alex even though you are scared. Reconnecting with him even in your fear is what will help you feel safe."

"You're right," Sarah responded thoughtfully.

"I have one more question for you," the therapist asked.

"Yes?"

"Alex told you he loved you, as more than a friend. Do you think you feel the same way?"

"I have always felt at home with Alex. He has been the one person I have always chosen to make time for. He is the face I look forward to seeing. So many things are so easy with Alex, the way I wish most of life was. But I mean easy in the best way, like I can talk to him for hours about what I love most, stories, saving the world one animal at a time, and music. But something has held me back. A part of me knew he loved me and I chose to marry someone else. Someone who I knew I didn't connect with. I can't ignore that choice."

"What about how you feel now that he's told you he loves you?"

"I don't know," Sarah responded. And she genuinely didn't. All she was certain of was that she couldn't stand the distance between her and Alex anymore.

"The divide I feel from him aches in a way completely different from the grief I have felt lately. Distance between Alex and I makes me feel sick. I have never experienced this feeling before. All I know for certain is that I don't want to feel distant from him anymore."

"So start with a single word. It's okay to find him."

Chapter 28

Sarah always knew where to find Alex. He was usually working at the bar. She found him there the next morning talking with Gabe. She saw the familiar golf pencil tucked behind his ear. He had on a light blue hoody with the word *Crooked* sprawled across the front as if it were spray paint in dark brown letters. Sarah noted that she loved the way he looked. She hadn't realized how much she missed him until she saw him smiling with Gabe. Alex had a smile that spread throughout his entire face when he laughed. He was charming. Most of the charming men Sarah had known accompanied their charm with arrogance. Alex wasn't arrogant. She remembered this about him as she stood in the doorway of Crooked and took in his presence in the moment. Speaking to him was going to take courage and nervousness flooded her stomach. She took a deep breath and stepped forward.

Alex immediately looked up as she stepped closer and straightened his posture. Without a word, Gabe exited to the office, muttering something about "balancing last night's close out sum."

Sarah approached Alex. *Start with a word*, she thought seriously. She decided to go with two. "Hey, Alex," she said as friendly as possible though she felt awkward.

He was overjoyed to see her, but afraid to show vulnerability. He wanted to feel right with Sarah again, and he knew he still loved her deeply. However, he was ashamed of his rage but had also realized when he saw her that he still felt angry. Although he expressed himself poorly, he realized he meant some of what he said about Sarah choosing Jesse. For a long time, he felt unheard by Sarah. She was the one who loved and listened to him the most. He knew in his heart that she wouldn't want him to feel dismissed, yet he couldn't ignore the feeling that she had dismissed him by choosing Jesse though he was never fully open with her until the night of their argument about feeling more than friendship for her. He wanted to just talk with her again, to feel the simple yet powerful comfort that they both gave each other so easily on most occasions. However, he wasn't ready to face the anger he showed her or the frustration he still felt. "What can I do for you?" He tried to sound kind, but the words came out stoic and cold.

Sarah was caught off guard by his coldness but was determined to continue. "Um…Well, I just really wanted to talk to you." She didn't know how to move forward or what the right words to say were to repair the damage done by their fight, but she had also never fought openly with Alex, or anyone, before.

"Alex, I hate this. I am sorry for some of the things I said to you and how I said them." She fidgeted with an old receipt sitting on the bar, folding it into smaller and smaller squares. "I can't take my words back or even say I didn't mean them. The truth is, I do believe you deserve more, and I do believe you're avoiding your music career." Alex stiffened when he heard her words. "But I shouldn't have accused you of avoiding your dreams or brought Sandy into the conversation." A part of Sarah felt like she actually should have brought Sandy into the conversation, the truth was that maybe Alex needed some honesty and a push, but she still regretted that she told him drunkenly. "I just want to fix this." Sarah didn't think about how to "fix" the part where Alex loved her; she had no idea what their relationship was going to look like, only that she wanted him in her life.

Alex sensed that she wasn't going to address the love he felt for her and barricaded himself inside politeness even further. "Sarah, I am your friend. I always have been. I will be here for you and talk through anything you need, but I don't need to discuss my music career, or lack thereof in your eyes." The last words had a bite to them. "I can keep my feelings and dreams to myself. I don't need you to fix them for me, and I don't need to rely on you."

The last words stung. Sarah was hurt. Thoughts raced through her mind. They had never had a blowout before, but surely Alex knew she would be there for him. His words felt one-sided and unfair. Just because she didn't respond to his feelings in the way he needed in the moment didn't mean she wasn't deserving of his honest friendship. How could she learn how to repair and how to respond to his feelings if he was just going to close himself off to her?

"Alex, what do you mean you don't need to rely on me?" she said, her voice shaking with fear that he would cut himself off from her.

"I mean, I will be your best friend. I will be there for you. I will talk through your thoughts as I always have, but I am not going to ask anything of you or talk to you about my 'lost dreams.'"

"How am I supposed to respond to that?" Sarah said, frustration filling her voice.

"Respond however you want. I don't understand why this is a problem or why you would be confused. You still get your best friend. We can talk whenever you want, and I am not going to ask anything of you."

"Do you really think I want the kind of relationship with you where you don't tell me how you feel?" Sarah's fist tightened around the paper she had been facing as she seriously met his eyes with her own.

Alex was closed and cold. The smile he had shown Gabe was nowhere to be found. He met her eyes too and said, "I told you how I felt, and you didn't know how to respond. I don't expect you to now."

"Alex, I wasn't expecting your feelings. I wondered, but I never actually knew. I, like you, have also been through hell recently. I am struggling to feel safe around anyone. Just because I couldn't give you the reaction you needed in the moment doesn't mean that we can't sort through our friendship or whatever we might be together. And maybe what I said about your music career was hard to hear, but I truly do want better for you. I don't think you want this life at the bar, whether or not you're willing to admit that you don't want it, and I want to help you figure out how to move forward." Tears filled Sarah's eyes as she spoke.

Alex wasn't going to budge. He refused to feel rejection from her again. "Sarah, I fail to see how this friendship doesn't work for you. This friendship will hardly look any differently than before, except that I won't demand feelings from you that you're not ready to face." There was a finality to his statement and Sarah was disgusted. The right words found her fairly easily; the hurt pushed her back into survival mode where she could find the words and behaviors she thought she needed to survive the moment. She still desperately wanted to connect with him again but saw that there was no breaking down his barriers now. Survival mode it was. "I have never desired intimacy with the coward who cannot face himself. And I am going to stop apologizing for the truth."

She thought of all the men who had ever disappointed her, people in college whose names she had forced herself to forget but came back to her now—Tim, Jason, Brandon, James…Jesse…Dean. Everyone seemed a coward. Everyone, in this moment, Alex included, seemed afraid to honestly face the words they said and their feelings. She wanted Alex to be brave enough to pursue what he really wanted, even if what he really wanted meant the unknown. He disappointed her, and she had to let him. She knew when someone wasn't going to move. She walked out of the bar after her last words, letting the door slam behind her. Her heart was broken though she couldn't admit it to herself. Jesse had hurt her, Dean had hurt her. She couldn't stomach Alex hurting her too. She had to move on, she had to go to work, she had to support herself financially. There was no room in survival for loneliness. She swallowed as she pushed back the tears in her eyes and forced herself to walk home. For now at least, she and Alex were done with whatever relationship they had.

Chapter 29

Alex felt instantly ashamed for closing himself off to Sarah, yet he had no idea how to move forward. He decided to continue with what he had started, playing the roles he was comfortable in. His thoughts raced as he wiped glasses and scheduled musicians. In between every thought was Sarah and her thoughts about his music. "Okay. I can fit this acoustic performer on Saturday at four…" "I wish I were the performer…" "Should I order more whiskey for happy hour or…or stick to Schnapps…" "I miss Sarah, I want to be around her again…" Something deeper in Alex knew that he wanted to pursue his music career. He wanted to leave the Midwest. He wanted more than to maintain a small business. He loved his grandmother, the customers, and the musicians he partnered with. But he loved creating more, and he loved Sarah with the same part of his brain he used to create. But there was vulnerability in both creation and loving Sarah. His music might not always enchant. There were certainly nights at the bar that his songs fell flat. Not every lyric he wrote would become a story others loved. Writing made him feel alive, but the process also made him feel stupid. Too often, he felt self-conscious about his own words, which is why he would just as soon perform a cover.

Sarah saw him more deeply and truly than anyone else, but she could also hurt him. With Sarah and creation came fear of loss and rejection. He didn't have to feel that fear inside the familiar. Sandy had been with him in one way or another his whole life. He didn't yet know how to live in a world where she didn't exist anymore, at least not in a way he understood. He certainly didn't know how to exist in a world where Sarah wasn't his best friend, but he wasn't ready to accept her as just a friend anymore. And he was still angry though he wasn't entirely sure who or what he was angry at.

Sarah is gone, at least for a little while, he thought. He knew he had hurt her too with his coldness. And he knew her well enough to feel certain that she was disappointed in him. Alex turned her words over in his mind. "I have never desired intimacy with the coward who cannot face himself..." He didn't like letting her down, which is why he always made sure he fit into a box that she could rely on. But both Sarah and Alex had outgrown that box. Alex was stuck in the space between pain and fear and progress and passion. He knew his life had reached a point where he had to move forward into greater accomplishments and planes of existence or settling. But for now, he simply froze.

Chapter 30

In many stories, characters close themselves off after they have been hurt one too many times by too many people, including those closest to them. They shut down and won't enter into any intimate relationships or potentially vulnerable situations because they are too afraid of others betraying them again. Such stories miss a very important human instinct that rears its ugly head too often in reality. Such stories miss that there are very dangerous ways of opening oneself after being hurt. After the fight Sarah had with Alex, Jesse, Dean, and the memory of all who had siphoned her strength or abandoned her, Sarah didn't close herself off. Rather, she opened a part of herself that had been lying dangerous and dormant underneath the blanket of disappointment she wore throughout her adult life. Sarah liked to believe she was protected by giving herself away in pieces. Since she was lying, no one could really hurt her. She knew she was lying to herself. She told herself she was satisfied with mediocrity. Underneath, Sarah wanted more.

She wanted Alex, but she believed he wasn't ready to face the things that held him down. But here's the truth Sarah didn't see, a lie that she believed down to her bones: every time someone she cared for disappointed her, she believed it was because she wasn't good enough for the treatment she needed from him. All of Sarah's beautiful pieces never snapped properly into the world's jagged, jaded, fucked-up puzzle. And Sarah believed she was wrong because she didn't feel like she fit anywhere.

Sarah was a strange dichotomy because she was confident and sure of herself enough not to change her honesty, bravery, and passion for the beautiful and forgotten things of the world. She was always still Sarah, even in her hurting, yet she was deeply anxious and insecure. Her therapist encouraged her to live in the present, and presently, she didn't feel she could rely on Alex anymore. For now, she buried the hope of ever being truly understood, seen, and loved for all that she was. When Alex, the one safe relationship she thought she had, let her down, Sarah quickly turned to a coping mechanism she developed from a very young age, compartmentalization.

Rarely are our struggles the lies we tell ourselves. Most of the time, we know we're lying to ourselves, that we're pretending. Sarah knew she was pretending with Jesse, but she learned that he could still hurt her. What she didn't realize is that there were more dangerous kinds of lies, those we take to be truths. The lies we were told young and always. The lies that wire our brain and push our bodies…and eventually numb us into apathy toward how we lie to others. And Sarah was numb.

One of Sarah's favorite parts of her job was connecting with the shelter families. She had an intuition about people and whether they were a good fit for the animals. She had worked there long enough to discern within ten minutes whether or not someone was worth the background check for adoption.

So she would be lying if she said that she didn't immediately see that Joel was the type to cheat on his wife. She knew he was from the moment he flashed his brilliant grin at her. His smile was intentionally charming, and he was intentional about asking Sarah questions she enjoyed answering, while also making sure to gently guide his wife through the shelter by lightly placing his hand on the small of her back.

"So, Sarah…" He made sure to use her name though she had only introduced herself once as she led them through the long hallway of Labrador-retriever mixes. "What have dogs taught you about the people you see? I'm sure you've seen a few 'interesting characters' make their way through here…" He met her eyes as he spoke, but somehow, she knew that he was looking at more of her while she answered.

"Well," she said confidently, not wanting to admit to herself his attention flattered her as she tried to address him and his wife, Erika, with her answer, "it's true that animals have a sense about people, but so do people…I find that those seeking a particular type of animal are usually trying to see something of themselves in the creature, however strange that might sound. So what have you both learned about yourselves that you are hoping to find here?"

Joel was impressed with her intelligence, and he made sure to acknowledge her charm and intellect as they spoke. He was a marketing manager for a local internet company. The corporate, marketing types were outgoing and knew how to make people feel needed and important. Hence, Sarah led them to the retriever section; nobody made their owners feel needed like retrievers.

"Ah," Joel said. "S, we're in the right section looking for retrievers then? Fun-loving, engaging, always ready to have a good time, right?" He put his arm around his wife's shoulders and gave her a goofy side hug that made her smile and brush his arm off like an annoyed teenager, but she smiled, flirting with him, and responded, "And predictable." Erika was about six inches shorter than Joel with black hair and brown eyes, similar to Sarah's. She was petite and wore a purple shirt and fitted leggings. Erika was intelligent but distracted.

Sarah learned that she was an ER nurse and her work schedule shifted, but she loved the job or rather said, "I couldn't imagine doing anything else," which might have meant something different. Erika seemed like the type of person who had to tell herself, "Well, I just haven't experienced that yet" rather than "I regret not doing xyz…'" Sarah also couldn't ignore the evidence that Erika and Joel had two kids, an eight-year-old son and twelve-year-old daughter wandering with them. They were a Midwestern "hockey family," and it was clear that any time not spent at work was devoted to the sport, as such a sport demanded. Erika and Joel added their birthdays to their applications, both were in their late thirties, which meant that she would have been in her early twenties when she had their daughter. These were all details that Sarah stored in her mind as she tried to get to know them though not for reasons she was willing to admit to herself yet.

Joel was handsome and tall. Sarah was used to being taller than many of the men she had dated, which she actually liked. But she was in a place where she wanted to feel sheltered. And she didn't want to admit that she desired to lose herself in the stereotype of "tall men" who somehow symbolized more of a protective nature. And in her experience, tall men often felt less pressure to prove themselves. Maybe the confidence that paired with being tall was a part of their privilege and toxic masculinity, but again, tall men were often less likely to try to outsmart Sarah or "make up for" what the world taught them they lacked in height with arrogant behaviors. Joel had dark eyes too, and his hair had silvered in a sophisticated way a little near the ears. Tall, dark, and handsome.

"Nothing wrong with a little predictability right?" Joel continued. "This world throws out enough shocking and, at times, horrifying surprises, yeah? Remember when Haley cracked her collarbone on the goalpost in that game against the Rangers two years ago? Sometimes, you think life is hard in the routine and then one wrench is thrown in the plans, like a broken collarbone or a flat tire, and before you know what hit you, stress stops time and the pressures of the daily grind don't seem so bad." Joel had a point.

"Well in the name of predictability," Sarah said as she unlocked one of the sliding doors to a kennel, "I'd like to introduce you to Cruiser. He's a two-year-old golden retriever-yellow lab mix." She clipped a long red leash to his collar as he casually walked out to Joel and Erika. Erika bent down and scratched behind his ears as he wagged his tail excitedly and greeted her with big, friendly brown eyes. Joel's eyes were fixed on Sarah while Erika was distracted.

Sarah continued, "He loves people. We don't know much about why the family dropped him off here, only that he was still fairly young and healthy, so the reasoning could have been as simple as not being able to care for him anymore. We love when his type comes though because his previous owners dropped him off before any kind of negligence appeared to occur." Cruiser stood as she spoke and leaned into Erika, bending his very large body into a shape that looked similar to a horizontal banana. He happily groaned (sort of the dog equivalent of a cat purring) as he leaned against Erika and she pet his belly.

Sarah chuckled and said, "We call those his 'hugs.' Cruiser is a gentle giant. He sometimes doesn't realize quite how big he is, or maybe he does and he just doesn't care and loves anyway." Joel smiled bigger as Sarah went on. "He's sweet, that's for sure. And predictable"—Sarah met Joel's eyes—"even in his struggles. He doesn't like storms or anything that reminds him of thunder. He will shake as long as the sound lasts, and sometimes an hour or so after the thunder ends. But at least you'll know you're in for some anxiety from him when a storm comes."

"Seems like a good fit. What are our next steps?" Joel eyed Sarah carefully as he said each word.

"I have your application. Our team will look over everything, and if we are a good fit, we will reach out." Sarah smiled.

"Great," Joel responded simply. "Well, hon"—he rested his hand on Erika's back as he spoke—"ready to go?"

"Yeah, yeah," Erika said as she patted Cruiser's back and stepped away. "How long does the application review process take? This is our guy."

"Two to three weeks," Sarah replied, "but we always prioritize families who seem like a good fit, so the response could be sooner."

"Okay, well, as soon as you can get back to us, please do. I love this guy." Erika gave him one final ear scratch before turning, calling the kids back to her. (They were distracted by a new pack of Bernedoodle puppies.) "Let's get back to the car. We'll go out for lunch down the road on the way home."

Erika pulled her sunglasses off the top of her head and slipped them over her eyes as she and the children filed out into the parking lot. Joel was close behind them but said something to his wife about needing to stop at the bathroom on his way out. Erika waved in acknowledgment as she searched her purse for the keys to their white Suburban.

Sarah was at her computer, processing notes from Joel and Erika's visit. She felt a presence approach and looked up to see Joel standing in front of her.

"Hi, Sarah." He grinned. "Listen, I appreciate everything you're doing here, and I can tell that you care a lot about the animals and people you work with. You have a beautiful heart." Sarah sensed something almost like sincerity in his voice. "If you…or your team decide anything sooner about Cruiser's home, feel free to text my business number." He reached into his wallet and pulled out a very organized, professional-looking business card. "I am a manager at my company, so I always have my cell in case my team needs to reach out about something." He pulled his black Ray-Bans out of his front hoodie pouch, placed them carefully and cooly over his eyes while smiling a charming, clever smile, and walked confidently out of the shelter.

Sarah knew why Joel had given her his business card. She was both disgusted and flattered by the way his eyes peered into her as she had spoken to him. He was looking for a side story, someone to lose himself in. Joel wouldn't be looking to adopt a dog, with his wife and kids, if he had planned on leaving her. Sarah knew that Joel wanted a piece of her, not even necessarily an actual piece in the sexual sense of the word. He wanted her intellect and conversation too. Sarah could tell by the questions he asked and the way he intentionally showed he was paying attention to her responses that he was looking to distract himself, and Sarah was a "fun" challenge.

Sarah was also lonely. As she turned over Joel's card in her hand and leaned on the front desk, she began to replace the feelings of betrayal she felt with excitement about what it might feel like to hang out with Joel. Sarah learned in therapy that Jesse's refusal to tell the truth about what Dean did hurt even more than the actual crime. His actions showed Sarah that she wasn't worth protecting, not even inside a marriage. At the end of the day, all that mattered to Jesse and Dean was the "consequences" men had to face, whether or not they deserved them. The stones in Sarah's stomach turned again, the stone of grief poking at her harder than the others as she thought more about Jesse.

As anger began to rise, she quickly ignored them and forced her eyes to focus on the numbers on Joel's card. There was no part of her that wanted to hurt Erika or contribute to any kind of family discord. The second she thought about how Erika or the kids might feel if she chose to text Joel, she blocked the guilt out of her mind. Before she could circle back to the flattery she felt when Joel expressed his attraction toward her, Alex, the person she wanted to avoid thinking of the most, creeped into her mind. All her thoughts raced. They were all connected though Sarah was not aware yet.

All Sarah knew was that Alex helped constitute the weight of all the stones now, alongside Jesse and Dean but for different reasons. His cold behavior had hurt her more than Jesse's betrayal ever could though she didn't fully understand why. The sinking stones all flared hot with anger as she felt tears filling her eyes and refused to feel vulnerable again. Life seemed like such a joke. She felt as if no one would stand up for her or defend her. No one close to her anyway. The people who she confided in the most during the assault were strangers—Natalie, Rachel, the SANE nurse, Detective Selena, and Attorney Corey. They were there, but they were strangers.

Alex wanted to be there for her, but he was so filled with guilt, she often didn't feel that she could share her feelings with him. Sarah realized in that moment how angry and lonely she actually was that she had felt forced to shut down the only honest relationship she'd ever had. She also realized she had to just keep running, keep ignoring the stones because who would be there to help them stop smoldering? She had openly entered therapy and not just for the assault. She wanted to face the anxiety that had always weaved itself in and out of her mind too, becoming a filter for all of her existence. Her therapist helped her see how anxious she had been her whole life without her awareness. She often felt pressured to finish her homework immediately in college, terrified of disappointing her professors. She chose an active job, one that would keep her moving and stimulate her brain to make connections between the animals' needs, people's needs, and all the needs fit together. Sarah was always moving. Therapy was growing too expensive and she had to quit, but she lived in openness with her therapist and the detective long enough to learn that honesty and strength were lonely places.

Tears continued to well in Sarah's eyes as she thought of all the ways honesty had let her down and left her feeling isolated. Her mind hardened, and she created a dam that would hold them so they couldn't spill all over her face. She couldn't fall. She decided to have one last moment of honesty with herself before she opened up to a behavior she never would have imagined herself engaging in.

She thought, *I have come to the conclusion that no one mirrors my strength, and it's not arrogant to believe so. I've faced so many wounds and pressed on through them. Sometimes, I allowed them to heal properly, and sometimes I bandaged them up with distractions and kept moving. I know of no one else who is not afraid of themselves. I am not afraid. I've been ashamed, but I wasn't afraid to see the truth about myself and why I've hurt or made those I loved vulnerable. I am not afraid, but I am agonizingly lonely. The world is so full of liars. Liars who are too cowardly to face themselves and all who have lied to them. They are drunk with illusion. The pain of sobriety is deep. I wish someone, anyone, could share my strength. But the truth is no one will. Betrayal is the way of the world, so why not embrace lies and stories while ignoring those I hurt along the way?*

Sarah pulled out her phone.

She entered the ten-digit number, sure to include the area code, slowly…

"Hi, Joel. It's Sarah."

He answered almost immediately. "I was hoping you'd reach out. I wanted to thank you for your help today. You have a unique way of really seeing people and expressing yourself. That doesn't come along often. I was pleasantly surprised."

"Well, it's no problem. I love what I do, and I care a lot about the animals I support."

"Your passion is clear." He included a smile emoji. "Listen, would you be open to meeting up for lunch to share a little more with me? About the adoption process I mean…"

Sarah knew that Joel meant meeting up alone and that his wife, and especially his kids, were not going to be a part of the meeting.

"Sure," she texted back. Then she told herself they were just having lunch, maybe a drink or two. *I just need someone to talk to for a little while*, she thought. *Maybe he does too. There's nothing wrong with meeting up with him.* She also slowly had to turn Erika into an apathetic enemy in her mind, though she actually knew very little about her or about the relationship between Erika and Joel. *Erika is probably working a lot. She's probably too distracted to notice if Joel has a long lunch. She has patients to keep her busy and work friends. Maybe Joel has felt like she hasn't noticed him for a while…*

"Awesome. I know a beautiful place downtown with a patio, lots of flowers lining one of the walls. Do you like flowers?"

Most people like flowers. The question was basic. But Sarah loved flowers more than most. Summers were always her favorite time in the Midwest, and she thought of the beautiful plants that grew near the beaches in California. Being surrounded by plant life was one reason she fell for Jesse, all their nature walks. So Joel choosing a place to eat surrounded by flowers was impressive to Sarah in a way it may not have been to others.

"I love them, actually."

"Perfect. How about tomorrow?"

"Done. I will meet you there."

Joel sent the smiling, blushing emoji in response.

Conversation with Joel was easy. He was witty and showed what appeared to be genuine interest in what Sarah had to say. He asked her questions she enjoyed answering and gave her his full attention, eyes locked on her in an endearing way. "So tell me about the dogs people haven't adopted. I can see why Cruiser is easy to love, but tell me about a dog that people haven't found easy to love?"

Sarah didn't even have to think of an answer. She had thought about the dog she was about to share with him a lot on her own already. Sarah's thoughts were a primary reason she was well-liked by Joel, Jesse, and others quickly...She was easy to talk to because she thought a lot. No matter what they said, she had something interesting to respond with. And she knew how to listen.

"Nox, the Doberman," she replied. "Nox is beautiful but angry. He will meet your eyes with his own but plant his feet and stand across the room. He will also likely run from you if you leave a door open too long. Openings are painful. Trust is painful. Most people don't have the resilience to see that his anger is trust and running is the result of letting it show. If you shelter him long enough to feel safe in all he feels, he will show you the strength I've come to know in him. He may even share it."

Of course, Joel loved what Sarah had to say about helping male symbols feel safe, and he knew she meant what she said about Nox. Sarah realized after she shared about Nox that she didn't have to close herself off completely to her honesty or what she loved in this distraction. She could draw a little bit from her heart, keep part of her true self alive and open.

Maybe this, whatever it was, with Joel could work, she thought.

"Damn," Joel responded. "He sounds like a hell of a guy. Do you think he would be better off just staying at the shelter with you? Sounds like he knows you pretty well, or at least, it's clear that you notice him and must have helped him feel safe."

Sarah sighed. "A shelter is temporary. A place to hide from something more cruel. But Nox can't thrive at the shelter. None of the animals can. They may find peace and comfort in staff like me or the fullness generic food provides after starvation. But no, he would not be better off living there. They've been abandoned, beaten, and some have flat out run away. A shelter is temporary comfort. What they need is a safe home to belong."

"Hm..." Joel looked at Sarah thoughtfully; he knew she would be interesting to talk to, but there was a light in her that he didn't expect. He knew that he wanted the light, at least some part of her brightness, and he would find the right words to make sure she felt like she was shining.

"You really care about each of them, don't you?"

"Yes."

"I could tell. I was impressed when you matched us with Cruiser. You notice people. You notice the animals. Everything. All their needs, quirks, and potential. The potential is probably the most impressive thing. You see what could be."

"Yes, I see potential, but I feel disappointed a lot too. You know, if a family flakes out on actually following through with an adoption. Or the tattered state in which some of our animals are dropped off."

"There's nothing wrong with being disappointed," Joel responded then paused to sip his beer. "Disappointment and frustration just mean that you want something better. Better for the people and better for the animals. We could use more people like you in the world."

Sarah blushed. Joel's appreciation for her passion took her slightly by surprise. "Well, thank you for understanding." She sipped her wine. "But what about you? I know...from your card...that you work for a local internet company. But how did you enter the marketing world?"

Joel leaned forward. He wore a white button-down and his bicep flexed as he folded his arms on the table. "People needed someone fun at my company." Sarah raised her eyebrows. "I know how that sounds," he went on. "But really. The corporate world can get ugly on the inside of the company and the outside customer base. I manage a team of door-to-door sales reps, and they deal with a lot of harsh statements and apathy from all angles. Sometimes, it's an angry prospective customer threatening to set their dogs on them. Or a disconnected member of upper management asking more of them and referencing 'core values' and the 'work family' and how 'we're all equal links in the chain.' Well, last I checked, the CEO wasn't being told to 'get a real job' and 'get the fuck off my property.' There's a wide disconnect between the corporate chain and the links that are out there collecting the clients. I'm sure you've heard the corporate story before and the difference between the 'working man,' so to speak, and the "higher-ups" in their office chairs. But the higher-ups know how to manipulate their people enough to keep making money for them. Some sort of 'Free 20 Friday' where they rain money from the ceiling or make a game out of cash prizes usually helps people forget they're making close to minimum wage."

Sarah nodded.

"Anyway," Joel went on, "sure, I am just middle management in a corporate machine with a lot of insincerity and corruption, but I like bringing fun into my team's world. I joke a lot with them, sometimes we'll play Spades, the card game, on their breaks. And I listen. Most of them just want to feel heard, like anyone. I get a lot of satisfaction out of helping the sales reps feel seen."

"Wow," Sarah said. A part of her actually was impressed with Joel. "There's a lot of strange systems in this world that we all have to work inside of. If people were responsible enough to care for the dogs and cats that they've domesticated, there wouldn't be a need for shelters. But the truth is that many people avoid their responsibilities, or don't want to clean up their own messes, so others have to try for them. If your company actually took care of their employees and paid them a fair salary, maybe you wouldn't have to take on extra tasks to boost morale. But I love what I do, and it sounds like you do too. We've both found meaning in cleaning up messes, so maybe humanity comes full circle."

Joel smiled at Sarah, infatuated with her. "Maybe it's fun seeing where some decisions can take you."

Sarah smiled back.

Chapter 31

Alex was lost in the routine. Nothing was going to stop him from the distractions. He didn't want to write anymore. He would play on live nights, but only covers. No more originals. Alex easily explained the absence of his own music with grieving over Sandy. Maybe playing the dead grandmother/guardian card was gross, but who hasn't used grief for their own advantage at some point?

Sarah weaved in and out of all his thoughts. No matter how much he tried to distract himself, he couldn't help but think of her. Stacking chairs, Sarah's hair. Pouring gin. Sarah's favorite hard liquor. Laughing with Gabe. Not as fun as laughing with Sarah. Sarah's smile. Sarah's eyes. Sarah's everything. She frustrated him. He had his own disappointments with her—Jesse, her own distractions of losing herself in the stories of others, and the thought he really didn't want to face, but the one that creeped in the most, that she made him feel uncertain of how much he meant to her. Or maybe if he meant to her what she meant to him. Alex was miserable without her. His life was by no means empty. He had a lot going for him, but his purpose was lost. She had always awakened something deeper in him, a part of himself he hadn't yet grasped on his own.

There were too many opportunities for Alex to be alone with his thoughts. The bar always emptied out at night. Gabe and the other staff returned home. Conversations with Pete ended or turned. Pete continued to bring him joy. He always had a fun story about a new fast-food place he tried on his route or new facts about beautiful places he'd seen. "The Grand Canyon has forests, Alex, and elk wandering around. Did you know that? Ya step outside and there'll be four of 'em just wandering. Didn't expect to see the forest in the desert. Life can be surprising I suppose."

Alex couldn't help but see metaphors in most comments people made, whether they meant to create them or not. Alex was always thinking in stories, something was always a symbol of something else. His mind made him creative, but the same creative thoughts that inspired the metaphors quickly turned to the anxiety he was trying to avoid. Vulnerability meant rejection. Alex hated the idea of being vulnerable to anyone. He only opened himself on particular terms when he was almost certain he would be accepted. Sarah's almost rejection, he'd realized he'd never actually received a clear answer from her about whether she loved him or not, was as close as he had come since he was a child to feeling rejected about a part of himself he actually cared about.

Alex was more similar to Sarah than he was aware. Though the connection and self-awareness started to creep in slowly, as much as he tried to push the thoughts out with distractions. Alex learned at a young age that the things he cared about the most—his creativity, writing, and music—could be very easily dismissed or not taken seriously. He had always written songs from a young age; but Sandy, as much as she loved and encouraged him to write, was too busy running the business to read his words, to live inside his creativity with him. The few times that his dad had stopped at home, Alex had tried to show him a few of his poems. His father dismissed the paper with an, "Eh, you're not gonna make any money doin' that," or "There's a thousand other 'starving artists' out there, what's so special about you? I see the 'dreamers' all the time in Vegas." Maybe Alex's father was trying to help Alex deviate from his own destructive path, or maybe he was a closed-minded asshole, Alex wasn't sure yet. Sandy was setting the example of a provider, maybe she never even had time for dreams of her own or thought she didn't. No matter their motivations, both Sandy and Alex's father taught him there was no place for creativity. And empty spaces are excruciating. As a matter of fact, the empty spaces that felt they had no place were just as excruciating for Alex as they were for Sarah.

Both Alex and Sarah woke up at night with the same feeling, though the feeling was one they had never acknowledged to each other or anyone. To acknowledge the feeling and hear the words out loud would mean it was real, and they both wanted to continue to pretend that it wasn't. Both would awaken in early hours of the morning, still wedged slightly inside their dreams, vulnerable. They woke up alone and devastated over what their lives had become. Alex and Sarah both felt that there was no place for their ambition. No one who could understand their dreams, the beauty of life full of learning, creativity, and truth. They felt surrounded by cowards like Jesse and shallow people at the bar, looking to run from reality. Those who glimpsed the precious nature of their dreams and sought to pervert them for their own selfish use.

When Sarah carved out Jesse's intentions, and now Joel's, she was empty and in excruciating pain. Alex felt the same when he thought of his words and music landing on the ears of anyone who hadn't already respected him because of his business. What if he played his music for actual artists in LA's music scene? Of course they wouldn't take him seriously. But was he really absorbing any sort of meaning from the crowds at his bar? Only for a few seconds of the morning when the sun peeked through the curtains, teasing both Alex and Sarah with the hope of light, did they feel the pain of emptiness within the tiny sliver that poked through the curtains. The thought of each other and the hope of finding a kindred spirit stabbed into the emptiness. Both had been too afraid to fully share themselves with each other. They didn't even fully know themselves. Patterns had trapped them.

Both Alex and Sarah had sought a love that neither had seen or felt as much as they found some comfort in each other up to this point. Who can set an example of being fully vulnerable, sharing thoughts, stories, and music that doesn't come from a corrupted world? True companionship. Sarah and Alex believed they longed for a love they had never seen or felt. They ached for something that they believed had never existed. And where was their power to find such a love when life had so many other demands? And if they could find true companionship in each other, who could they look toward to acknowledge they were on the right path, a trustworthy path? God? Religion? The universe? Simple biological chemistry drawing them in? There. Was. No. Answer. Only a longing for something they were not sure they would ever find.

But Alex and Sarah didn't give up on the idea of finding themselves and companionship. Sarah and Alex both lied to themselves. They found jobs that were sheltered versions of what they really wanted, jobs where they could feel passion and create but never had to be truly vulnerable to anyone. Clearly defined roles. What Alex and Sarah didn't realize is that both of them were living truthfully with each other in their conversations and whenever they chose to allow their hearts to speak. Alex's choice to write songs and poetry kept his creativity alive. Sarah's openness to the animals, the way she saw them and the families, kept her passion alive. They didn't have to exist perfectly to release their light in the world and find something of real love. They both were still too afraid to live fully authentically for the very real ways that too many others proved that love could be taken advantage of or ripped away. But the lesson that both Alex and Sarah needed to learn was that cruelty doesn't take root so deeply and widespread that love couldn't grow beside it.

Alex remained quiet and worked hard. He responded to others when he needed to, for business, and kept everything running smoothly. He even laughed and joked with the patrons when he could. He refused to let much of his creativity to the surface and didn't want to face the shame he felt. He also continued to read. He followed many musical artists on social media. Christina Perri had always been one of his favorites. He loved how her voice rang when she sang. She could punch words out in songs, capture grief, and hold villains accountable in a smooth manner unique to her. "Who do you think you are? Running around leaving scars…Collecting your jar of hearts…" Brilliant. He had been scrolling on social media late one evening, trying to distract himself somehow outside of work and ignore the creeping thoughts of Sarah and that "what would have happened ifs" when it came to music school when something Perri had posted caught his eye.

He knew that Perri was no stranger to anxiety and grief. She had lost a baby and suffered a miscarriage, a unique grief that no parent should ever know. Perri had grasped wisdom in the chaos and pain of one of the ugliest cruelties this world has to offer, the death of a child. At first, Alex wasn't sure why, but he stopped scrolling when a few of her words caught his attention, starting with "All the feelings…" He slowly read her summary of losing her children but then started to notice how she gave anxiety a name and learned to embrace "her."

> Every day was filled with an anxiety that hummed;
> sometimes very loud and sometimes very quiet.
> It was always, always there;
> always reminding me what could go wrong.
> I listened to her and accepted her.
> She had a job to do in case I forgot the grief.
>
> In every breath, standing hand and hand with me was fear.
> I learned to walk with her too.
> I learned to accept she wasn't going anywhere.
> she was there to protect me;
> in case I forgot about the pain,
> but she didn't win.
>
> The fear actually could never win because she wasn't stronger than the joy.
> Behind every corner, there was joy.
> After every doctor's appointment there was joy and relief.
> Inside every conversation with Carmella (her surviving daughter) there was joy and fulfillment.
>
> With each kick and wiggle, there was joy and new belief.
> Inside our marriage we found joy and understanding.
> Inside every person's eyes who knows and loves us, there was the biggest joy.
> We walked through it all.
> We did it together…

So no matter what happens in the next couple days,
I promise I will look at this pregnancy with an endless gratitude.
I have learned a new surrender, so profound, I'll never forget it.

This darling baby girl inside me has already changed our lives for the better.
She represents all the possibilities we can only achieve
if we're brave, intentional, open, trusting, and only if we try again.

Try again at things that broke us.
Try again at things we still want.
Try again at people we still want to be and try again at dreams we still believe in…

"'Surrender,'" Alex thought. "'I learned to walk with her.'" Perri spoke of anxiety as if it were an enemy and a friend, all at once. She did not arrive at a perfect realization. She was afraid and brave at the same time. She had accepted all parts of herself. She didn't want to run. She stood and sank into all she felt.

Words had a way of sinking into Alex. One word could change his mind. He sat with Perri's words for a long time. "Try again at things we still want. Try again at people we still want to be. Try again at dreams we still believe in…" Alex had believed for a long time that time wasn't on his side, the likelihood of success with creative pursuits wasn't on his side, and there were too many demands in his life for him to pursue creativity in a vulnerable way. He decided his own future. He projected a vision of himself into the future, an old man working the bar while Sarah had eventually married some rich, Australian billionaire who helped her finally get her own veterinary business started. In his mind, a future that didn't exist became the truth. But he took Perri seriously. Now, each time he had a thought about Sarah, about his own "failures," he didn't run from them. He started to allow himself to feel each fear. Maybe if he kept feeling, he could start to learn how to exist vulnerably, maybe Sarah would forgive him, maybe he could be honest with her, maybe there was a future he hadn't considered…step one.

Chapter 32

Cheating is easier than most people think. All one has to do is tell a story to themselves about the person they are hurting (their significant other or the lover's significant other). If people don't see the person they are hurting, if they don't have to face them, they can easily justify their actions. Sarah never saw Erika after the day she met her at the shelter. Joel blended partial truths about his whereabouts with actual lies. "A meeting with a client ran late." The meeting indeed ran late, but he added an hour or two of "car time" with Sarah. Sometimes, he was "taking Cruiser on a walk." He was, but he wasn't on the walk alone. Sarah usually met up with him. And Joel was particular about choosing a time when he knew Erika would be tired from a late ER shift and might be less likely to think about how long he was actually out.

Sarah was used to telling herself stories. Joel himself was a story. Her mind slipped easily into compartmentalizing her time with Joel. She wasn't in the business of imagining other women as villains. She never thought that Erika "deserved" to have her husband cheat or that "something was wrong" with Erika. Sarah never told herself there was something "Erika wasn't doing" for Joel. The truth was that Sarah did her best to pretend Erika didn't exist, or she told herself that Erika wouldn't care about what Joel was doing. "Their marriage problems were bigger than her." Sarah was more focused on what her affair with Joel did for herself than what the affair did to Erika.

The affair distracted Sarah from the truth that she was agonizingly lonely. Deep down, she knew it. She was also in pain. But it was much easier to make witty comments to Joel and impress him with her intelligence than to face how much she missed Alex or the fear she had of truly being vulnerable to anyone. Her mind had been trained to give away pieces so that no one could break all of her. She had to slip into survival mode to navigate her way through the "justice" system without allowing the pain of Jesse and Dean's actions to swallow her whole. Therefore, her mind slipped easily in and out of the person she needed to be to cheat with Joel.

What Sarah didn't yet understand is that living inside stories always comes at a cost. Sarah didn't see it, but she was slowly chipping away at all the bright pieces of herself and willingly handing them to Joel, as she had done with Jesse, who both attempted to use her pieces to mold something resembling beauty in themselves. Sarah didn't see that she was breaking because she knew she was lying. Sarah was aware that Jesse was not the love of her life, neither was Joel. She knew who both of them were and what they were — liars. But she thought her own lies empowered and protected her from the truth she didn't want to see, that no one could ever understand her. At least, it was a fact she buried inside herself and believed to be true. So in her lies, she thought she found power. But the piece she didn't understand is that her lies were so bold and beautiful that they were almost an art in themselves. They were a sponge Jesse and Joel used to mask the smell of their own insignificance. Joel, like Jesse before him, had recognized the gift that existed in light in her eyes, but he wanted it for his own selfish purposes. And even though Sarah was lonely with Joel, she made an art of telling herself she wasn't.

One of the easiest and funnest ways to avoid feeling lonely with Joel was to spend time on his boat. His family owned lake property an hour north of the city area, and he and Sarah occasionally spent weekends there. He would drive his speedboat around the lake, beer in hand all afternoon. Sarah felt the familiar comforting warmth of sun on her skin and the breeze on her face. The breeze felt especially refreshing when Joel would intentionally speed the motor up to hit the wakes of other passing boats. He was careful with his boat, as the machine was crucial to his ego, but he couldn't help but occasionally play with the thrill that came from jumping waves.

Joel kept his boat at the lake property during the summer, so Erika wouldn't have noticed it missing from their garage. He soaked up his afternoons with Sarah and loved the distraction. Sarah would ask him about the topics he loved discussing most. She had discerned that Joel was bored with his job, but he loved feeling needed. He loved playing the role of the boss everybody liked and wanted to rake in high sales numbers for. Sarah could see how Joel truly did make work fun in the corporate world. He was fun. She learned a few things from him too.

"So how do you make door-to-door sales fun?" Sarah asked one particularly sunny afternoon as she leaned back on the boat's back white pleather seats.

Joel smirked. His smile stretched wide as he spoke, "You might already know the answer to that." He sipped his beer as he waited for her to respond.

"I 'might' know a lot of things, but I am still curious."

"Fair enough," Joel went on as he continued smirking at Sarah. "People like talking about their lives outside of work. My reps have hobbies and friends. I learn what their hobbies and friends are then make similar jokes. I'm sure you do something similar with the families you connect with."

"I suppose you're right. People like to be seen for more than the tasks given to them or boxes they check on paper…" Joel knew Sarah meant more with the last statement, but he didn't shy away from the tiny pieces of truths she let slip to him. He saw her honesty as refreshing and challenging, a strange but very real irony that existed within their twisted affair.

"Maybe that's why I will probably never be upper management. I can't see people as numbers. I can't see them as worth only what they produce." Sarah eyed him. "I know, I know. That's literally what corporate America is, profit and production, it's the business I'm in. But I don't know, I guess my reasons go back to our first conversation, 'Things coming full circle.' I know that what I do has very little meaning in the wide world and that I work for corporate greed, but maybe there's some sort of ethical victory in showing the frontline employees that they have more value than only that which they produce."

For a split second, Sarah saw the sun reflect off the water as Joel said, "That which they produce." She thought of Alex. He had the ability to produce beauty every day and had. Music and words that made the world better in mystical ways. Alex's music brought Sandy's mind back to life even if just for a few moments. There was real power in that. The thought of Alex and all that he could create made Sarah wince.

"You okay?" Joel asked. "Your eyes looked strange for a second."

"Of course." Sarah shook her head and smiled. "How could I not be all right? Look where we are."

"I thought maybe we could do a fire tonight. Maybe cook some dinner that way?" Joel was excellent at cooking over campfires. Sarah loved the nights she spent with him, eating smoky potatoes and watching the stars. She could see so many more at the lake, and they shined all the brighter farther north, away from the city lights. She started to notice that she enjoyed the beauty around her—the sun, lake, sky, and creativity of the food—more than she enjoyed Joel himself. He was interesting for a while. But she spoke nothing of the stories she loved to read or that she thought she might try writing. These were creativities that only awoke in her when she spoke to Alex. She thought of his eyes and her own mind briefly as she stared at the stars and winced again. Joel didn't see her wince in the darkness, but the ache Sarah started to feel was getting harder to ignore, regardless of the levels of the light.

Chapter 33

Perri's words sat with Alex as he sat at his own bar, twirling the pencil he kept behind his ear casually and perfectly around the space between his thumb and index finger. He was finally slowing down for a minute. Perri's vulnerability encouraged him to be vulnerable. Alex had known for a while that his best work was created when he was in the most pain or had something vulnerable to say or feel. So many of his beautiful poems and songs were born when he found a moment in the thick of whatever he was thinking or doing to bring them to life. He felt a lot of anxiety around Sarah and at the thought of her. She had certainly hurt him. However, the anxiety was about more than pain. He was anxious because Sarah had always encouraged him to exist openly, to allow the creative parts of him that he had been taught had "no practical purpose" in this world.

Alex could never fully abandon his creativity, which was why he chose to play at the bar. He began to realize that he had never truly run from his music or abandoned that path entirely. He had allowed his creativity to exist at the same time that he ran Sandy's business. For the first time, he realized there was some power in that allowance. Maybe creativity didn't have to exist perfectly. Maybe he didn't have to be the perfect artist, always existing in some profound mindset. He had been an artist and a business owner. He had written music while caring for Sandy. He had loved Sarah despite not expressing that love as he could have. Everything was gray.

He thought back to his first conversation with Sarah about *Avatar: The Last Airbender*. Her favorite character was Zuko. An imperfect ruler who had spent much of his life chasing a toxic "honor" that didn't belong to him. Yet a more humble, vulnerable power had slowly grown within him while he chased someone else's dream. Zuko allowed that power to grow by willingly surrounding himself with humble, wise leaders such as Iroh who put others first.

Alex realized he could keep taking steps toward himself, that he could keep growing, even if he did so imperfectly. Maybe he could work through the anxiety he felt when he was around Sarah and begin to feel safe instead. He could "try again at something that broke him," "try again at something he still wanted," just as Christina Perri wrote. He could try again at his music. He could try again at pursuing school. He could try again to tell Sarah he loved her and share his words in a way that better expressed how he felt (i.e., sober and articulate).

So step one, he thought, *is acknowledgment of all I feel. Done. What is step two? I can't reach out to Sarah yet*, he said to himself. *First, I need to address all she asked of me, and all that I should have been asking myself. Do I want to go to music school? Do I want to create?*

"Do I have it in me to sell Sandy's business?" he said the last question out loud.

"You are asking the wrong question," Gabe said.

Alex was startled. "Shit! Dude! I had no idea you were there."

"I'm always here, almost as much as you." Gabe smiled.

Alex dropped his shoulders and relaxed. "I suppose that's true. You have been here for years and watched me ask and answer a lot of questions. So which one should I be asking?"

"Is there another way you could carry Sandy's legacy on?"

Alex frowned, puzzled.

"Why does Sandy's legacy have to be the business?" Gabe asked. "And who says the business wouldn't continue to thrive in someone else's hands?"

Alex pursed his lips. "Ah, so you're speaking as someone who has a vested business interest?"

"So what if I am?" Gabe smirked. "Maybe my interests could help you work out yours too. Things have a way of coming together."

Alex had known for a while that Gabe had been interested in becoming a part-owner with him. But he never pushed Alex too hard or stepped outside any boundaries that set Alex as the leader and primary decision-maker when it came to The Crooked Picture. Not until now, anyway, but now seemed to be the right time.

"You have my attention, Gabe. Where are you going with this?"

"Actually, let me back up…I have known you ever since you took this business over. You moved so quickly and never stopped. From barback to owner, your business sense was fluid."

"Well yeah, I grew up around this business. I watched my grandmother run everything since I was young. Keeping a place clean and friendly seemed simple."

"When you took over this business, is that what you wanted? To own and run it?"

Alex frowned. "I never thought about what I wanted. Taking over the business seemed like the right thing to do. And I guess I knew I didn't want my grandmother to feel like I had abandoned her and the place she built from the ground up. She worked so hard to create Picture. This business meant everything to her."

"To her," Gabe responded.

"And? What?" Alex questioned, beginning to feel flustered.

"Sandy found fulfillment in this business. The business was her creation, her legacy. What if it's not your responsibility to carry on her legacy?"

"Of course carrying on her legacy is my responsibility," Alex said, frustration clear in his voice.

"Why?" Gabe raised his voice, challenging Alex.

"Because I owe her!" Alex's voice was raised too, as tears filled his eyes.

Gabe let the silence ring after Alex's words for a few moments then responded more softly, "Why do you think you owe her?"

"Because she spent her whole life being financially responsible for me, taking care of me. If I don't help with the business, she might think I am ungrateful."

"Did she ever tell you that she thought you were ungrateful?"

Alex thought then answered honestly. "No."

"Then why do you feel responsible for her feelings and legacy as if they were your own? Why do you work so hard to say and do the right thing for every person who walks in here, god forbid they feel uncomfortable."

"Because if I don't take responsibility for their feelings and well-being, then no one will."

"Why do you think that?"

"I guess, if I am being honest, I felt like my dad abandoned Sandy. She never told me I was a burden, but I felt like one. I never felt like I was good enough for him or Sandy. If I was enough, why would he have left? Why did my mother and her family never want anything to do with me? Why was gambling more important? I know my grandmother loved me, but her love doesn't take away the sting of my own mother and father choosing a life without me. I wasn't enough for them to stay." Tears spilled out of Alex's eyes.

"And if you don't stop moving, you won't have to feel that."

"Yes. Owning this bar is easy. There is no part of me that can be rejected by anyone, at least not anyone I care about. How could my dad be disappointed if I run the bar his mom started? How could Sandy ever feel that I wasn't enough if I just kept taking care of her and what she made? Maybe if I made sure that what mattered to her was taken care of, she wouldn't ever have a reason not to believe in me."

"And now that she's gone?"

"Now, I feel frustrated about how cruel life can be. The last few weeks, I've had nothing but time to think, and I have come to understand that I am anxious. I am afraid of risking love because, god forbid, love gets ripped out from underneath me. I am so sad, Gabe, because at one point, my heart was fully open to love and belonging. I was real and vulnerable to love, and it was snatched away. Life taught me that I should be afraid. My father left, my mother left, and my grandmother became a stranger and died. People who should have protected me either chose not to or they were no longer physically able to. It made more sense for me to be dutiful, to take on responsibility. The business, caring for my grandmother, providing for myself. My mother and father sure as hell weren't going to do any of that. I adopted this "if I don't, then no one will" mindset. The only place I feel like my actual self, not myself just surviving, is when I am playing the songs I write or writing in general and, sometimes, when I speak to Sarah. But those are spaces I sometimes fit into life's demands. I love Sarah and I want to be vulnerable with her, but life has given me too many reasons to be protective. Life has given her the same logic. Even if I were to allow myself to be fully vulnerable with her, how do I know if she would be willing and able to do the same after all life has thrown at her?"

He paused and tried to take a deep breath before continuing, "The worst part is, I am aware that my mind is trying to help me survive, that I won't allow myself to be truly vulnerable with Sarah because I am afraid of losing her. I am not only afraid of the loss, but that she will take too many pieces of me with her. I hate that at one point, my heart was open and someone took advantage of that love and burned me. Now that I may have a chance at true love and belonging again, my mind won't allow me to see the difference between safety and danger. I exist in the space between awareness of my fears yet feeling powerless to harness them."

"It's exhausting," Gabe responded. "I can see how exhausted you have been. Most people don't understand that survival is a lifestyle. You learn how to survive once, your mind teaches you how to survive always. There is no room for vulnerability because it's dangerous. To lie and take control is so much safer. Control is predictable. You never have to be a victim. Never to another and certainly not to your own feelings."

"My own feelings are the most exhausting part of all of this. I don't know where to put everything—guilt, grief, and fear—and not just about one topic, about several."

"Have you tried writing again?"

"Recently, I've thought about trying."

"Do you think writing would help?"

"It has in the past. Sandy and Sarah always encouraged me to. But I don't have a name for this. I'm not sure what to call any of it."

"Maybe there doesn't have to be a name for all you feel. Maybe you just need to give voice to the truth that all of these feelings can exist at once, that life really isn't black and white…That you can find your path in the gray, or maybe the gray is the only path as long as the right people are with you."

"All this advice for a business, Gabe?"

"Alex, it's not a secret that I've wanted to co-own this place with you, and of course, I could use the money. But for me, learning the business from you means more. I feel energized when I am here, even when I 'fail.' If I fuck up inventory or overshoot the amount of Schnapps we'll need for holiday weeks, I feel better when I get the order right the next time. I love the story of this place. I love that Sandy started it. I love the events we host here and the people we draw in. My passion is here. I've seen the circles that have formed under your eyes, even before Sarah was raped here." Alex winced at Gabe reminding him of the event. "Sorry…What I mean is you are good at running this place, but the business is taking too much. The only time I see you truly passionate and happy is when you are performing and when Sarah is here. Why don't you consider selling to me? You know I will give you a fair cut of what it's worth, and you can use the cushion to pursue what you actually want or spend time trying to figure it out."

Alex had always trusted Gabe. He was his friend and business partner. He grew up in Sandy's neighborhood and was passionate about the town. He belonged there. He was starting his family there. But Alex didn't realize until that conversation just how much of him Gabe actually saw. With the exception of his performances, he was often in business mode while working. It never occurred to him that Gabe paid attention to how Alex might be feeling or the kind of energy he used while running everything. In that moment, he appreciated Gabe more than he knew how to express. Maybe what Gabe was teaching him was that he didn't have to express guilt-inspired gratitude all the time. Maybe existing with Gabe as he was, was enough. Gabe had accepted and loved him as a friend in his imperfection without Alex even realizing he had the acceptance. Since he was always in business mode at the bar, he never stopped to think that Gabe had seen and accepted him in the anxiety he felt. He paused a moment, before continuing…

"I can't remember the last time I thought about what I actually want. There have been traces of that part of me, when I think of my love for Sarah or when I create. But most days, I just want to push fast forward, which makes each day feel agonizingly longer. I want to fast forward to a time where I can sleep through the night. I am up every hour. Most of the time, I wake up remembering a nightmare from the ten minutes of that sleep that finally found me. I am plagued with grief for my grandmother. The empty feeling of irreplaceable loss is pitched like a tent in my stomach with no clear indication of how long it will camp inside me. I hate camping by the way."

Gabe smirked as Alex smiled for a brief moment and went on, "The sadness and guilt of failing to save Sarah sits in bags under my eyes. The exhaustion of the friend I should have been to her haunts me. If I was there, actually present in the bar at her reception, I would have seen her with Dean. I know I would have stopped it. Not 'could have.' I know myself and I know I would have. I had already sensed that there was something dangerous about him. There was a dormant but certain aggression in his eyes. He knew what he was going to do the moment he realized he wanted Sarah. I know he purposely chose her wedding. Succeeding at raping her fed his narcissism all the more. From what Sarah said about him claiming he could 'be her escape,' he probably saw himself as a gift. That's fucking twisted, I know, but that's how it always is with rapists and narcissists, the illogical becomes logical. Somewhere in his mind, he convinced himself that he needed her to feed his ego and the opportunity was something she wanted."

He breathed deeply again and continued while Gabe quietly listened. Like Alex, he was used to listening to all the pieces of every story. The ability was natural and necessary in their line of work. "I think the more she said Jesse's name while he raped her, the more he realized she wanted someone else. That's why he let her go. He couldn't stomach the thought of Sarah wanting someone besides him in that moment. I don't know, it's my understanding of people like that I guess. You see and hear a lot of the sick secrets men share when you're the one supplying them alcohol. When the alcohol is flowing and inhibitions are to the wind, a lot of depraved truths come out. I've seen the same look Dean had in his eyes in more of our patrons than I'd like to admit."

Alex paused as Gabe replied, "You're right. Too many."

"Anyway, I've become too anxious to see Sarah since we argued after our vacation, you remember that?" Gabe nodded. "The grief I feel for my grandmother, the guilt about Sarah, and the anger I showed her in that guilt have all piled up too high. I've hit a point where I've spent too much time and energy fighting my own feelings. I know what happened to Sarah isn't my fault, but I can't help but FEEL that it is. I harbor this strange, instinctive anxiety that sets me on edge around her. I feel like she should hate me for her own feelings of grief and sadness, and I can't stomach her anger. I still love her deeply, and I can't bear the devotion I have to her along with the crippling sense that she would be better off without me. Every word of grief she has shared, I blame myself for because I wasn't there to stop the horror that crushed her. She doesn't blame me at all for her feelings, yet I can't shake what feels like a truth that I am responsible. I fight my own mind and instincts all day and night, while grieving, and I don't know what to do with myself. I can't look in her eyes without feeling so angry that these are our circumstances. It's not her. It's all the feelings, and I just need some space from them."

Gabe took a deep breath and responded to Alex with a look of genuine concern, "It can be confusing to figure out if the right relationships are supposed to be hard." He paused, choosing his words carefully. "Often, people fall in love without knowing all the risks they are taking. They just know how they feel when they meet the right person. Sometimes feelings can be trusted and sometimes they can't. Think about the anxiety you feel now, probably just your body making you fearful of nonexistent threats. Yet the feeling deep in your chest that simply tells you Sarah is different, that she is meant to be your companion should be trusted. Both of you are honest with only each other. You haven't just been honest about how you feel, you've been honest about who you are. Those actions are hard. Personal growth often accompanies honesty and vulnerability, which can also be difficult. When you add traumatizing events and grief, strains you didn't know would be on your relationship, the sense of rightness can be especially confusing."

"So then, how do you know when things become too hard? How do you know if someone is actually right for you or not?" Alex asked, a desperate sadness in his eyes. "My relationship with Sarah has become difficult. I can no longer guess how she feels about a person or topic, and she has begun to hide some of her feelings from me, and I hate that I assume the worst when she does."

Gabe sighed. "You and Sarah have both been through some incredibly painful experiences lately. Some that never should've happened. Death and assault are some of life's most raw and horrifying portals into reality. Rape should never happen. Death is so mysterious and misunderstood that it feels like it shouldn't happen, or maybe simply that shouldn't exist. Both are different and both can lead to growth. The question you have to ask yourself is whether you want to grow in the difficulty and differences together? Is the growth driving you apart or bringing you closer together? Sometimes anger and pain can be signs of becoming closer. Not if you are staying in those feelings to hurt the person, but whether you are finally trusting someone enough to release them. Do you feel like you can with Sarah?"

"Lately, I've had to ask myself if Sarah is truly the right person for me. This chance to pursue her is probably my last, and in the anger and sadness I've felt, I've been so uncertain. Somehow, more uncertain than when I loved her silently from far away. And in many ways coming to terms with my feelings for her and that I could somehow be with her has been harder than obstacles like Jesse and whatever else she might be doing now that we've been divided."

"Since I've known you, Alex, you've always struggled with understanding that something right doesn't have to be something perfect. You have never allowed yourself to make mistakes. You have always fulfilled obligations such as taking over your grandmother's bar when she got sick, putting aside your creativity when your songs improved. Even stepping out of Sarah's reception after you felt too emotional during the 'I'll Be' song you sang to her. That might not have been your original, but the way you delivered the melody was more beautiful and raw than anything I've ever heard you play here. And it's not your fault that you weren't there for Sarah. You were simply taking a moment to acknowledge your emotions though I know the guilt eats away at you.

Gabe continued, sliding his thin-framed glasses further up the bridge of his nose as he spoke, "The realest and most important things in this world are vulnerable and imperfect. They are the most important because they are real. What 'perfect' thing in this world actually exists? Nothing. The very idea of perfection was created by insecure people who are power-hungry. People who will create any ideal standard either to feel above others or profit from them. Nothing real is perfect. Nothing right is perfect. You need to accept yourself as you are and understand that the feelings and behaviors that you perceive as weakness and shame in yourself are the very tools of growth that you can use to change this world. Start with Sarah, just be fully honest with her even if she's hurt you. I've seen that she loves you just as much and feels just as afraid. She probably has more reason not to trust than most people, but that doesn't mean that you can't show each other how to feel safe. So long story short"—he smirked—sell the bar to me and use the money to get out of here and finally write your music. Or at least take a few days to think about it and write again. You know creating will help you sort things out."

Alex smiled and poured a glass of sauvignon blanc for the two of them. Then, he lifted his glass to Gabe and said, "Well, cheers to love and grief existing all at once." As the both of them lowered their glasses and sipped, Alex knew Gabe had been right about pretty much everything he said. It was time to be bold enough to let go of the guilt he felt about keeping his grandmother's place. He had to create his own space. Sandy never wanted him to live out of fear and obligation to her. She was the very person who encouraged him to find his voice.

A song started floating around in his mind. Words that embodied the painful beliefs he had carried so long started to string together; the belief that if he worked hard enough for those he loved, did exactly as they wanted, and kept his feelings to himself, they wouldn't leave. They wouldn't leave because he didn't ask anything of them or demand too much. He didn't realize until that moment that such fear was what kept him from being truly honest with Sarah and himself most of his adult life, fear that if he felt and asked for too much, she would leave and he would feel ashamed.

"Thank you, Gabe," Alex said as his eyes finally began to dry and he sipped again. "There is something so peaceful about finally hearing a comforting truth and allowing the words to sink in. I believe you are right, and I know you have a lot to gain from keeping this business booming." He smiled, only half-joking. "But that doesn't change the truth that you are right and the business and my music would be better off if we moved on. We've been too sheltered here. I think it's time I seek out California again. There was a spark that I discovered there when I visited with my grandma. I want to see if I can light a creative fire with it."

Gabe smiled in return. "You know I will take good care of the place."

"Of course," Alex replied. "I just have one last question before I step out."

"Yeah?" Gabe asked.

"You think Sarah would go with me?"

Chapter 34

Sarah was caught by surprise when Erika walked into the shelter on Tuesday afternoon. Sarah had been seeing Joel for about two months at this point, finishing out the summer with him. A couple families were meandering down hallways, browsing, led by another shelter employee. Sarah was just finishing up some paperwork when she heard the *ding* of the shelter entrance doorbell, indicating that someone had walked in. This was a familiar sound, but her heart dropped into her stomach, next to the stones, when she saw Erika. Erika's hair was down, long, straight, and black, similar to Sarah's. She removed her sunglasses and slid them up on top of her head, pushing her hair back. Erika was petite, and pretty and she had bags under her eyes, slightly darkened divots where years of sleep deprivation from her job and her kids left its mark.

"Oh, hi!" Sarah was caught off guard and stood up straight, not knowing what to do with her hands as Erika approached the front counter. Erika stood confident but guarded, gripping the strap of her purse for stability as she confronted Sarah.

"Do you remember me?" Erika's question was very straightforward. Her words carried significant weight.

"Um, yes, of course I do," Sarah responded. "Cruiser's mom, right?"

"'Mom' is not my name. Do you remember my name?" Erika's voice was controlled but anger began to seep into her words.

Sarah was operating out of shock, so she simply followed what her body told her to do, as she had in the past. *Answer honestly,* instinct replied inside her. "Your name is Erika."

"And how often have you thought about my name in the last two months? While you were sleeping with my husband?"

"I..." Sarah waited for her instincts. Before she could piece together a sentence, Erika interjected.

"I know what you must think of me. Tired, bored nurse/mom, looking for a dog to fill some family void. Husband must be bored with her..." Erika paused but Sarah's instincts told her not to fill the pause with words of any sort.

"You know my name, but how much of my story are you actually familiar with? You saw me for an hour on a Sunday with my husband and my kids. You saw me on paper. What do you know of my life?" Sarah was at a loss for words. She just looked into Erika's eyes, at least giving her the respect of meeting them.

"I am not so oblivious that I didn't see how Joel looked at you when we first walked in here. And you would be ignorant to believe you are the only woman he has ever looked at that way." Sarah had a feeling what Erika was saying was true but had never wanted to acknowledge that truth since meeting Joel. Of course, Joel laughed, joked, and turned his attention toward other women. Sarah already wasn't the only one; Erika, his wife, was there too.

"I also saw how you looked back at him," Erika continued, trying to take deep breaths as she spoke. "And I saw how you looked at me. It's your job to get to know people fast, and there is probably some truth to whatever you think of me. I know that you aren't the reason Joel cheats. Our problems are bigger than that. But while you were writing whatever fantasy novel you fancied with Joel, at our lake house, I was working twelve-hour shifts, providing the primary income for our family, and taking care of our kids and Cruiser, in between."

Sarah gulped. She couldn't help but feel ashamed of her relationship with Joel. She was never supposed to see the consequences of the affair. She was only supposed to see the story she was writing with Joel. Cheating was so much easier when Erika was just the "busy wife who didn't care." Now, Erika had a face and feelings that were felt right in front of Sarah, and she couldn't lie anymore. The only words she could think to say were a question. "How did you find out?" she asked more with shame than frustration.

"Do you think you're the only one who walks Cruiser at that dog park? People talk there. That's all they do. I figured it out after a few of the regulars there said, 'Oh yeah, I saw your husband here with your sister.' They probably assumed we were related since you and I really don't look all that different. From there, it wasn't hard to figure out you were. This honestly isn't the first time my husband has cheated. He changes his phone codes, and I always figure out the new ones, eventually." Sarah nodded. She let Erika steer the conversation.

"Anyway, Sarah, I know your name too. I am not here to talk about Joel. I am here to talk about myself. I want you to see my face, and I want my side of the story to be interwoven into whatever 'memories' you have created. This isn't a game to me. It's my life."

Sarah was still in shock, but she knew she owed Erika the respect of her time and attention. She said, "Okay. Can we sit in the back room though? I'll have someone cover out here."

"No. You were out in public with my husband, so I am going to be out in public with my story. You can face me here."

Sarah was embarrassed that this conversation was happening at her workplace, with her coworkers potentially listening in the background (they were), but there was nothing she could do. Erika had a point.

"Fair enough," she responded.

"I just want you to know that there is more to me than 'bored and busy.' I am passionate about what I do. My life isn't boring. I am an ER nurse. Every day, people come into my own place of work with everything from bizarre, hypochondriac mindsets to serious medical emergencies. I get to be there for it all. I get to be what they need for it all. I have conversations with my coworkers, and I get to be 'Erika.' Not wife. Not mother. Erika. Maybe that work identity is tied to being a nurse, but people actually ask me questions there unrelated to where their socks are and when I can pick them up from their friend's or I am getting the kids from practice, right?" Sarah nodded again, opening space for her to continue.

"I can also tell that you are smart. Cheating with my husband must have been calculated for you. And just as you know there is more to me, though I'm sure you told yourself there wasn't, I know there is more to you. So I am going to give you the respect of telling you why I married Joel. The story is more for me than it is for you, but I believe you're intelligent enough to understand what I mean. I am sure you have wondered why we were married in the first place?"

"I would be lying if I said I hadn't, and we are beyond lies now," Sarah responded, her survival instincts had kicked in by now and each step, each response that she should give was clear to her.

"Yes, we are beyond lies." Erika continued, "I married Joel because I got pregnant when I was twenty-two, shortly before we both graduated from college. That part of the story isn't interesting. Irresponsible, drunken sex is fairly common among college students, and a lucky few of us have long-term consequences. My family called me crying when they found out and said I had betrayed them. They were deeply religious." Sarah understood this part of the story more than Erika knew.

"According to them, my private sex life was an offense against them and their religion, and I was somehow responsible for how they felt about an unwed pregnancy. For days and days, the pressure continued. And Joel is all about image. He didn't want to be the guy who was known for ruining some young girl's life. Offering to marry me was charming and noble on the surface. And of course, I said yes. I hate to admit it, but my family got to me. I did feel ashamed. And how do you think that family would feel now if we got divorced? The same people who helped out with pickups and drop-offs at hockey practice and invited us to big meals on Christmas Eve. They are clueless about all that goes on underneath the surface.

Erika continued as Sarah silently listened, "Joel is charming. He has charmed them too. They don't care about the real story as long as the one they tell themselves, that we did the right thing by creating a stable home with two heterosexual parents, fits their understanding of the world. And I am in too deep, at least for now, to lose that image. I have never feared that I couldn't support myself and my kids alone, as I said, I am the primary wage earner in our home. I fear losing the image we have built. I worry about disappointing my family, and yes, we have been together so long that I have no idea what I would look like alone. And I don't know if I'll ever be ready to find out."

Erika took a deep breath as tears filled her eyes. She gripped her purse tighter, and Sarah felt this was the moment to speak. Erika was vulnerable with her. Vulnerability always spoke to Sarah, regardless of whatever walls she had built, and she knew the right thing to do was respond in kind.

She took a deep breath. "I owe you more than an apology. I owe you the truth. You have already discovered the truth of our affair on your own. My story shouldn't matter to you, and I am not telling you this to gain any kind of sympathy. I know I don't deserve that. I am telling you this because you deserve the truth of my situation and the vulnerability that comes with honesty."

Erika was quiet but continued to make eye contact as Sarah continued.

"My ex-husband's best friend raped me. On our wedding night. I've pieced together that maybe you didn't fall in love with Joel, not really, and I don't know that I ever truly loved Jesse, my ex-husband. I married him for a story too. He distracted me from the truth that everyone I had ever loved, or hated, disappointed me. It was so much easier to lose myself in my time with him than to face the pain and disappointment of feeling like I didn't fit in anywhere with anyone. Now, it seems, I am repeating patterns with Joel. But if I am really honest, the pain of what my ex-husband and his best friend did, whether I loved him or not, justified whatever I did to ruin someone else's marriage. Marriage had disappointed me too, and men had hurt me in horrifying ways. When I decided to have an affair with Joel"—Erika grimaced for a second as Sarah said the words *decided* and *affair*—"I told myself you didn't care, but I justified my actions because of the pain that had been inflicted upon me. If marriage was going to burn me, I would make sure it burned others too. I feel disgusted with myself now that I am facing the truth of my thoughts, the thoughts I tried to ignore. But what do I have to lose at this point, now that you're in front of me, in my place of work?"

She glanced over her shoulder for a moment...Sarah was certain now that at least one or two of her coworkers were listening from the back room. Sarah faced Erika and continued, "As I said before, you deserve more than an apology. I am not telling you about the rape to gain your sympathy. I am telling you because the thoughts tied to what happened to me are the truth, and I used your husband and your life to run from my pain. I now realize an affair really isn't an escape. And whatever story I told myself about you, and about Joel, was never the entire truth."

Erika took a deep breath and responded, loosening her grip on the strap of her purse but not letting go as she spoke, "Too many of us think we know the truth about someone else's life based on details we don't understand. Then, we tell ourselves a story about them that makes us feel better about ourselves. You saw me once and drew conclusions about me. But the truth is, you know very little about me, and I know very little about you. I will never forgive you for adding fuel to Joel's ego fire and whatever distraction he is trying to create for himself. But I appreciate your honesty. And I don't think I have to ask you to stop seeing my husband."

"No, you don't," Sarah said seriously.

Erika pulled her sunglasses down from where they perched on her head and put them on, covering her eyes. "I won't ever speak to you again, and I am going to ask that you at least give me the dignity of keeping what I have shared with you to yourself."

"Of course. You won't ever hear from me or any part of your story told back to you in a twisted manner from someone else." Sarah meant what she said.

Erika nodded, turned and walked out the door.

"Well, shit." Sarah heard the declaration from the back room. Then she turned and leaned toward the register, bracing herself with her hands. Her phone dinged, notifying her of a new message, likely Joel's usual afternoon check-in. Sarah took a deep breath. It was time for the distractions to end.

Chapter 35

Alex had decided he wanted to try out music school. There was one fairly near the beach he had visited with Sarah. The school also had a connection to local beach restaurants where the students could play live gigs, a taste of home for him. He had calculated everything. He could make enough money on the sale of the bar to help him find an apartment and pay for school until he could find another job. He hadn't planned his entire future, just the first few steps, and they felt right. He even lucked out when he called a few of the restaurants and asked if they had any open mic nights where he could start playing some of his originals, maybe even try some new stuff. He needed to be in front of an audience again.

He also desperately wanted to talk with Sarah. He needed to apologize for his coldness, he wanted to tell her he loved her (sober and articulately), and most importantly, she was his best friend and he missed talking to her. He couldn't wait to tell her how excited he was to finally pursue his music and that he had found the courage. He hadn't spoken to her since their fight at his bar. He had no idea what she had been doing; his pride had kept him from reaching out. But he realized that he would need to try to contact her first if he had any hope of mending and moving forward. A text seemed too informal, a phone call might be a little better, but face-to-face would probably be best. Then she could see him. She would know he was serious. He decided to stop by her work that afternoon. He remembered her schedule and knew that she would be there.

Chapter 36

Sarah was rethinking everything. Seeing Erika face-to-face and confronting her affair with Joel forced her to realize that she couldn't justify self-destructive behavior, no matter how much others had hurt her. Ultimately, she wanted and loved Alex. She missed him. She thought about the ache in her stomach when she woke up every morning feeling lonely. She knew that she had a connection with Alex that would make that ache go away, but neither of them had been ready to risk the vulnerability that accompanied feeling something real for another. In the meantime, Sarah was done avoiding herself. She decided she needed to leave the shelter for a while and reevaluate what she wanted to do with her own life. She had called Alex out on refusing to pursue his creativity, yet she had settled for a job that was less than what she had originally dreamed because of the barriers to building a business, and her own student loan debt. There had to be some way to become a veterinarian, or something like one. Maybe she needed to reevaluate her dreams entirely.

Regardless, the shelter didn't feel like the right fit anymore, and that wasn't just because several of her coworkers had inevitably heard that she was having an affair though that knowledge didn't feel great. She hadn't thought about the reflection of her behavior on the shelter. She represented the business. Her manager would be furious that she had slept with one of the customer's husbands, regardless of her reasons. She owed Jamie the courtesy of an apology and the firsthand telling of her interaction with Erika. Sarah went back to the step 1, step 2 process she had used to make it through the assault and court process. She was certain of three things, all of which she wanted to try to use the step process to pursue:

1. She wanted to apologize directly to her manager.

2. She wanted to live her life honestly, even if that meant pain and loneliness. Distractions weren't working.
3. She wanted the space to figure out what the next step was for pursuing her own dreams.

She needed to find a place outside this town. Sarah had been so overwhelmed with fear about turning a corner and running into Jesse or any of the court officials. Her identity was deeply tied to the trauma she endured, and she no longer wanted the associations to run her life. She worked hard to harness her anxiety and reframe her thoughts. However, she also knew the power of an entirely new place with entirely new faces and sights. Somewhere new could be the answer. She thought of the last place she felt safe or where she thought she might feel more like herself. California. She was going to return to the same beach she had visited with Alex.

There was so much beauty there. The palm trees, the ocean, the sun. I could feel again and sort out my thoughts, Sarah said to herself. Just as she was thinking, her phone dinged again. Joel. She texted him back and asked him to meet her at a park nearby, not the dog park…

"Well, hey there, stranger," he said, knowing he was ironically cheesy. He sat on the bench beside her. He looked around and attempted to drape his arm around Sarah and squeeze her shoulder affectionately. She inched away from him, a serious look on her face.

Joel's smile dropped; he felt confused about Sarah's rejection. *Erika must not have confronted him*, she thought. *It made sense. Erika had caught him cheating before. She probably didn't want to waste her energy on expecting more from him. His patterns were clear and created.*

"I am here to end this, Joel," she said factually.

He pulled the sunglasses off his face and placed them on top of his head, just as Erika had. "What? What do you mean?" he responded. His voice sounded worried.

"I mean what I said. I am here to end this."

Joel took a deep breath. His unfiltered reaction over. He was ready to turn on the charm he was so used to pulling off the shelf when he needed it. "Sarah? We have something good going here. We support each other, you know, unwind from this world. Why would you want to end us?"

Sarah was not going to tell him that Erika found out, that was Erika's business to share. Instead, she would tell him her own reasons, unfiltered.

"Because I have outgrown 'us.' Maybe 'us' never really fit who I am in the first place. I finally realized I can't do this and be myself. I can't live a fractured version of who I am. And more importantly, I don't want to."

Joel wasn't going to give up his distraction easily. In his own twisted manner, he had grown to care for Sarah. He loved the conversations he had with her. She was the perfect, challenging escape. "Okay…Is it that guy you told me about, Alex? Who is he anyway? Where has he been the last couple months?"

Sarah was frustrated that Joel had brought Alex up. She realized in that moment that she didn't like him talking about Alex. Joel trying to "one-up" Alex felt gross and wrong.

"My decision isn't about that guy," she said, unable to mask the frustration in her voice. My decision is about this, 'us.' We are not sustainable. We both have other lives."

Joel frowned, as if feigning mild disappointment in one of his employees, trying to minimize how Sarah felt. "Come on. We've been sustainable these last few months. We've been communicating better too, you know? We've both been more honest about what we want."

"Honest?" Sarah was angry now. Now that she refused to see Joel through the eyes of escape, she actually saw him and was disgusted. "What about what we're doing is honest? Do you share how we're communicating better with Erika?"

"Ah, of course not." Joel leaned back and smiled. "But this isn't about her. It's about us."

"You're right, this conversation isn't about her. And it's not about me either. Whatever we are talking about now and whatever we are is all about you. This is whatever feels easiest to you."

"Sarah, that's not fair. You know you mean more to me than that." He tried hugging her again, and she moved back even farther but made strong, determined contact with his eyes, in the light. She had enough of the games. She thought of the honesty she shared with Erika and decided to expose Joel to some too. She had a feeling he was a creature of habit and wouldn't change his patterns no matter what she said. But if nothing else, she was going to extend the honesty for Erika and for herself.

"And who are you to me, really? You're a story. An escape. I know you won't leave Erika. I know you wouldn't run from your life. You have too much to lose. I'm a story for you too. An escape. The only difference between you and I is that I know what I am running from. I know who I am and what I am afraid of. I am afraid of vulnerability. I am afraid of exposing my heart to someone fully and experiencing the rejection of all that I am, especially the weaknesses in myself that I loathe. I guess that is the ultimate vulnerability for me, the appearance of weakness. But it's something I've never had to show you because I don't actually care. I have only ever felt weak around one person, Alex, my best friend. 'That guy.' It's a strange irony that the person who should know and love me truly is the one person I am actually afraid of being loved by. I've shown so many weaknesses to him already, and he's loved me all the more. What am I really afraid of then? God, do old wounds have a way of fucking up the present. I don't know how else to fight them other than taking the first step in stopping this. So you can take your 'team' mindset and fuck right off, Joel. I hope, for your wife's sake, that you actually find yourself and what it is you truly want. If not, I guess you're in the right place. This world is made of lies."

Joel didn't want to give Sarah up, but he wasn't about to face himself. "I'm sorry you feel that way," he said simply, put his sunglasses back on, and walked away. Sarah knew enough about men like Joel to piece together that he would probably reach out via text about a month later when his other options thinned. She blocked his number as soon as the door of his Suburban slammed shut.

Chapter 37

Sarah arrived in California the next morning. Steps. She had an open conversation with her manager about the affair. Since she chose to come directly to her manager with the truth and Jamie was close enough with Sarah to extend some empathy, she shared that the required suspension for her actions could be called a sabbatical, and she needed to be away for at least two weeks. Sarah booked a hotel on the ocean and allowed herself to sit and think on the porch outside her room, under the sun, a place of clarity for her.

Sarah was searching for the balance between vulnerability and safety. As she sat and allowed herself to feel Jesse, Dean, and Alex, all the actions and words that had sunk into her, the stones returned to her stomach. She remembered their names: grief, disgust, pain, isolation, and anger. All tied to individual actions and words said and done by the three of them and many people before. All individual, yet connected. And in her anger, she chose to hurt someone else, Erika. While she was with Joel, she was able to ignore the stones though they never disappeared. Now that she was alone with herself, she couldn't help but feel them.

Sarah felt happy and warm under the sun. She was able to live at peace and enjoy the present. But with that enjoyment came acknowledgment of all the feelings she tried to ignore. *Why did I ignore them?* she thought to herself. *What am I really afraid of? And what do I actually want?* As the noise of the distractions slipped away, Sarah could finally hear herself. She concluded that she was afraid and ashamed to show vulnerability. It didn't matter if the vulnerability was shown to the men who heard her voice in college, lost friends, Jesse, Dean, Joel, or Alex. She was ashamed to feel vulnerable around anyone. Especially Alex. She felt that trusting men with the things she cared most about—books, her views on the world, her care and concern for people—meant that they had a hold on her, that she had something to lose.

And a part of her had been vulnerable with Jesse and Joel, even if she didn't want to admit it. She could never fully shut herself off completely with anyone, no matter how hard she tried. So what of the stones in her stomach? They never disappeared. Maybe she felt them less when she was distracted, but they were never gone. She got up from the patio and chose to walk with her thoughts around the resort complex. There were beautiful pink, red, and purple hibiscus everywhere; and Sarah loved looking at them.

She walked throughout most of the afternoon. Her body wasn't used to all the sunshine, no matter how much she loved the warmth, and she felt exhausted. She slowly lay down and rested her head on the soft pillow of the condo bed. Only a couple minutes passed before she slowly drifted off to sleep, breathing deeply. Then she had a very strange, beautiful dream. She was walking along the ocean shoreline, surrounded by beautiful oval stones, about the size of golf balls. The stones were made of many colors—blue, purple, teal, pink, and sparkling silver. But there were gray and beige stones too, just as beautiful. She picked up a large lavender, translucent stone.

As Sarah held the stone, she noticed a few people on the beach, including a woman who appeared angry at everyone around her. She waved her arms back and forth in frustration and was yelling something Sarah couldn't hear. Her head was covered in a red shawl, and she was cloaked in gentle, billowing maroon along with bright red scarves. As Sarah glanced back at the stone, she lost herself in its beauty for a moment. Then looked again at the angry woman, but this time, in her eyes. She was angry at the world, but she understood Sarah; she stared back and her anger softened. Sarah stared then looked down and continued admiring the stone, turning the lavender one over in her fingers. Then, though she wasn't sure why, she looked down at the purple stone, pressed her lips against its smooth surface, and sang a simple tune, one that was extremely familiar to her, yet she knew she hadn't heard the music before.

Almost instantly, Sarah sank into the water, pulled by the stone. The rock pulled her body as if it were a speedboat and she was dragging behind, underneath the surface. But she wasn't afraid, there was something thrilling about the water, and miraculously, she could breathe. Then, the dark ocean water tugged her arm and pulled her up and through the surface. She sped along the top of the water, lying down and creating a small wake. As she quickly drifted, the woman's face appeared in her mind again, like a guide, and whispered to her, "You spoke a language she could understand." She, meaning the sea. Sarah wasn't afraid as she was pulled along by the stone. The sea was calm, and she knew she was in no danger of drowning.

As the dream came closer to ending, the sea dropped Sarah on shore near some apartments, not far from where she had found them. There was an angry man out on his patio, yelling at someone inside. She felt afraid. She wasn't sure why the sea brought her there. *Maybe she just needed to show me she could make me move*, Sarah thought. Still, she felt nervous. She didn't want the angry man nor anyone else around to see her. There was something mysterious and beautiful that had captivated Sarah, and she didn't want to lose it. She dropped to her stomach, in the sand, to sink below the sight line of those in the apartments. Her purple stone lay near where she was first pulled away. She longed for the stone's lavender softness but grabbed a small, beige, smooth stone in its absence. She pressed her lips against the tiny stone. But instead of a song, she whispered, "Take me back." She dropped the stone in the water and was instantly tugged back to the exact spot where she had found all the stones. Instantly, she was awake.

She didn't know what the dream meant, only that she awoke with strong feelings of longing, wishing she could grasp them again. She remembered how powerful she felt whispering to the stones. There was something comforting about holding on to them but moving at the same time. Then, Sarah thought of the five stones in her stomach. When she imagined them in her hands, in all the beautiful colors she had just seen, they didn't feel so heavy. She could feel their purpose, to protect her. Sarah spoke her next thought aloud, so she was certain to hear herself, "maybe I need to accept that protection, but find a new place for such a shelter. I need to accept all of myself and believe there is something strong enough to ground me."

Stones can feel secure. They are something to grasp and hold on to. But they can also be moved. She got up and decided to walk along the shoreline and sink her toes in the sand, watching the shell fragments fill in the spaces between her toes. Sarah walked the rest of the afternoon and watched the sunset along the ocean shore and stared at the crashing waves into the night.

As she stood in the darkness and saw the white caps of the waves crash over the navy water beneath them, she felt overwhelmed by the ocean's power. Under the light of the moon, she could barely see the ocean's movement, but she could hear the powerful crashing and sinking of the waves. Standing in that power was terrifying and treacherous. But Sarah felt free. Such vast darkness but, simultaneously, such power. In the darkness and the brave waves, Sarah was finally brave too. No one could see her in the dark, and she didn't have to try to hide. She could face the pain she felt about Jesse and shame she felt about Joel. No one had a voice but the waves. They cared not for whom she married, what she'd lost, nor the degenerate unkindness done to her by Dean. The waves cared for themselves. Crash. Pull back.

Crash. Maintain life. Sarah picked up a small, round stone in the sand, unaware of what color the stone was. Then, she had an idea, inspired by her dream. She imagined the stone she grasped was the lavender stone in her dream, and the first of the five stones that sat in her stomach. She decided to whisper to the first stone, the one that represented grief. She held the small, quarter-sized rock to her lips and whispered, "Loss means that you have something to lose. Grief means you are alive and you are seeking to hold on to the life that you find in others. Jesse offered you the life and beauty of the natural world. It's okay to grieve the loss of exploration you found with him and to seek that beauty elsewhere." She slowly pulled the stone away from her lips and tossed it into the ocean. Instantly, her stomach felt a little lighter. She realized the powerful waves were strong enough to hold her grief. There was a place for all she felt. Sarah watched the first stone land in the water, hearing just the smallest *plop* among the crashes.

Then, she picked up a second stone, similar in size to the first but jagged and sharp. This was the stone of disgust, mostly disgust she felt toward herself. She carefully turned the stone over in her fingers and thought of how sick she felt about sleeping with someone else's husband and the predatory look she remembered in Dean's dark eyes, empty, as he raped her. Finally, she thought of the void of emotion Jesse revealed as she desperately told him the story of what Dean had done on their wedding night and how he blankly stared back at her. Disgust at how selfish humans could be, herself included, sliced at her. After she allowed herself to accept all that made her feel disgusted, she held this stone to her lips, careful not to allow its sharp edges to cut her and whispered, "Growth can be found in the ways we let ourselves down and the ways that others let us down. Disgust does not have to become shame. I can learn from repulsive behaviors and seek out those who would show me differently. Focus on those who would comfort and help me—Alex, Detective Selena, Attorney Corey, my inner self. Me, the one who told Erika the truth. All of this exists too…" She threw that stone into the water as if it were a tiny frisbee, watching just the slightest shadow of its jagged edges spinning in the darkness. The ocean caught this stone too.

Next, Sarah picked up a fat, round stone, the thickest she had found so far, almost the size of a baseball. Pain. This was the biggest stone Sarah had felt in her stomach but also the one she tried to ignore the most. The pain took up so much space. With each sinking feeling the pain had caused her, she tried to avoid it with distractions. This stone of pain went all the way back to her college days. From the first time she was labeled a "feminist" by the boys in her class. She was made to feel that something was wrong with her because she simply suggested that women didn't have to be treated as second-class citizens. Nobody else spoke up in class. Nobody defended her opinion. She was made to feel wrong, and that hurt. Ever since, she had avoided expecting that anyone else, men especially, might believe that the oppressed people of this world deserve better. Sarah realized that the moment she was made to feel ashamed for speaking out, she only allowed herself to become "close" to people that she ultimately knew would disappoint her (Jesse). Having high expectations hurt too much.

Sarah watched her own bicep flex as she held the round, fat stone of pain. Instead of feeling the weight of the pain, she instead focused on her ability to hold the stone. She focused on the strength she had developed since then. The pain was heavy, but she was strong, despite those who would seek to weigh her down. She whispered to the fat stone, "There will always be those who oppose you, who would seek shelter in their own traditions and the familiar. What matters is that you have grown, and there are those who would grow with you. You can allow the pain to move you forward." She lifted her arm and threw the stone of pain as if it were an actual baseball, using all the strength she possessed. The ocean caught it, like a friend, and Sarah was flooded with relief. Only two more stones.

Isolation was next. Isolation had a way of following pain. Sarah picked up a smaller round stone, one that easily could have hidden behind the thick stone of pain. She was reminded of the mornings she woke up in agony, feeling that she had no one to share her deepest thoughts with. Sarah learned during the period of silence she experienced with Alex, and the empty distractions that she lost herself in with Joel, that she was the happiest when she could share the thoughts that mattered most to her. She wanted a place for her passion, she needed to be able to express it, and when she couldn't, she felt agonizingly alone.

She whispered to the small stone of isolation, "There is always a place for your creativity and always those who would hear you. Alex hears you, even if he doesn't listen perfectly, even if he has growing to do. And growth is not a negative path. Growth is what reminds us that we're alive. His soul hears yours. You can trust that your ideas and passions will find companionship in him, and in the satisfaction of knowing that you see people, that you see the world, and may be making waves just as powerful as those you see now without even knowing it." She tossed isolation gently into the ocean and watched the stone land among the waves, no longer alone.

She finally came to the most powerful, consuming stone—anger. This was the stone that formed in the wake of all the others. If Sarah was angry, she had felt something else first that turned and burned into rage. She picked up a stone that fit perfectly in the palm of her hand; it almost felt comfortable. Anger often masqueraded as safety. The stone didn't burn her hand, but in the darkness, she imagined that the stone was one of coal. That's how it felt in her stomach, slowly smoldering, burning her from the inside out. She thought of all the times she spent with Joel, under the stars, feeling the wind on her face in the boat, how the wrinkles in the corner of his smile annoyed her, so cocky. She thought of Jesse and his betrayal, the time he spent with his friends partying instead of defending her, she fumed. She thought of Dean. So sick that he sought power and validation by raping her at her own wedding, but almost just as bad, all the stolen glances he gave her, seeking silent validation that he had caught the attention of a strong woman. She thought of Alex and how he had disappointed her. She was angry that he wasn't braver because she knew he deserved better and she wanted to grow with him.

By the end of her thoughts, she noticed that her breath had become short and high and her shoulders hunched as she gripped the stone. Anger was what she needed to let go of the most. Anger drove her to the affair. Ultimately, she was angry that the world wasn't better, that justice was not always done. But in gripping her anger, she burned only herself and lives that had nothing to do with her pain (Erika). Sarah thought of the perfect words to speak to her stone of anger, words that would accept and calm its fury. "You have protected me. You wanted better. You were the driving force behind my ability to speak to the detectives and seek justice for myself when no one else sought it for me. You encouraged me to speak up in class when others spewed comfortable lies and sparked the passion that animals deserved better. That the creatures of this world who are taken advantage of and used should be respected and cared for, even if they communicate differently. You helped me want more from Alex. I have needed you, but I have to let go, or the passion will turn to bitterness and the fury to apathy." Sarah tossed the stone into the water, as if waving goodbye to a friend she had outgrown.

Her stomach was empty. She accepted and removed the stones. Sarah sat in the darkness and emptiness. She felt relieved to simply be empty. To let go. She sat in one of the beach chairs that had been left in the sand and continued to watch the waves crashing. A final thought occurred to her. *We can find pieces of ourselves in dark places. Many fear who they will become in the darkness or what might consume them inside it. But the darkness can help us find the freedom to understand the pieces of ourselves that we can't see, that even others can't see. In every dark piece, there's a purpose. Collect the piece you need there and allow it to take shape in the light.* Sarah was confident that, soon, she would find her light.

Chapter 38

Alex felt nervous as he approached the glass doors of the shelter. He hadn't seen Sarah in months. He believed that the right thing to do was find her in person. He knew he owed her the respect of speaking directly to her. It was not lost on him that he had hurt Sarah with his silence at the bar last time they spoke. As he pulled on the handle, the nervousness he felt increased.

What if she's still mad at me? What if I can't find the right words to express how I feel again? What if she rejects me... Friendship or... otherwise? he thought. *I don't know if I could handle feeling rejected again.* Alex took a deep breath and opened the door. *No matter how she responds,* he thought again, *life is worse without her, and I don't want a life without her.* He believed that reaching out was better than being cut off from the one person who made him feel like there was more to life than obligation.

He approached the counter and saw Sarah's coworker, Layla, filling out some paperwork. Layla had a long, brown braid that rested over her shoulder as she wrote. She looked up when she heard the door shut. "Alex?" she asked, looking surprised. Most of Sarah's coworkers knew him. He had visited her enough in the past that he was well-known as her best friend.

"Hey, Layla," he responded, awkwardly fidgeting with his hands. He couldn't decide if he should put them in the pocket of his jeans or cross his arms.

"Um... Is Sarah here?"

Layla dropped the pen and had a concerned look on her face. She glanced from side to side then stood on her tiptoes to look behind Alex and make sure that there were no customers coming

"Have you talked to her recently?"

Alex looked awkwardly around and then said, "No, actually, I haven't. That's why I'm here."

"Oh, um, some stuff went down."

"What do you mean?" Alex quickly responded, worry clear in his voice. "Is she okay?"

"Well, safe, yes. Okay? I'm not so sure..."

"This is getting cryptic, Layla. Can you tell me where she is?"

Layla glanced around again before speaking. "I only know pieces of the story, not her exact location..."

Alex stared, annoyed, waiting for her to continue. He realized she knew more than what she was saying.

"Okay, listen," Layla said. "I know that she's on a 'sabbatical' for a couple weeks and something about California."

Alex frowned, taken aback. "California? Why?"

"Well...something happened with one of the customers. I'll be honest, the only reason I know is because I overheard part of it. I know you're her best friend, and I am a little worried about her. So I'll tell you..."

Alex listened intently, unaware that he had started holding his breath.

"A woman came in one day while Sarah was working. She spoke to her at the counter. She must have been in here before with her husband and family. She told Sarah that she knew..." Layla looked down for a moment and hesitated. "She knew Sarah was having an affair with her husband."

Alex continued to listen, his serious expression unchanged.

"Anyway...There wasn't screaming or name-calling like you might think. The woman was oddly calm but direct about how the affair affected her. I don't know, it's just my opinion from the other room, but we get a lot of different people in here and the woman didn't sound super angry. More than anything else, she sounded sad. Sarah did too. It was the first time I heard Sarah sound sad in a long time. She's been strangely witty lately. She joked around a lot. I guess now that I think about it, Sarah was the type to talk about serious things occasionally, but up until the conversation with that woman, I haven't heard her say anything serious in a while."

"What did Sarah do when the woman left?"

"Just finished out her shift, quietly, and left. I obviously wasn't going to ask any more about the conversation. She knew that I overheard. I might have let an 'Oh shit' slip. I mean, what else can you say in a scenario like that? And I knew Sarah felt bad. She said something to the woman about pain, and it was the first time she talked about...the incident...since she first told our manager and took time off. I don't know, Alex. Something was just, different, with her after that conversation. And I don't know if that difference is good or bad. Maybe neither. Maybe both."

"But you know for sure she's in California?"

"Yes. Our manager is supposed to keep confidentiality. But humans are humans and even the best of people let gossip slip. There's probably something empowering about having information."

Layla realized the irony of her last statement and cleared her throat while standing up a little straighter and said, "Anyway, Alex. I hope there's a way for you to check in with her. She's given our manager enough information to know that she's safe, but we don't really know anything beyond that."

"I do," Alex said. "Thank you, Layla."

Layla nodded as Alex hurried out of the shelter. He fumbled with his keys and headed toward the airport.

Chapter 39

Alex's flight wasn't scheduled for another week, but he found a way to switch his ticket and get to California that evening. He was in absolute go mode and the anxiety he felt about reaching Sarah helped him find solutions, the right things to say to the right people at the airport so he could leave earlier. His mind continued to race as he sat on the plane, wishing he could speed up the engines. All he wanted to do was see Sarah. Somehow he knew that she had gone to the same place they visited together. It was just a feeling he knew he could trust, and he had been trying to trust his intuition more lately. He wanted to text her and call her, but he didn't have the words. He was flooded with so many feelings he didn't have a place for.

Steps, he thought. *Isolate each thought.* He tried to slow his mind and freeze each thought, as if it were a TV show playing in his mind. He didn't care that Sarah had an affair. "I mean, I care for Sarah, but I don't judge her for choices I wasn't there to see and a life that doesn't belong to me." Alex had seen enough affairs, live and the story version, at the bar. He knew there was always more to everyone's story. Very few people wake up and decide to blow up a relationship with infidelity. Of course, cheating was not okay. It never is. But Alex knew that cheating was symptomatic of something bigger. And in Sarah's case, he suspected her reasons were tied to grief. People made all sorts of self-destructive choices when they were in pain, when they believed they had nothing to lose. More than anything, he was worried about Sarah, and he just wanted her to know she wasn't alone.

Although Alex was growing to accept that he didn't have to save everyone in every moment, he couldn't help but feel a twinge of guilt again for not being there for her. He wanted her to feel seen. He wanted to help her find a name for her pain so she could work through what she was feeling before the hurt ate away at her even more. He knew Sarah well. She was self-destructive, but she was reflective too. If she had a face-to-face conversation with this man's wife, she would have let everything she learned from that conversation sink in.

Maybe Sarah has already found a name for her own pain. Maybe I don't need to. Her feelings are her own. I can listen, I can support her, but I don't have to take her experiences on as if they are something I should be ashamed of, for not being there for her perfectly. Alex continued to think but realized he wanted to name something for himself. He pulled the pencil out from behind his ear and lowered it to the page of his notebook. He began writing furiously.

Sarah was ready to relax. Acknowledging the trauma she had been harboring was exhausting, but she was slowly feeling lighter too. The morning after she had thrown all the stones, she slept well then slowly awoke to the sun. After a short walk on the beach, she simply sat in the sunlight and listened to the waves. Each crash and pull reminded her of the freedom of movement and unexpected outcomes. Knowing that she didn't have to control the story she was in made her nervous, but that knowledge also helped her realize that she could be honest and creative. The sound of the ocean helped her live presently in a way that the cold heart of the Midwest couldn't. She needed new sights and new sounds, and she was certain that she felt more at home here, under the sun, near the waves.

Sarah thought about her dream of becoming a veterinarian. In college, she believed she wanted to open her own business. She took the shelter job because building such a business was way beyond what her four-year degree salary and student loan debt could afford. For a moment, she stripped away all obstacles in her mind and thought about opening a business in California. The cost of living was high, and she definitely still had debt. But maybe she could create a new dream. It was clear to her that she had outgrown her job at the shelter, long before the affair with Joel. California was new. There was a lot of ocean and climate to explore, places, plants, and animals she had never seen before. Maybe, instead of a shelter, she could find a job at a local aquarium.

My experience with animals, and my degree, should give me an advantage when applying, she thought. *Maybe I don't want to own a business.* She remembered all of the on-call hours her manager, and sometimes she, spent responding to crises or reintegrating animals that people had decided they couldn't take on. *No, I don't want to own a business, I don't even want to manage one anymore…But how can I grow? How can I feel like I am creating and helping others?* Creation was one thing that Sarah was certain of. She loved the relationships she had created between the families and the animals. She loved creating safety for the creatures when they had known only danger. The passion of creation is what kept her around the shelter so long.

Then, she thought of Alex. She thought of his talent for writing, and she thought of how much she loved to read. *Maybe I could write too.* The ocean inspired her. *Maybe I could try out journalism and document my new experiences here…I could see new forests [California had plenty], rivers, bays, and mountains and write about all of the animals there?* California housed many ecosystems, as she had learned on her trip with Alex. She could see and write a lot without having to travel too far. *Maybe I could even try writing a fantasy novel too. There is so much beauty here.* Sarah's dream of the stones taught her that her imagination could thrive. *That's what I am going to do. Dreams and steps. I've got enough saved to rent a small place here and find a job. The beauty of writing is that it's free. This is manageable,* Sarah thought. She didn't know where her dreams would take her, but she knew they felt right and she knew how to take the first couple of steps.

Another thought occurred to her. *I want to share my life with Alex. I am tired of living without him.* She realized that in the past, she thought that she and Alex were too busy to "truly date each other," as she had shared with Pete. Whatever that meant. But now that she reflected on her life and time spent with Alex, she noticed that she put energy toward sharing almost every spare moment of free time she had with him. She didn't have to wait for the perfect scenario where they had all the time in the world. Some obligation or challenge would always come up. The important thing was continuing to find the moments with him that she could in the midst of the chaos of whatever life was throwing at them. Only a couple of months had passed but each day without him felt like she wasn't acknowledging the part of herself that longed to share the things she cared about most. Sarah was worried about what Alex might think of her affair with Joel. She wanted to be honest with him about everything, not because she felt she owed him an explanation, but because she needed him to love her for everything she is, including the pieces of herself that formed in dark places.

"I'm going to call him tonight," she concluded. "But first, dinner."

Chapter 40

Alex had arrived around midnight from his evening flight. He was able to rent a car and get to a nearby hotel. He was exhausted. He fell into the bed at the hotel and was asleep almost as soon as his head met the pillow. He awoke late the next morning to a notification from a local restaurant on the ocean, not far from where he had eaten and danced with Sarah. "Open mic night!" When he decided to try out the local spots, he turned notifications of their events on his phone so he wouldn't miss one.

Shit, he thought, *it's tonight*. His original plan was to rest up, call Sarah, and let her know he was in the area and wanted to see her. He still felt worried but didn't want to lose an opportunity to play. He was trying to get better at realizing his own dreams and remembering that although people needed him, it wasn't his responsibility to save them. *I can call Sarah tomorrow. I've got time and I know I want to take this musical opportunity*. Alex was beginning to experience the freedom of not being tied to a business at all hours. He could ease into the day and his plans, no need to respond to an ordering crisis. However, he was definitely rusty with his guitar. He needed the day to practice. He sat up, pulled his guitar from the corner of the room, and strummed a few simple, familiar chords: A minor, C, B minor… And he began to put sound to the words he had written on the plane. He stumbled awkwardly through some of the chord progressions at first, but then the music started to flow.

The restaurant would allow him to play a single song. Usually, when Alex performed live, he had rehearsed the covers, and especially his originals, several times before playing them for others. But the more he practiced his new piece, the stronger he felt that he should perform this new song tonight. *What do I have to lose?* he thought.

Well, potentially a lot, I guess. He was trying to make a name for himself in California, and a botched performance could prevent that progress. *But what are dreams without risk?*

Alex realized he reached people most deeply when he sang from his heart. He thought of how he played the last song for Sandy and the song for Sarah at her wedding. He remembered how tears had filled Sandy's eyes. He thought of how he felt when he was writing vulnerably. Maybe his audience could feel that vulnerability too. Maybe they could relate to the feeling. "New song and open mic it is."

Sarah decided on dinner at random. "I'll walk along the beach until I find a place that looks interesting." She loved the spontaneity of the trip. She was in a small, beautiful beach town so restaurants lined the streets, most of which had patios on the coast. The sun was setting as she walked and the ocean waves moved calmly, easing into the evening. She saw the restaurant where she ate and danced with Alex, embracing the memory. She took a deep breath and chose a small bar and grill a few paces down from where they had spent time together. She was craving french fries. Then, she saw a small sign that said, "Open mic night!" She smiled when she saw the sign and realized how much she missed live nights at The Crooked Picture. Maybe the open mic night would be a good opener for her conversation with Alex. She could tell him about the music she heard there and ease back into her conversation with him.

She was seated at a table near the middle of the room, a few of the tables in front of her blocked part of the stage, but she could get a clear view of the microphone. She ordered a glass of cabernet and sipped slowly as she watched the first set of performers, a partnership of two young women who played folksy music as a duo on their guitars. Their music was fun, the kind you could easily tap your foot along to. They ended with a beautiful song about loss and death but finding hope in the spiritual part of the person that remained on earth in the beautiful things that remind us of life daily.

By the time the women were finished playing, Sarah had finished her second glass of cabernet and had to pee. She stepped into the restroom as the applause rose and the break began for the second performer to get set up. She looked into the mirror of the bathroom at her eyes and her hair, beginning to see the beauty in the light that her eyes carried. She saw that her own gaze had the appearance of someone who had seen more of the world than they should but had the resilience to continue to see what beauty exists beside the cruelty. She loved the green-and-brown colors of her irises and how they swirled around each other in an unpredictable pattern. The more Sarah looked, the more she realized that, although she felt wonderful about accepting herself, she may have a slight buzz. She snapped out of her haze when she heard a few test chords being strummed on a single guitar outside the bathroom. She quickly washed her hands and heard a familiar voice just barely over the sound of the paper towel dispenser. He spoke only a sentence, but she had heard that voice enough to recognize him. "This song is called 'Sheltered'…"

Sarah dashed out of the bathroom and into the dining room. She couldn't get back to her table without interrupting, but she could see Alex from the back. *How?* she thought. *When? Why?* A million questions raced through her mind, but her thoughts stilled as he began to play a song she had never heard. She knew instantly that it was a new original.

So what does life mean
When I choose to write the scene?
Am I better alone, where there's no roller coaster?
I only coast.

Uphill and downhill with
you but I am certain I am alive.
My mind is my enemy and
My best friend, my protector, and a liar
desperately seeking truth.

I live here, aware but sheltered,
protected from the gifts of vulnerability.

The only freedom is creativity.

Uphill, downhill, open to life's cruel and swift turns.
I choose to embrace what I see and make
a beauty of my own.

Nothing is ever certain,
Even when I believed
I could create my own safety.
I was never safe inside a world of familiarity
and "control."
Same people. Same faces. The same stories.
People lying, people scheming, but mostly people running
from the truth of the pain others have shown them
and the hurt they've caused.
Unaware that their pain is in every word they
speak and
dead roots give life to dry dreams.

But even the cruelest of evils in life
cannot prevent love
from growing beside them.
So I will be this anomaly, maybe a
constant contradiction of what I "should" be.

I will be everything, all that is honest and real in me
that I can't explain.
All that could allow me to hurt.

Music is the voice I've needed to listen to all my
life and
I will finally sing loudly enough that I can hear…

I don't need to be afraid, I need not seek
shelter. I did not deserve to be abandoned and I won't
abandon my chance.

I am not too old.
I am not too afraid.
I am not too weak.
I am not too damaged.

I am my own creation, and I can embrace what I
have been handed

I need not seek shelter.
I need not seek shelter.

I am the storm.

Alex repeated "I need not seek shelter" three more times then faded into "I am the storm" again and ended the song on a beautiful minor chord. The entire time he sang, he was looking toward the audience but didn't actually see them; his mind was captivated by the music his body was creating. He hadn't scanned the room until the end, searching for his audience's reaction to the song. As he looked around the room, he saw a familiar set of eyes watching him from the back. They were filled with tears. His own had filled with tears as he sang. He allowed one or two of them to fall when he saw *her*.

Sarah asked to move outside to the patio and for another chair. As they sat down together, once again near the ocean, Alex explained that he had stopped at the shelter looking for her, and her coworker shared that she was out in California. Sarah's eyes shifted nervously as he spoke; she knew that Alex was likely aware of her affair. He then went on to share that he was planning on coming out to California anyway and he'd explain why later.

"First though, I want to start a different conversation if that's okay?" Sarah nodded. "There's a million things I want to say to you and fill you in on, but I guess wanting to start this conversation is the point." Alex confidently met Sarah's eyes in a manner that he never had before as he spoke. "From the moment I met you in high school, I started a conversation I never wanted to finish." Sarah's eyes continued to fill with tears. "I am sorry for how I treated you last time we spoke. I was hurt, and I didn't know where to put my pain. I spent so much of my life protecting myself from rejection, from ever feeling like I couldn't measure up to the expectations of others, even though I still felt unworthy underneath everything the entire time."

Sarah continued to listen. In most of her conversations with Alex, she tended to speak more. She was mystified and surprised by his song and the words he was speaking now. He had written the song for himself. He was speaking up for himself. Alex had never written a song for himself before, and she was so happy that he did. He had something to say, and she wanted to hear him.

"I realized how afraid I was of being vulnerable and how guilty I felt for something as simple as being taken care of. I have believed I was a burden to others, so I did everything I could to take care of their needs first, pretending like I didn't care about my own. I didn't realize how miserable I actually was running the bar all those years though I don't regret them. I met a lot of people and played a lot of music there. People and music that is intertwined with who I am now. I don't want to regret or reject any parts of who I am anymore. Ultimately, I realized that I've never believed we are at 'war' with ourselves. Inherently, I've never wanted to harm myself or work against my own good. Rather, I've been at war with every lie told to me by my family, Western culture and, hell, the world. My mind and body have always sought to become and protect my true self at the same time that I felt so insecure. The world is what has given me reason to feel threatened."

"We're good at jumping right back into it, huh?" Sarah said, smiling. "There's so much I want to say to you too, and I know we left things awkwardly…" It was at this moment that the server chose to refill their water and bring Sarah's fries…making sure to create an uncomfortable, unintentional silence as Sarah was in the middle of an important thought. "Anyway," Sarah continued as she tucked her hair behind her ear and spoke, "neither of us are innocent when it comes to the argument we had and the tension after. We both were misunderstood and spoke hurtfully. I am sorry for those who've hurt you and that I didn't see how much you were hiding before. I know I can get lost in my own convictions a lot. I am really sorry for the ways I didn't see you. I want you to know now that I am in awe of you. You found your own voice though I've heard it weave in and out of the music you've played before. But tonight? That song was for you, but I know that the words found a place in the hearts of all who listened. We all seek shelter." A couple of the tears spilled from her eyes as she looked at Alex. "Anyway, in the interest of avoiding shelter, can I share a few thoughts with you?"

"Always."

Sarah breathed deeply and spoke, "I've never been afraid to face the darkness in me, or at least, some of the things that were difficult to feel. I rode into some of my trauma headstrong. Throughout the prosecution process with Jesse and Dean, I exposed every inch of my pain, desire, and panic and all the consequences that accompanied them. I faced every single shadow that accompanied the darkness that Dean forced upon me." Alex nodded and encouraged her to continue.

"I'm aware that you must know I had an affair. I will own it. I did it. There's no excuse I want to give to try to 'justify' sleeping with someone else's husband. I was honest with his wife when she confronted me, and I'll be honest with you now. I was tired of feeling guilty about how I coped with the way the world was, Alex. Therapy, honesty, and all the bills that came with healing. After the rape, I wasn't afraid to face the horror that was done to me and my own thoughts about it. Never. Straight out of the hospital, I went to therapy. I chose to. No one had to coerce me. I followed simple advice. Why wouldn't I want to heal? And maybe I did heal from Jesse and Dean. But on the other side of trauma, there was empty hole. And feeling distanced and hurt by you grew that emptiness.

"Once I carved out all the rotten remains of the selfish drives and desires of Jesse and Dean, I was left feeling like I lost all the creative pieces of myself. Soon, the empty ache was filled instead with heavy stones of grief. I thought I was healing, but when we fought, I was afraid I would never find anyone who would want to heal with me. Who could follow me to the other side of all the world's done to them and remain whole enough to exist as someone creative, genuine, and brave? No one, or so I thought. I didn't want to feel overwhelmed with heavy grief and emptiness all at the same time, so I convinced myself that filling that void with lies would give me the relief from loneliness that I was so desperately seeking."

"I can understand that," Alex said. "I filled my life with my own lies too. Maybe not an affair, but a life where I was lying to myself about what I actually wanted. I lost myself in the stories of others too. My head was full of them every night at the bar. Stories told to me by patrons or stories I created based on judgments I made about them. All the while pretending that the fear of rejection hadn't cut me off from the people and interests that mattered most to me."

He sipped some water and looked at Sarah as she continued, allowing more tears to fall from her eyes. "I don't want to admit that he hurt me. Jesse. He was supposed to be something I could control. No one ever wants to admit they were trying to control someone else or a situation. But I was. I was trying to control him and the outcome. I wasn't trying to control him in an abusive sense or as if I had power over him. No. It was more like I controlled him and us because I was never in a situation where I couldn't help how I felt. I knew how I felt about Jesse from the beginning, from the second I saw him again in that bar. And I knew exactly what he was. A coward. A douchebag. A big ole bag of dicks. He wasn't brave enough to live his actual life, and I was his escape. I was a tiny, hypersexualized corner of his brain. A part that had complete control over him when I wanted it, and I allowed myself to be his beautiful, intelligent, and artistic trophy. I never loved him, you were right. But the piece that I learned is that I could never cut myself off from who I am completely, and I grew to care for him and expect respect from him. I don't like to admit it, but I was vulnerable enough that he could hurt me."

Sarah reached for Alex's hand. She had never held it before, but she hoped that his touch would help calm her and that the gesture might help her discern if he still loved her. Either way, she knew she loved him and wanted to tell him. Sarah had learned that honesty with every part of who she was and who she loved was the only peaceful way to live, even if she had to feel pain or risk rejection. Alex lightly grasped her hand in response as she spoke.

"I was going to tell you that you've turned me into a romantic. But I don't think that's the truth. Romantic tendencies have always been dormant inside me. Guarded when, in my vulnerability, a coward sought to snatch my power. Remember that? Philosophy class November '06? Kyle Weathers."

"Oh god, yes." Alex rubbed his eyes with his free hand, remembering the frustration of that conversation.

"When I brought up deconstruction theory about Nietzsche and that true strength is found in humility, especially for men, he told me that 'to glorify feminism is to emasculate men.' That I was 'denying them their godly roles as leaders.' Jesus. I tried to get my point across but knew then that they wouldn't hear me. The hardest thing to do was lay aside power for empathy, to entertain the idea that understanding and supporting another was actually a challenging task, requiring muscles of another kind. I spoke aloud, in front of our entire class that true strength was to unlearn bias and internalize reconciliation. As if such a task is for the weak. Anyway, when I said that, I was thinking of Simon from Golding's *Lord of the Flies*. You know, the empathetic, observant, thoughtful one?"

Alex nodded.

"The only one on the island whom, in their fear, they ripped to shreds within days? When I shared under the umbrella of what I thought was an educational institution full of a wide open sky of minds, I had hoped that our class could create a new story of strength. Real strength. Empathizing with others. Reconciling bloody pasts. But Kyle was the same as the past. That toxic, stagnant pillar piercing our society and refusing to bend, to see that there was a world beyond the place he chose to tower over others, seeing only his high-up view. So I sunk back beneath him. Romantic endeavors are an empathetic joy too beautiful and painful to remain exposed above a stubborn earth. I didn't realize it then but Kyle, and those like him, encouraged me to slowly suppress the part of myself that would be loving and vulnerable. But I've had a lot of time to think lately, and I realized that your creativity restores my passionate vulnerability. You inspire me to hold on to and continue searching for the bright pieces of myself. You've shown me that there is always a place for my creative thoughts, even if there are those out there who would seek to suffocate them. And I want to tell you, now that I am willing to live in fear and bravery at the same time, that I love you."

Alex gently slipped his hand behind her ear, intertwining his fingers with her hair and pulled her in, across the table for another long kiss, just like the one they shared together the last time they were in California on the dock. "Of course I love you too, Sarah. A few sour conversations and hard feelings can't change that. I don't fear conflict or rejection from you anymore. You inspire me, you help me grow, but I am not afraid anymore of feeling hurt by you. I don't like to hurt. I don't like to argue with you. But I never would have faced myself, and the frustration that was eating away at me if we hadn't. Frustration just means we want something better."

Sarah smiled and wiped her eyes, tasting Alex's kiss as it lingered on her lips. "So what exactly are we both doing here again? And what do we do now?" They both laughed gently in response to Sarah's question.

"We do what we've always done. Share our dreams with each other. I think the difference now is that we are both brave enough to learn how to live them."

Sarah and Alex walked together on the beach in the night, holding hands and making plans of creating together. The ocean waves rolled powerfully beside them, the light of the moon guiding their path. Nothing was certain, nothing was planned forever, but they had the first few steps, both finally believing wholeheartedly that they could take them together.

About the Author

Jenna Dill is a debut author and high school English teacher from the Midwest. She is grateful for all the stories that enter her life from her students, family, and friends. Every day, she is inspired by the beauty of words and how they have the power to shape, build, and add value to human life and the earth. Her passion for teaching and learning is the same passion that drives her motivation to write. One of her favorite authors is Trevor Noah who stated, "Love is a creative act. When you love someone, you create a new world for them." She hopes that readers will always find the courage to learn how to love others and see the power that their stories have to shape another's future.

Printed in the USA
CPSIA information can be obtained
at www.ICGtesting.com
LVHW051154310124
770460LV00046B/571